Related Kaplan Titles

CPA Workbook
GRE
Guide to Distance Learning
Kaplan/*Newsweek* Graduate School Admissions Adviser
Kaplan/*Newsweek* Law School Admissions Adviser
LSAT
Résumé Builder and Career Counselor CD-ROM
Scholarships
Student's Guide to On-Campus Job Recruitment

Other Resources from Kaplan and John Douglas
Available in Spring 1999

John Douglas's Guide to the FBI Exam
John Douglas's Guide to the Police Exam
John Douglas's Guide to the Chicago Police Exam
John Douglas's Guide to the Los Angeles Police Exam

Guide to Careers in the FBI

by John Douglas

Simon & Schuster

Kaplan Books
Published by Kaplan Educational Centers and Simon & Schuster
1230 Avenue of the Americas
New York, NY 10020

Copyright © 1998, by John Douglas. All rights reserved.

All rights reserved. No part of this book may be reproduced or transmitted in any form or by any means, electronic or mechanical, including photocopying, recording, or by any information storage and retrieval system, without the written permission of the Publisher, except where permitted by law.

For bulk sales to schools, colleges, and universities, please contact Vice President for Special Markets, Simon & Schuster Special Markets, 1633 Broadway, 8th Floor, New York, NY 10019.

Kaplan® is a registered trademark of Kaplan Educational Centers.

Project Editor: Donna Ratajczak
Cover Design: Cheung Tai
Interior Page Design: Michael Shevlin
Interior Page Production: Doreen Beauregard and Jobim Rose
Desktop Production Manager: Michael Shevlin
Production Editor: Maude Spekes
Managing Editor: Brent Gallenberger
Executive Editor: Del Franz

Special thanks to: Enid Burns, Alison May, Kiernan McGuire, and Sara Pearl.

Manufactured in the United States of America
Published simultaneously in Canada

October 1998
10 9 8 7 6 5 4 3 2 1

Library of Congress Cataloging-in-Publication Data

Douglas, John E.
[Guide to careers in the FBI]
John Douglas's guide to careers in the FBI: the complete guide to the skills and education required to be a top FBI candidate / by John Douglas.
p. cm.
ISBN 0-684-85504-6
1. United States. Federal Bureau of Investigation—Vocational guidance. 2. United States Federal Bureau of Investigation—Officials and employees—Training of. 3. United States. Federal Bureau of Investigation—History. I. Title.
HV8144.F43D68 1998
363.2'023'73—dc21
                                                                98-35527
                                                                CIP

ISBN: 0-684-85504-6

Contents

About the Author

During 25 years with the FBI, John Douglas became a leading expert on criminal personality profiling. Early in his career, he served as a recruiter for the Bureau; later, he conducted the first organized study into the methods and motivations of serial criminals, and became known as the pioneer of modern criminal investigative analysis. As a consultant, he continues assisting in criminal investigations and prosecutions throughout the world. An Air Force veteran, Douglas holds a doctorate in adult education, and is the author of numerous articles and presentations on criminology. He coauthored two landmark criminology texts: *Sexual Homicide: Patterns and Motives* and the *Crime Classification Manual*. With Mark Olshaker, he's coauthored several best-selling nonfiction books: *Mindhunter: Inside the FBI's Elite Serial Crime Unit; Unabomber: On the Trail of America's Most-Wanted Serial Killer; Journey into Darkness: The FBI's Premier Investigator Penetrates the Minds and Motives of the Most Terrifying Serial Killers;* and *Obsession: The FBI's Legendary Profiler Probes the Psyches of Killers, Rapists and Stalkers, and Their Victims, and Tells How to Fight Back.* He lives in the Washington, D.C., area.

Dedication

This book is dedicated to all FBI Special Agents—past, present, and future—who make the ultimate sacrifice in the line of duty.

Acknowledgments

I'd like to thank all the former Special Agents who shared their insights and expertise; this book could never have been written without their generosity and good humor. Paula Klaris deserves special thanks for her invaluable editorial assistance.

PART ONE

Introduction

CHAPTER 1

Special Agents Tell Their Stories

You're going to get a lot of just-the-facts-ma'am information in this book. You're also going to get a look at just what it's like to be a member of what I consider the finest investigative agency in the world. The information here comes from the Bureau itself, and from the experts—former FBI Special Agents. I worked with most of these guys and I have a lot of respect for them, as agents and as people.

I'm giving you their stories here for two reasons. First, you'll see a range of the career opportunities open to you as a Special Agent of the FBI. Second, I want you to get to know the men I interviewed, because they're the ones who are going to let you "walk in their shoes."

One thing you should keep in mind: Most of these guys joined the Bureau in the late '60s and early '70s, about the time I did. That was a time when the Special Agent force was pretty much all-male. Things have changed tremendously since then. The Bureau has made a real effort to change the composition of its workforce, so it reflects American society as a whole, and they've done a good job of it. (You'll get more information about that process later in the book.) So as you read these guys' stories, don't think you have to be a guy to follow in their footsteps.

GREG COOPER

I met Greg Cooper while I was teaching at the National Academy. He came up and introduced himself and said, "I really want to be a member of the profiling unit." Well, lots of people, inside and outside the Bureau, say that to me all the time. I just said something polite and moved on.

But Greg was serious. He made it his business to do everything he could to prepare himself to be a profiler. And as I got to know him, I realized that he really was talented and he would be an asset to the unit. And I was right.

I guess I first became aware of the FBI from watching that television show with Efram Zimbalist Jr.—*The FBI*. Me and who knows how many kids in the '50s. But I remember back then I used to daydream about being an agent.

But I first got seriously interested in law enforcement when I was going through Brigham Young University and the Provo police chief taught a criminal justice class I was taking. I was very, very impressed with him—the image he projected and the experiences he talked about. This was someone I could look up to and emulate.

I went up to him after one of the classes and asked if there was some kind of a part-time job down at the police department. He said, "Well, there's a position as a part-time cadet in the detective division." So I went down and applied and was accepted. I worked in that capacity while I was going to school full time, working on a bachelor's degree. I was twenty-one, sort of the baby detective.

I was just enthralled with it. And having an opportunity to work with detectives at that young age was impressive to me.

After about 18 months, the detectives talked me into taking the test for the full-time position as a police officer. I took that test, passed it, went through the interview process, and then was offered a full-time position.

So now I'm working full time and going to school full time. I graduated from BYU, then went to the Provo Police Academy and graduated valedictorian. My first six months I worked undercover as a narcotics officer.

I was still looking at the chief as my role model. He was a reflection of what I wanted to be, what I could attain. During the time I was undercover, I realized I needed a graduate degree if I was going to make any real progress, do what I really wanted to do. And so I decided to go back to school.

I got into the Masters of Public Administration program at BYU and continued to work full time as a police officer. It was a killer. I wouldn't recommend that to anybody. I'd start school at 8:00 in the morning and have to be at the department by 2:30 to start shift. It was midnight by the time I got home, and I'd have schoolwork to do. It just didn't let up. By the end of the first year I'd wake up in the morning not knowing what day it was. I'd have to look at the calendar to figure where I had to be and when I had to be there. It was terrible.

I finished the master's degree, still with my eye on being a police chief, but I was also open to other things. I applied to the FBI and went through the testing process and did well. But they weren't hiring at that point.

Then about six months after I graduated, a job opened up—police chief in a little town called Delta, Utah. I applied and was hired. I was about 26—I think I was the youngest police chief in the state.

About 18 months into the job, I attended an FBI profiling school—one of the "road school" sessions they put on, a three-day profiling session in Salt Lake City.

I just had one of those *ah-ha* experiences. "This is for me. This is what I'm supposed to be doing." And that became the focus.

Within a few months, I got a call from the Bureau. They were hiring Special Agents now and they were wondering if I was still interested. April 1985, they offered me a position and I went for it.

While I was at the Academy, John Douglas gave a profiling class and, again, I knew this was what I was supposed to be doing. I was, of course, very impressed with him and just became even more convinced I wanted to become a profiler.

So I went on and graduated the Academy and was sent to the Seattle Field Office. Then I was in a two-man resident agency in Olympia, Washington. It covered five counties and four Indian reservations—just a huge territory.

I started teaching interrogation courses because I realized that I had to set myself apart if I wanted to become a serious contender for that specialized profiling unit. I was teaching all over the State of Washington for the Police Academy. I'd been through the Bureau's GPI, or the General Police Instructor course, which certified me to teach. I put that interviewing course together myself, and worked with another agent, who'd been an attorney and a police officer in New Orleans. Now he's assistant U.S. attorney back home in New Orleans.

So anyway, we're teaching this class. And the Bureau says, "Have you been back to this in-service on interrogation techniques?" No. "Well, we need to send you back there." Okay, great. I'm thinking this would be a great opportunity to meet John Douglas. And that's how things really start rolling. I go back there, make an appointment, tell him what my goals and ambitions are.

He outlined the things that would be necessary for me to become a candidate. One was to become a NCAVC coordinator—the National Center for the Analysis of Violent Crime. Each FBI division has a coordinator that functions as a liaison between the local police and the NCAVC in Quantico, and that's where they look first for profilers.

So recognizing that, I immediately went back to Washington and tried to make inroads. I had no luck, because there's only one coordinator in the Seattle division, and he was very, very protective of his position. Very frustrating for a young guy who's trying to climb. So I continue to teach and maintain contact back East.

Then one day I get this phone call from my supervisor, who knows what my interest is. And he says, "Guess who's coming to town?"

"Well, who?"

He says, "John Douglas. Would you be interested in picking him up at the airport?"

Yeah, I'll pick him up. I'll polish his shoes, carry his bag, whatever he needs.

So I picked John up at the airport, and talked to him about my ambitions. He said, "Look it, guy, you've got to be with the Bureau at least five years before we can give you serious consideration."

I said, "Five years, John? I've been in the Bureau just coming up on three. I've still got to wait another couple of years?"

"Yeah, sorry. Those are the rules."

After that, I maintained contact with him. He'll probably tell you I called him every week, just to make sure he'd remember who I was. And I just kept plugging away. Eventually, we got a new ASAC, Assistant Special Agent in Charge, in that division. And I went to visit with him and told him about my situation, and he opened the doors up. I became the NCAVC coordinator, continued to teach interview interrogation, and kept working at the resident agency, which was fascinating. I mean, in a small RA like that, you have an opportunity to work every case that comes into your area.

Pretty soon, I came up for a transfer, and ended up going to the Resident Agency in Santa Ana. They've got about 67 agents there—huge for an RA.

I realized I still had to maintain this coordinator spot to get where I wanted to be. So I proposed to create a coordinator spot out of the Santa Ana resident agency to service Orange County. And it sold. I functioned in that capacity for almost exactly a year and then I got a phone call from Quantico. John had just been promoted to unit chief, which left a profiler's position open. I then became a candidate for that spot, and almost exactly five years after that first profiling seminar, I headed back to Quantico.

That was probably the best professional experience of my life. John's not intimidated or jealous of anybody else's talents at all. He tried to amplify the talents of anybody who wanted to make a difference and achieve his own goals and ambitions. So he would facilitate opportunities for people. Three weeks into my training, he asked me to write a chapter on interrogation for the *Crime Classification Manual*. I felt like I was really being recognized for some of my accomplishments.

So I had a year of training, then about three years as a profiler, and acting as John's primary relief supervisor. After he retired, I was acting unit chief, also the Violent Criminal Apprehension Program manager, still profiling, and also teaching a couple of classes for the National Academy. It was way, way too much.

During that time, the Oklahoma bombing occurs, and we're asked to conduct the assessment profile on that. It was quite an experience—a lot of intensity, and a lot of pressure.

Then I got a phone call from the Provo police chief. He was retiring and wanted to know if I'd be interested in coming back there. This was the chief who hired me as a cadet, my original role model.

I applied for the job and within three weeks, I made the jump—moved back in August 1995.

In terms of the case load, it's been kind of a rest, but I do a lot of teaching and consulting on the side. It keeps the interest level and involvement up. My priority at this point is to teach as much as I possibly can because the tools belong in the hands of local law enforcement. They're the ones who need the tools and use them. Doing that brings a lot of satisfaction.

PHIL GRIVAS

Phil is the kind of guy you always hope is going to run any organization. He's smart, he's hard-working, and most important, he never forgets what it was like to be one of the troops. Phil's now enjoying a well-deserved life of leisure with his wife.

I was born and raised in New York City. I attended local schools in Manhattan. And then at the age of 14, we moved to Queens, and I attended a local high school there. I graduated in January of 1963. And then from '63 to '64, I worked in a large office in Manhattan, in the mail room. In 1964, I joined the United States Army. I served there for two years. I was discharged in the March of 1966. And then I was appointed to the New York City Police Department on August 1, 1966.

I'd planned on becoming a police officer ever since I was a very, very young fellow. I grew up without a father. My parents were divorced, and for a great deal of time it was just me, my mother, and my sister.

All through my childhood, the policeman on the corner, the neighborhood beat cop, always represented a kind of role model for me. A strong male figure. Everybody in the neighborhood always had a great deal of respect for him. So that's what I wanted to do when I grew up.

I was very methodical about it. In those days policemen were drafted just like anybody else was. So I knew the smart thing would be to get my military obligation out of the way before I went into the Police Academy. That's why I joined the Army.

Then while I was in the Army, I studied for the police exam and flew home to take it, about six months before I was discharged. I passed it, and so when I came out of the service, I just continued along with the rest of the process—medical tests, physical tests, psychological exams, things of that nature.

I'd researched exactly what the requirements were. And I made sure that I had everything that was required.

At that point the FBI was something totally alien to me. I first really became exposed to the Bureau after I'd been with the police force about two years.

One day I was on patrol, and a woman came running out of an apartment building and said, "Somebody's breaking into the mailboxes."

So I said, "Okay, stay outside." I walked in with my partner, and sure enough, there was a junkie, trying to pry open the mailbox, to get Social Security checks, whatever. We grabbed him and brought him back to the station house.

Breaking into a mailbox, that's a federal offense. The Postal Inspector came, took the prisoner. I gave the Inspector a statement. Then I was subpoenaed to federal court, to testify against this man.

While I was in court, and waiting to be called, I struck up a conversation with the man sitting next to me, who happened to be an FBI agent. I don't know his name. I don't even remember what he looked like. But we talked for about a half hour. And I asked him a lot of questions about the FBI. And I was just so impressed by his answers, how he presented himself, how he presented the Bureau. I was really taken by it.

The next time I was downtown, I stopped off at the New York office of the FBI. And I'm at the reception desk, and I said, "My name's Philip Grivas, I'm a police officer, and I'd be interested in what the qualifications are to be an agent."

"Oh, sure, just have a seat."

An agent came out to meet me, and the first thing he said was, "What is your degree in?"

And I said, "Degree? I don't have a degree."

The guy looked at me like I fell off a truck. And he says, "Well, look. You have to have a minimum four-year college degree before you can even be considered for a position with the FBI. And then you need a couple years of investigative experience, and this and that."

I said, "Okay, thank you very much."

I went home, and I spoke to my wife about it, and started getting geared up for this new goal.

The next month I signed up for classes at the John Jay College of Criminal Justice, and graduated in three-and-a-half years, still working full time as a policeman. At one point, I took fifty credits in one year—21 credits in one semester, eight over the summer, and 21 again in the fall. It just seemed like every week that went by, I just got more and more drawn to this idea, becoming an FBI agent.

My wife was very supportive, and so were my friends. They all said, "Well, Phil, this is what you wanna do, good luck." But there was no guar-

interview. Then there was the oral exam, the written exam, the back-ground check. But I just had to give it a shot.

My wife had been working at a bank, and the last year I was in school she got tired of it, and was kind of undecided where she wanted to go. So I said, "Well, why don't *you* apply for the Bureau? Maybe they'll have some administrative assignment there."

She said, "Well, why not?" She applied, and she was accepted. She became a clerical employee in the New York office.

Now, she was kind of cute. *More* than kind of. And she still is. So they put her at the reception desk. The Assistant Director in Charge of the New York office, Mr. Malone, had his office on the same floor. Every so often, he'd be in the reception area, waiting for the elevator or something, and he'd just engage her in conversation.

One day he noticed she had a little miniature version of my shield on her sweater. Malone recognized it, and said, "Whose policeman's badge is that?"

She said, "Oh, that's my husband's. He's a policeman up in the Bronx. He's going to school now. He's interested in applying to the Bureau."

So he says to her, "He is? Well, when he's ready to graduate, you let me know."

As far as I'm concerned, this was like winning the Lotto.

When I was a couple of weeks away from graduating, Malone stopped by her desk again, and said, "Well, how's your husband doing?"

"Oh, he's doing very well. He graduates in a couple weeks."

"Really? Did he get his application in?"

"Yes, he did."

"Okay. Have him see me Monday morning."

She comes home, and she tells me this. My heart almost stopped.

I call up one of my close friends, and we sat down. I said, "Look. This guy's gonna ask me questions. I wanna be prepared. I want you to throw questions at me, anything you can think of that he might ask me. I don't want to sit there—flat-footed, mouth open."

We took a long walk, for a couple of hours. And he would just shoot questions at me, quizzing me on everything from political science topics to my knowledge of current events. Law enforcement issues. Anything we could possibly think of that might come up.

And my friend says, "I've read that when they conclude an interview, they'll sometimes ask, 'Is there anything you'd like to say?' You should have something prepared for that."

So I went into the office, and I took the written examination that was issued at that time. And then I was escorted into Malone's office. Very prestigious-looking office. Huge desk, paneled walls. I was really taken by it. I was thinking, "Boy. I can't believe I got this far."

He asked me a bunch of questions about the police department, and this and that. And then he asked me, "Well, Philip. Is there anything you would like to say, before we conclude this interview?" And oh, I was really itching.

I looked at him, leaned forward, looked him in the eye, and said, "Sir, I really believe that if given the opportunity, I can make a positive contribution to the Bureau."

He leaned back, big smile. And then he said, "I believe you will, Philip. I believe you will."

I was sworn in on September 11th, 1972, and then I was transferred to St. Louis for my first office.

It was kind of a culture shock. A former New York City policeman—I had to tone myself down a little bit. Not that I was overbearing—never have been, I don't think. It's just that New York City, the Bronx, is a very different place from St. Louis, and the work of a policeman is very, very different from the work of an FBI agent.

When you're a cop, you're in uniform. Often you're patrolling in a high-

you've got your eyes going all over the place. You're very aware of your surroundings. Anything can happen at any time. And when you're out there in uniform, you're it. And all eyes are on you. You're expected to respond immediately. As an FBI agent, you're more like a detective. You go to the scene *after* the crime has been committed. There isn't the same type of tenseness and stress associated with the job.

So in St. Louis, that was when I first found out I had to pull back a little bit. Relax a little bit. Just take things a little bit slower. Learn the administrative requirements, as well as the practical investigator procedures. It just took a little time, like when you start out in any job. I did have a big leg up, having the experience that I did, dealing with certain elements and handling myself on the street. That was a plus, a *big* plus.

We started out working in applicant matters and general criminal matters. I found myself being very attracted to fugitive cases, and I ended up working mostly fugitives while I was there. I was just better suited to going after those kinds of people, rather than people who were committing white-collar crimes—bank fraud, embezzlement crimes, organized crime cases, loan sharking, things like that. Fugitives are individuals that commit felony violations, mostly violent crimes. They've been identified by the local authorities, and warrants have been issued, and they've fled the jurisdiction in order to avoid prosecution.

From the beginning, I've wanted to catch the bad guys. And these, to me, were the bad guys, and the people who were doing the most harm to people. I've always been more comfortable on the street, dealing with certain people, a certain element. There's the physicalness of it. When you're dealing with certain people, they respect strength. And they respect people that know how to act, and stand up.

I never did, nor will I ever, take anything away from the guys or the gals who handle surveillance work, or espionage work, or organized crime, or white-collar crime. Those crimes are out there and they need to be dealt with. But early on, I learned that I was drawn to the more active, more physical aspects of the job.

So I was in St. Louis for three and a half years. I was transferred back to New York in July of 1976. I stayed there for 20 years. Finished out my career there—I retired in 1996.

When I first got back, I was assigned to the the Weathermen Fugitive Squad. The Weathermen were responsible for a lot of violent, criminal behavior during the Vietnam War era. They had a hand in a bombing at the University of Wisconsin in Madison—the math building was bombed, and one person was killed.

So for a couple of months, I was on that squad, helping track some of these people who'd fled prosecution. And then I was assigned to the bank robbery squad. I worked the bank robberies for five years, and then transferred to the fugitive squad for about five or six years.

In 1987, I was promoted to supervisor, and I was made the special assistant to the Assistant Director in charge of the New York office. I remained in that capacity from 1987 to 1994. And then the last few years I was in the Bureau, I was the supervisor in charge of the Operations Center in the New York office.

I really enjoyed working fugitives and bank robberies. I got a great deal of professional and personal satisfaction out of that. But I think there's a natural progression in a lot of people's careers. You get to a particular point in time, you say, "You know what? I think it's time to do something else." That was when I was approached by the Assistant Director in charge of the office, who asked me if I'd be interested in coming up and working with him.

I'd never thought about it before, going up the administrative ladder. But gee, when you get an offer from the number-one guy in the office—I've got to be honest, it's very flattering. I mean, there are 1,100 agents in the office. To be asked to do something like that was something special to me.

That was a big change. You have more responsibilities as a supervisor. You don't just have your own cases—you have everybody, and their cases. And if you're the kind of individual who's conscientious about your

new supervisors do. First thing you learn is, you can't expect everybody to work at your standard. But there should be a minimum standard that you, as a supervisor, can be happy with.

I had other positions, too. I was the commanding officer of the SWAT team, and I was also the agent in charge of the hostage negotiation team. And for 17 years I was in charge of the security detail responsible for escorting the last five U.S. attorneys general whenever they were in New York, *and* the last three FBI Directors when they were in the city.

The first time I was asked to do it, I was in the bank robbery squad—William Webster had just become FBI Director at the time. The ADC called me in the office and said, "Phil, the Director is coming in tomorrow and I want you to pick him up and escort him and stay with him and make sure he gets in and out all right."

Well, I went home and I told my wife, "Honey, you're not gonna believe this. All these agents in New York and the boss asked *me*." And then it dawns on me—if anything happened to this guy, it'd be on my head. *Lots* of pressure. It's kind of a Catch-22 situation. If you do a good job, which takes a tremendous amount of work, you're always gonna be asked to do it again. If you do a lousy job, well, not only are you not gonna be asked again, but you could get fired. When I'd recruit people to work with me on the detail, I'd say, "Look. I was selected and I am selecting you. And this is completely voluntarily. These people, they're very high profile. They're very, very important. If anything ever happens to them, you can't imagine the pressure we're going to be placed under. So, let's do a good job. Let's be professional. Let's keep our heads up. But you'll go places. Accompanying these people, you'll do things and see things that you'll never have the opportunity to see or do without them."

Of course, handling both the AG and the Director, it got hectic sometimes. I'd be at home and get a call: "Phil, the Attorney General is coming in with an entourage and they're spending the weekend in New York. Handle everything."

I had to make hotel reservations, get guys lined up to handle the escort, contact the airports, go over their complete itinerary, send advance teams out. This is all on top of my normal responsibilities at work. Then the Director would come in the next week, and I'd get to do it all over again. That took an enormous toll over the years.

Sometimes what drove me nuts wasn't so much the possibility of a dedicated terrorist effort. If that were the case, not only would the AG or the Director be dead, but I'd be dead, too. But trying to prepare for and deal with the normal stuff that happens in New York City—that was what really got to me. The crazy cab driver, the guy running out of a store firing a gun. Any of the things that can happen on any day in a city of eight million people.

Still, it's a kick, in a way. "Wow! These people must think I know what the hell I'm doin'!" And I'm honored. But boy, it doesn't come without a price. A lot of sleepless nights. A lot of, "Did I do this? Did I check that right? Did we plan for that?" And we were the people they relied on for *everything*. "I forgot to pack my tux shirt. I need a shirt for my tuxedo." They come in and it's a crazy, wild town: "Phil, can we do that? Phil, can we do that?" And your planning goes out the window.

When you're doing this for a long period of time with people, you develop a rapport with them. I mean, they're still the Attorney General, the FBI Director, and you're still just Agent Phil Grivas. But when you see them for the twentieth time that year, it's "Hey, how's your son, Phil?"

And you become privy to a lot of information. I made it real clear to my guys and my gals that we would *never* repeat anything outside of our own circle. That was just one of the ground rules. You're around these people so much and you literally have to stand close to them all the time. You can't protect somebody from across the room. The trick was trying to stand close to these people without them noticing you or feeling you. So you're standing there with a little earpiece in your ear and people staring at you, eating hors d'oeuvres, drinking wine. And they're in tuxes and you're in a dark suit.

I was so grateful when I left and I looked back and said, "I can't believe it. Nothing happened. Seventeen years I did that and I never had

BRUCE KOENIG

One of the finest forensics experts I ever worked with was Bruce Koenig. Whenever we had any kind of audio problem, we knew that if anything could be done, Bruce and his people would do it. The strength of the Bureau's forensics, engineering, and other technical support departments makes a huge difference to law enforcement agencies across the country and around the world.

I'm probably not the typical FBI agent. I never thought about being in the Bureau; I never played G-man when I was a kid. What happened was, I got my undergraduate degrees in physics and math. While I was in school, I worked for the Bureau of Commercial Fisheries, feeding rats. Which, incidentally, counted toward my federal pension when I retired. Not that I'd planned it that way—it's just a job that came up.

I graduated during the Vietnam War era, and I served in the army. I went in under the officer candidate school but got in and said, "Well, I don't think this is going to be my direction, to be a military officer for life." So I didn't go to officer, just became an enlisted man. I actually ended up sitting in Fort Campbell, Kentucky, doing photography and being a clerk there. My wife always says they took a look at my physics degree, got as far as *"P-H"* and said, "Well, that must be photography."

When I was getting ready to leave the service, I started applying for jobs in the aerospace industry. Well, this was the late '60s, early '70s, when the space program was being cut back, and the aerospace industry just wasn't hiring. They were laying off guys with Ph.D.'s. Somebody I talked to said, "Oh yeah, the FBI's hiring. They want science degrees." Well, going to work for the FBI had never occurred to me. But if they were hiring, I figured why not. I applied and took a test and got in. This was in 1970.

I didn't come in thinking that would be my career. I thought I'd be in the FBI three years, aerospace would open up, and I'd go there. But once I got in, I changed my mind. I loved the job. I never thought about leaving until it was time for me to retire.

When I first started with the Bureau, I didn't plan to end up in forensics. I mean, it was in the back of my mind that I might be sent back to the lab. But once I got in the field, I really liked the field work. My first posting was in Atlanta, and then I went to Detroit.

I spent four years in the field, handling a lot of fugitive work. Selective Service violators—this was when the draft was in effect. And in Detroit, we handled extremist matters. The Ku Klux Klan, the violent faction of the Black Panther Party. We weren't interested in the groups' ideology, just the violent actions. I very much enjoyed my time out there—it was, get in the car and go out and do good things.

After about three years in the field, I was getting pressure to move up and become a supervisor there in Detroit. I realized I'd probably be behind a desk for the rest of my career, and I wasn't sure that's what I wanted to do. Then the engineering section, which was part of the FBI Laboratory at that time, offered me a supervisor's job in Washington, D.C. I thought about it and said, "Well, I think I'd rather go be a supervisor in Washington than be a supervisor in Detroit."

That was when I got into doing tape work and really enjoyed it. I started publishing papers in technical journals and really pushing the envelope of where we could go. And, lo and behold, I became the Bureau's tape expert. I didn't set out to do that; it's just that the work was so fascinating that I kept at it, kept exploring what could be done.

Early on, I worked on some tape, analyzing the Kennedy assassination. When John F. Kennedy was killed, I was in twelfth grade, so obviously I didn't investigate the assassination at the time. But in 1979, after I'd been working in the engineering section about four years, a group called the Stokes Committee released a report on the Kennedy assassination. They'd analyzed some audiotape of the event, and came out and said there's a 95 percent or greater chance that there was a second shooter from the grassy knoll.

The Department of Justice asked the FBI to look at it, and the project was assigned to me. I went through what the Stokes Committee had done and wrote up my report, which was published by the Department of Justice. Basically, I couldn't say whether they were right or wrong, but that there was no scientific support for their conclusion based on their own studies.

And then the project went over to the National Academy of Sciences, and I worked with them. They were gracious enough to actually mention my name in their report, which rarely happens.

The Stokes Committee had isolated some sounds on the tape and identified these as gunshots from a second shooter. We were able to show conclusively that the information area they were looking at actually occurred well after the shooting. The President's limousine was already out of Dealy Plaza on the way to the hospital. Whatever they were pointing out as these other shots had to be something else; the time just didn't add up.

I noticed that the *Washington Post* put the original story about the second shooter on the front page. But when the National Academy report came out, it was on the fifth page back. News showing a story was wrong doesn't sell papers. Every paper in the country did the same thing. I still run into people who talk about that second-shooter report; they never heard that it's been proved wrong.

There was one interesting sidelight to that case. Earlier, I'd worked on a shooting down in Greensboro, North Carolina involving the Ku Klux Klan and the Socialist Workers Party. There'd been a march, and the two groups were across the street from one another. Shooting broke out, and several of the Socialist Workers group were injured, five or six killed. The Klan was accused of opening fire on the SWP, who said that they hadn't fired back.

I did a big gunshot analysis, and I was able to show that both sides fired approximately the same amount of shots. I was able to take the echoes off the buildings and actually pinpoint, usually within two or three feet, where each shot came from. If you look at the videos you rarely see anyone firing. Someone in one group would shoot, the cameras would swing over to that side of the street, and they'd stop firing. And then the other side would fire, so the cameras would swing back. You only saw a handful of people actually firing. But based on analysis of the audio, often you could match up the source of a gunshot and the shooter, based on the person's position in the crowd.

Anyway, when I was working on the Kennedy case, I noticed that one of the waveforms from that audio looked exactly like one of the waveforms from the Greensboro case. We put it in our report just to show that by itself, this kind of waveform analysis isn't very conclusive.

When I retired, I was the project manager of the audio-videotape division, which is fairly high up. But I was pretty good at getting the paperwork out of the way, so I was keeping the administrative stuff down to 30 or 40 percent of my time.

The rest I spent in the lab. I like doing things. Hands on. And when you're in management, if you try to push too hard, you can actually mess everything up. And so I avoided that step. If I hadn't retired, they probably would have made me a unit chief. I don't think there had been much doubt about that. So instead I retired and opened up a consulting business. I still spend two or three days a week working at the Bureau. I still do most of their complex audio cases.

There's such a range of what you can do with tape. First, you can enhance it, make it more understandable. That's probably the easiest exam in the tape group, and the biggest bargain. When I left, I'd guess that was about 60 or 70 percent of the work. Another big area is voice comparisons. It's not conclusive as a means of identification, but it's a systematic way of comparing voices.

I spent most of my career and I still spend most of my time now doing authentication: Determining whether a tape has been altered or not, whether it's original or not; and signal analysis. That's by far the biggest amount of work I do now. It's a complex area; it usually takes about five to ten years work in the field to start really being comfortable with it.

The harder parts are things like gunshot analysis—how many shots were fired, or whether they are gunshots.

I remember we worked on one case where a guy got hit over the head with a baseball bat. The sound of the impact was recorded on a 911 call, and a bat was found on the scene. We had to determine, by the sound, whether that bat could have been the weapon. And the bat matched.

That's one of the things I love about this work. You never know what's coming up next.

JIM McFALL

Jim's forgotten more than I ever knew about firearms and weaponry. I first got to know him when we were both teaching at the National Academy, and I've always had a tremendous amount of respect for him. He's now the Executive Director of the Society of Former Special Agents.

My interest in the FBI came about in 1964 when I'd returned from service in the navy. I'd gone back to my old company and was working at my old job. I was generally happy doing what I was doing but I was also a little bit bored. I was a licensee engineer for an electronics manufacturing company in Philadelphia, and I handled the overseas licensees. It was a good job, a great company, a great boss, but something was missing. I'd been a naval intelligence officer during the Cuban Missile Crisis, and civilian life didn't have the same flavor as it did when I was in the navy.

So I started looking around, casually, and one of my friends mentioned that the FBI was hiring. I wasn't a lawyer or an accountant, but I thought I'd make an inquiry anyway. I just walked into the Philadelphia office of the FBI and was introduced to an agent. I gave him my background and we had a great conversation. We hit it off right away. He said that I was eligible to apply under the modified program, which I did.

I was accepted, and entered the new agent class that started training on January 25, 1965.

My first posting was Atlanta, Georgia. Reported there on May 1, 1965. For the most part new agents did background investigations on applicants, a process that we'd just been through ourselves, and we handled "car cases"—interstate transport of motor vehicles. We learned how to inspect and search recovered stolen vehicles for evidentiary material, and conduct an investigation to find the person who transported the car. And then gradually we'd be assigned more and more complicated cases.

In July of 1965, there was a great deal of civil rights activity in Georgia and in all the Southern states. I was sent on a series of special assignments to investigate violations of the federal civil rights law. Some of those assignments would last two or three days, or they might last two weeks, until the case was fleshed out. Then I'd go back to Atlanta.

Generally there'd be a team of FBI agents and whenever possible we'd cooperate with the local officers. In some areas—not all, but some—we encountered great hostility. On more than one occasion, I've gone nose-to-nose with deputies and sheriffs and ranking officers in police departments and told them flat out that they were dangerously close to obstruction of justice and interfering with a federal officer in the performance of his duty. Not a threat—a statement of law, a statement of fact.

If they persisted in hindering our investigation they could face federal charges. For the most part they'd back off, and we'd go on with our jobs.

You have to appreciate the time and the location. We're talking about the mid-'60s, the deep South, generally the most rural parts. There were police officers and deputy sheriffs who were as upset as we were about some of the violations that were being committed. But these officers in these local areas knew these people committing the violations. They had a certain conflict, as it were, in their role as a law enforcement officer, and their role as a friend, a neighbor, a relative.

Being from the North, I got my share of comments. One gentleman made a lot of disparaging remarks about the FBI and "damn Yankees." He finally said to me, "If you think it's so bad down here, why'd you ___

investigate violations of federal law. And in some places, things were so bad I saw violations occur right in front of me.

I saw one young fellow in a town called Newton, Georgia. He was leading a group down a sidewalk around the Baker County courthouse. There were maybe 15 people in the group, and this young fellow, about 19 or 20 years of age, this young fellow was carrying a sign calling for equal rights and the right to register to vote. Of course there was a crowd of locals watching. One of them broke out of the group across the street and ran over and hit this kid right in the back of the head with a maul handle. This is like an ax handle, only round. A real weapon, a club. The kid did a flip in the air, actually did a flip, and landed flat on his back. Just lay there. I was sure he was dead. Then the guy who hit him turned around and ran away.

In a situation like that, you're torn between two things. One, render aid to the victim, and two, catch the guy who did it. I rendered aid to the victim first. Then we got some help and went looking for the guy who hit him. Well, he lost himself in the crowd. All the rednecks would stand shoulder to shoulder so you couldn't get through. They wouldn't grab you—they knew better than that—but they'd just keep stepping in front of you.

23

It took us a few days, but we identified the assailant. We just kept talking to people, going back and asking questions over and over again. You can't let go and you can't ignore it. If you ignore it, they'll do it again.

I went all over Georgia on civil rights cases. It culminated in July 1965, when I was assigned to a Bureau Special. That means a team of agents on a particularly sensitive assignment, under the supervision of an Inspector from the Bureau headquarters. I ended up on a roving team: We went to Natchez, Mississippi, and worked on Klan cases there, especially the Silver Dollar group. These were dedicated Klansmen with a propensity for violence. Then the team moved over into Louisiana, working with resident agencies under the New Orleans Field Office to assist them in intensifying the investigation of the Klan in those areas.

I was in the Resident Agency from April 1, 1967 to April 1, 1971, and then I was in the New Orleans Field Office, assigned to various squads. I became the bank robbery fugitive coordinator, then supervisor of the bank robbery squad, then supervisor of the white-collar crime squad and the political corruption squad.

With the fugitive investigations, we used to feel that New Orleans was a prime location to find fugitives because it's a playground. The fugitives, especially in the wintertime, would come South and go to New Orleans to play and we'd find them. They had the Jefferson Casino in Jefferson Parish, and they had gambling over in Algiers, which is a section of New Orleans. It was a party town for the bad guys.

Later on, when I was in the white-collar crime–political corruption squad, we had a saying that Louisiana is the only state in the union where the citizens do not tolerate bad government—they *demand* it. There was one old politician there, years ago, O.K. Allen. His claim to fame is he built a bridge to nowhere—from nowhere, to nowhere. It's called the Sunshine Bridge, and when it was built there was no road leading to it, no road leading away from it. But O.K. Allen wanted a big bridge built in that parish and they built it. Later on they did build roads to it, but for years it just stood there.

In 1979 I was transferred to the FBI Academy as a staff instructor, and I remained there until I retired. I taught a wide gamut of students. New agents, of course, and in-service agents who came back. I taught police officers who were attending the FBI National Academy, which is a graduate school for police officers. Foreign police officers would also send visitors in.

After I retired, I went back to the Bureau to do a lecture for police officials in Kazakstan. I had a very good time working with them, and was offered a job at their training academy in Almonte, Kazakstan. The guy who offered me the job is the deputy chief of their police department—it's called the PMD, I think. I forget what the initials stand for. I have still have the guy's business card, but it's in Cyrillic. Anyway, I said I would think about it, then I talked to another guy on the staff who had been to

That was one of the things I truly enjoyed about the Academy—I had a wide variety of people to talk to, to work with. I was in the firearms training unit; I'm an expert firearms instructor, and for several years I was the Bureau's expert on less-than-lethal weapons and chemical agents. As a matter of fact, I introduced oleoresin capsaicin, or pepper spray, to the Bureau. I got it from a company in Florida who sent me samples and said "This stuff is better than sliced bread and vanilla ice cream. Try it out." I tried it out and, man, it'll knock your socks off.

All those years on the fugitive and bank robbery squads, all the armed-and-dangerous apprehensions I've been involved in, I was never shot, never hit. *That* happened at the Academy. I was teaching on the range and got hit by a ricocheting round. That was three days before I retired. A round came off a steel target, hit me right in the face, sliced through my lip and lodged in my upper gum. I had to go to the hospital and have it dug out. At my retirement party I had a great big swollen lip and a black eye from the impact.

The Bureau really puts a focus on training. What you do in training is what you'll do on the street. If you hesitate when you should react, you're going to get hurt. You might get killed. You might get other people killed.

I've been away from the Academy for several years now, but I know they're constantly upgrading the training they offer so it correctly reflects the current laws, the current social situations. The Academy really makes an effort to put the agents through scenarios that are essentially the same as what they'll face in real life.

Of course, that's not always possible. Laws change, society changes. And no matter how hard you try, training isn't going to be exactly like real life. I remember I was teaching one new agents' class and I told a war story to make a point. One of the trainees took exception to the technique I employed in the story. That trainee wrote a letter of complaint to the Assistant Director of the Training Division. I got called in and was asked to explain. I said, "What do you mean, explain?"

"Well, you told these agents that you did thus and so, blah blah blah."

I said, "There's no problem with that, is there?"

"Yeah, there's a problem."

"Well, I don't know what it could be; I didn't lie."

The guy said, "You *did* that?"

"Yeah, I did."

"You can't do that!"

I just said, "You can't do it *now*. But at the time I did it, it wasn't illegal. And I made that clear to the class—the difference between the situation then and the situation now."

I don't want to go into detail—let's just say it was an aggressive way of handling a situation. What I did was perfectly within the law. People who have never been there and never handled such a situation might find it surprising, they might even find it alarming, but that's the reality of it. You've got to be prepared to handle the situation—within legal limits, but sometimes forcefully.

Sometimes I wonder if that trainee ever reached a moment in his career and thought, "*Now* I see McFall's point."

BOB McGONIGEL

Bob was my very first partner out of the Academy. There we were, on the streets of Detroit, looking at each other and saying, "What the hell are we supposed to do now?" Well, we figured it out. Bob was a terrific partner—focused and no-nonsense when that's what the job called for, but a guy with a great sense of humor, too. He stayed on the streets all of his career, doing some really top-level organized crime work. Agents like Bob are the backbone of the Bureau. He and his wife are now living in Oregon, a place that Bob assures me has the best weather in the country—he did the research on it.

I'm a native of northern New Jersey, and while I was in high school, I

ity, attend school, and graduate. If the FBI felt you were qualified, they might hire you as an agent.

I wasn't really completely set on becoming an agent at that point, but I knew I had to pay my own way through college, and that seemed like a pretty good way to do it. So I went to work for the Bureau in the Newark Field Office on July 16, 1962. While I worked there, I went to Rutgers and got a degree in history. I felt that was a good preparation for law school, which was what I still had in mind as an option. There was no guarantee I'd be hired as an Agent, and being an attorney would be a good fallback. More profitable, too.

But having worked in that law office, being a lawyer looked like a lovely career, but rather mundane and boring. The FBI didn't seem like that at all—no two days would be the same. And I was right. I was really able to observe what the agents did. It got to the point where becoming an Agent interested me so much, I forgot all about the pursuit of the law degree.

Those first years at the FBI, I was a combination security guard, teletype operator, radio dispatcher, file clerk, and complaint taker from the public. I got to see it from all different angles, how everything worked.

That was a great education, a great opportunity. And there were a lot of young men and women who worked there while they went to college. It wasn't an official program, there was nothing laid out. And above all, there was no guarantee that you would become an agent. As a matter of fact, at certain field offices around the country, being a clerk lessened your opportunities to be an agent. The Special Agent in Charge at Newark the whole time I was a clerk didn't like people going that route.

But I made it anyway. I was sworn in as a Special Agent on September 25, 1971. My first posting was Detroit, Michigan. In training school, I'd guessed that I'd be assigned there. We had a pool based on where we all thought we'd be sent, and I won the pool. I just had a feeling.

Detroit was a good town to learn the business of law enforcement. I was rather a liberal in college. Naive, as most young people are about the world. When you're in law enforcement, you're out there trying to do a good job, trying to right the wrongs. You think of yourself as being on the side of right, so of course people are going to help you out. Then you go out in the field and realize that no, people aren't necessarily going to cooperate with you. Lots of doors slammed in your face, calls not returned. Kind of shocking. But you have to adjust quickly if you're going to survive.

You develop persistence, get an insight for human behavior. And you do it fast. At the time I was there, the Detroit office had an awful lot of brand-new agents, and not many seasoned agents to teach you the ropes. John and I—many, many times we would go out into the field and discuss what we were going to do before we actually did it. "All right, how does this sound? Okay, and then you'll do that, okay?" We'd pretty much proceed on a lot of common sense, and a little bit of the manual of rules and regulations. All our cases were reviewed by a supervisor. But we planned our own day-to-day activities.

When John and I first got to Detroit, there was a very large raid direct-ed at members of organized crime, bookies and betting and so forth. But at that point, I didn't do much with organized crime. Like most young agents just starting out, I worked pretty much general criminal cases:

bank robberies, fugitives, and thefts. Interstate shipment of stolen goods, which were largely tractor-trailers, and things like that. Vietnam was still going on, so we handled deserters and draft dodgers. That actually provided us with an excellent opportunity to do the basic things that law enforcers do. You just had the warrant, and you went out and got the body. We got to make a lot of arrests. Lots of hands-on experience, going out and doing it, doing the investigation, doing the footwork.

I was in Detroit for a little bit over a year. For my good work, I was rewarded with a transfer to Cleveland, Ohio. Cleveland was a lot like Detroit, only a little smaller.

I was in Cleveland for about two years, until February of 1974. Then I got a transfer to New York City. No one wanted to go to New York, but I'd

My tour in New York began the day that Patty Hearst was kidnapped. I spent a little over three years there, then I requested a transfer to Newark, New Jersey. I got that one, too. The Bureau's transfer policy was loosening up, and it was easier to move around. Particularly if you asked to go to what the pool of agents considered to be an undesirable place. And Newark's considered an undesirable place by a lot of people. The majority of people. Can't imagine why.

So I moved on to Newark, New Jersey and worked there until January of 1981, when I went to Atlantic City. In October 1983, I went back to Newark. I'd been stricken with colon and bladder cancer, and I wanted to be nearer the hospitals in New York City. Then in May 1989, I went back to New York, and finished out my career there.

That's sort of the thumbnail sketch of my career. All along, I traveled to other divisions to work on particular cases, for a month, two months, six months at a time. I went to St. Louis on a terrorist case for a couple of months. I went to Miami on an organized crime case for a couple months; Buffalo on another organized crime case.

Early on, I started developing a lot of experience on organized crime cases. Growing up in Newark, there were many organized crime figures in my neighborhood. And, of course, my father was a policeman, so organized crime was something familiar from a very early age.

I'd go in, help set up surveillance of suspects, interview suspects, help analyze the material, determine promising suspects, promising leads. I enjoyed that organized crime traveling work, and I did a lot of it, but I'm really a jack-of-all-trades. If you name a violation of law, somewhere or other in my career, I've worked on it. And that's exactly what I wanted. When I was a clerical employee, I always was frustrated by the fact that I wasn't out of the office doing these things. I was reading about it. I was hearing about it. But I wasn't doing it. And that's why I never really was interested in advancing to the supervisory level in the FBI. Because I didn't want to read about it, and I didn't want to hear about it. I had already done that for enough years!

One of the worst cases I worked on was a bombing at LaGuardia Airport, in the '70s. I'd certainly seen corpses before, but that was the first time I'd seen such devastation. The smell of death hanging in the air.

I was home at the time. It was about 7:00 at night. I was in graduate school back then, and I was working on a term paper. I get a phone call, and it's the office. There's been a bombing at LaGuardia, several people killed. There'd been an agent injured. He was an out-of-towner, coming into the New York office, and he just happened to be walking by the site.

I wasn't a bomb expert, but I was on a squad that had investigated several bombings and bomb scares in the city. At that stage, I was just helping at the crime scene. Sifting through the rubble, gathering evidence.

I have to say, I was very impressed with the New York City Police Bomb Squad. A fine bunch of professionals. I was really impressed with their skill. I also worked with their arson-explosion squad on the subsequent investigation. It was a great experience for me. You always hear about rivalries between different agencies and departments. That's true, there are some petty jealousies, but when a major case occurs, the line people really come together because their only goal is solving the case.

As it turns out, I don't think that bombing was ever solved. Well, the guys investigating it had a pretty good idea who was responsible, but there wasn't ever enough evidence to prosecute. Which is very frustrating. In some cases you get closure, even if you're wondering if you have the whole truth. When you're picking up some guy's fingers out of the bomb rubble, you want to at least get some closure.

JIM O'CONNOR

Jim was a member of the team who designed the training programs at the FBI Academy. He's a sharp guy, determined to keep the Bureau at the cutting edge of investigations. He was one of the early supporters of profiling,

the Marine Corps. But then I got an assistantship and went in for my master's degree in English, and I decided to go into college teaching. I took a job at what's now Gannon University—it was Gannon College then—in Erie, Pennsylvania. I taught there for three years, and decided I needed to go back for my doctorate. I started teaching part time at Hunter College, part of the City University of New York, and working on my doctorate in English at the same time.

While I was there, I started to realize that academic politics was not going to be my forte. I had met some people when I was teaching in Gannon, one individual in particular, who had gone into the FBI and said it was a great career, I'd find it interesting, and so forth. One day I was at Hunter and finished teaching a class and was really thinking about a career change. I just walked over to the FBI office over on 69th Street and asked for an application. I filled it out and then after I put it in, I decided to just go head and make a career change. I took a job with Merrill Lynch Pierce Fenner and Smith as an executive recruiter. I think I was with them about four months when the FBI called and wanted me to start going through the exams and interviews and so forth. That following June, June of 1965, I was sworn in as a new agent.

My first office was Indianapolis, Indiana. I did fugitive work, some applicant work, primarily organized crime and vice. We handled a few white-slavery cases (white slavery is the transporting of women over state lines for immoral purposes) and gambling cases there. I was in Indianapolis a little over a year, then I got transferred to Charlotte, North Carolina.

In Charlotte, I was on the road mostly. This was during the civil rights days—I worked a lot of Klan matters, school desegregation matters. Then I was transferred to the resident agency in Durham, North Carolina. There were four of us there, handling five counties. We did all the criminal security, racial matters, everything in those five counties. It was quite an eye-opening experience.

In 1968, I was transferred back to Quantico. There were eight of us selected for the Planning and Research Unit to plan the new FBI Academy, which opened in 1972. We were chosen primarily for the variety of backgrounds: firearms, defensive tactics, arrest techniques, sociology, forensics, accounting, law. I was called because of my experience in college teaching, and my area was basically communication research.

One of the first things we did was find a university for the National Academy Program to affiliate with. We ended up with the University of Virginia. That means every class at the National Academy qualifies for academic credit, some undergraduate, some graduate.

Our primary focus was training for police. All during the time we were planning, we were also teaching police community relations all over the country. And most of us were sent back to graduate school, too. So we weren't just sitting there.

In 1972 I was transferred to the Academy as a Supervisory Special Agent. I taught the education and communication arts unit: interviewing, interrogation, education. In 1974, I finished my Ph.D. at Catholic University. The next year, 1975, I was sent to the Police Staff College in Bramshill, England. This was when the FBI was really beginning to push the international aspect, and I was the first FBI representative sent to that course.

Essentially, Bramshill is the equivalent of the FBI Academy. It's where they select and train their future chief constables through England and Wales. There were 24 of us in that four-month course: 16 from the United Kingdom, and eight from the rest of the world. We had Egyptians, Danes, a Singaporean, an Australian, a guy from Trinidad. Two Americans: a captain from the NYPD, and myself. This was an executive-development type class, so we talked abut administration, managing major cases, and that kind of thing. Not specific investigative techniques, as much as running a department. You were dealing with people who were expected to move up.

It was interesting. As they say, England and the United States are two nations separated by a common language. And the policing system there is significantly different from ours. But of course there were certain things

Canadian police college.

After Bramshill, I went back to the Academy for a year, and then got transferred to the Inspections staff, as an Inspectors Aide. I spent roughly a year in 1976, '77, going around the country, inspecting FBI field offices. What we're looking for is effectiveness, efficiency, and economy of operation. Compliance with the attorney general's guidelines and the federal laws. You look at the entire investigation and administrative operation of a field office.

When I first joined the Bureau, these were surprise inspections. You didn't know these guys were coming, and all of sudden they arrived. When I was an inspector's aide, there was no surprise about it. They had all kinds of interrogatories that they had to prepare for us, before we arrived. Profiles, caseloads, priorities, statistical data. What was the overall budget, and how was it spent.

So we'd fly in for an inspection, and they would meet us at the airport. And then we'd go through the two most polite lies in the Bureau. The guys from the Field Office would say, "We're happy to have you here," and we'd say, "We're here to help you."

And then I got transferred back to the Academy. I was a section chief in charge of academic affairs, which is where I stayed until I retired, in 1989.

Since then, I've been head of the criminal justice program at Northern Virginia Community College. For three years, Northern Virginia shared me with George Mason University, and I was the head of the program there.

I still go back to the Academy, as a student. I try to stay current with what's going on. You can't ever decide you've learned all you're going to learn; you've got to keep an open mind to what's happening. Nothing stays the same for long. Not even the law. Every term the Supreme Court comes down with new decisions, and you better be up on those decisions and know what they mean in terms of the rules and procedures for law enforcement.

I think we're seeing more and more breakthroughs in other areas, too. Behavioral sciences, forensic sciences. It's almost staggering once you start thinking about it: DNA analysis, all the things that are being done today that couldn't be done just a few years ago. You've just got to keep up, if you're going to do any good at all.

DOUG RHOADS

Doug was a fine agent, someone I wish I'd had a chance to work with directly. Doug designed the FBI's recruiting program. I knew him by reputation, and I'd run into him at the Academy. And every once in a while, when I was watching a college football game on TV, they'd show one of the refs and I'd say, "I'll be damned—that's Doug Rhoads!" Doug's been an NCAA referee for over 20 years. Since retiring from the Bureau in 1994, Doug's worked as chief for a county sheriff's office in Virginia.

I grew up in Miami, Florida, attended public high school there. At that time Miami was more of a sleepy southern town than the big, international, cosmopolitan area it is now. I was born in 1944, so I'm talking about 1950, '51, '52. I always was interested in law enforcement, and we had a neighbor who worked for the FBI. He had the whole white shirt, button-down collar, snap-brim hat look, and I was impressed. Then when I was in eighth or ninth grade, we went up to D.C. and took the tour of the FBI headquarters. That was when I made my mind up that if I was going to be in law enforcement, I want to be on a national level. I think that was really where it started.

I went on to undergraduate school at the University of Florida, in Gainesville. In those days there was a perception, mostly accurate, that the Bureau recruited only lawyers and accountants. They hired others but the recruitment effort seemed to be directed at lawyers and accountants. I graduated in 1966, during the Vietnam era. I'd taken an ROTC commission but got a deferment to go to law school. Of course, the only rea-

Then I decided, "No, I'll take my commission, get that out of the way." So I went into the military, went to Vietnam. I got out in 1969, as a captain, and re-enrolled in law school. My only real interest in law school was to get into the FBI. It was just a means to an end. And even to this day, ten or 12, maybe 15 percent of the new agents have law degrees.

But pretty soon I realized that the FBI had expanded their modified entry program—meaning modified from law and accounting. Now, they'd accept three years' work experience in a field the Bureau was interested in. Well, I had three years as an officer in the military, so I applied through the Miami Field Office, and joined the Bureau in October 1969.

That was really a heavy hiring period. The Bureau's jurisdiction was expanding: there was the Safe Streets and Crime Control Act in 1968, the Omnibus Crime Control Act in 1970, and the Bureau needed people on the streets. The Bureau probably hired 2,000 new agents from 1970 to 1972. All that growth, there was a new agent class every two weeks, 52 agents each class. It was almost an assembly line.

But to be honest, given the times, given the rapid growth, given all that was there, the Bureau did like always: They rallied and did a good job. Got people through and got 'em out. When you graduated, they pretty much just gave you six bullets and said, "Get out of town, and don't get into trouble before you get where you're going."

I remember tearing open the envelope and reading "Dallas, Texas." I'm thinking, "Man, I'm from Miami, I've been to Vietnam, I'm here in Washington, I've been around a little, traveled some, but I've never been to Texas in my life." I figured at least I'd see a new place. I was married then—no children—so my wife and I headed off to Dallas. It was the best thing that ever happened to me.

I was placed on a fugitive squad with a total of eight agents; half of them were veterans, half of them were new guys like me. You got paired up and went out and learned how to do the job. I can tell you every arrest I was in on, every guy on that squad. I loved every minute of it. This was something I'd wanted since I was 14 years old. I was almost like a little kid. "I don't want everyone to know how much I really like it, so I'm going to bitch about things like everybody else—but I *really* like it."

After I'd been there about eight months there was an opening in a Resident Agency in Lubbock. What a place. You could roll a bowling ball from Lubbock and it'd go all the way to Minnesota. I remember snow with dirt in it. Twenty-five, 30 consecutive days with the temperature over a hundred degrees. But you know what? The way people in Texas treat law enforcement, you felt like a million bucks.

West Texas was a great place to be. The weather might have been a little weird, but the people were good. And because the RA was so small, I handled everything. They say, "These five counties are yours." You look at the map and you say, "Garza County? Where the hell is that?" So you drive down to Garza County and you walk in and say "Agent Rhoads, FBI, I'd like to meet the sheriff." You sit down and talk to them, you go to lunch with them, you share information with them, you develop a relationship with them, then you go down to Snyder and you do the same thing.

I was in Lubbock for just about 11 months. Then in March of '71, I tear the old envelope open and it says, "You're going to Richmond, Virginia." I get a phone call about five days later, it's the Special Agent in Charge in Richmond. He'd been the assistant to the Special Agent in charge in Dallas, so he knew me. He said, "Hey, I got a couple of RA openings, one in Charlottesville and the other in Roanoke. I want a guy who's experienced in an RA. What do you think about either of those two?" I said, "I'll take Charlottesville." That was it—very casual, almost conversational. So we packed up and drove 1,700 miles from Lubbock, Texas, to Charlottesville, Virginia.

Talk about a bird's nest on the ground. There were two veteran agents there, very distinctly different personalities. One was a former police officer from upstate New York, just an affable, friendly, hardworking, easygoing guy. The second one was an Irish Catholic from Boston, previous

He was telling me how to get to the office and he kept saying, "You go down Mockit Street." Well, I can't find this Mockit Street, so I finally say, "Is that 'M-o-c-k-i-t?'" Well, no. He's saying *Market Street* with this thick Boston accent. I imagine he took some getting used to for those Virginians.

Both those guys were just great mentors. I don't think they even realized they were being mentors to me. It was like, "Hey, here's the third guy on the team." And we worked that way together, very informal, loosely structured. But when something had to be done—when the bank robbery happened, everybody went. When the major surveillance happened, everybody did it. When the big fugitive lead came in, everybody went.

That's where I really developed the love of the resident agency. I enjoyed working with all the different divisions of local law enforcement. You have to rely on the state and local police a lot more when there's only three of you and you're covering 12, 13 counties. I met some great folks, and just loved it. I would never have left, and didn't leave until I had to.

I remained in Charlottesville from 1971 to December 1983. I eventually became the senior RA there. The senior RA when I started retired and then we closed a small office over in Stanton and added it into Charlottesville's territory, so we were up to five agents.

In December of '83 I was transferred back to FBI Headquarters in Washington. William Webster was director then, and they'd taken a look at the staffing issues and decided they needed to diversify their work force, and set up a more systematic way of recruiting. That's where it started: "Hey, design a program for us." It was fun, it was challenging.

So 1983 to 1985 was the research phase, and 1985 to 1990 is when it really got going as a program. Then in 1990, there was an opening down here in Charlottesville for a senior resident agent. To take the job, I'd have to take a pay cut. I'd been a unit chief, and I'd go back to a street agent. It took me about 45 seconds to decide I wanted to do it. I wanted to go back to the street, back to working cases, back to being a part of a small Resident Agency.

So October 1, 1990, I finished up seven years of the executive management thing and now I'm back making drug arrests, working bank robberies, locking up fugitives. I got right back to it: Get your car, get your gun, get your badge, get your cases. It was the best decision I ever made in my life.

FRANK WATTS

I joined the Bureau just about the time Frank retired, so I never got the chance to work with him. I wish I had. Agents like Frank did some important, frontline work at a time when it wasn't easy to do.

I grew up in the little town of Wiggins, Mississippi. We had maybe a thousand in population. Only two celebrities ever came out of Wiggins—that's myself and Dizzy Dean, the Hall of Fame baseball player. Growing up, I never had any idea of becoming an FBI agent. Never even thought of it. In fact, I never even knew what an FBI agent was.

Shortly after I graduated from University of Mississippi, I was working as an office manager for a utility company, United Gas Corporation in Gulfport, Mississippi. Even though gambling was completely outlawed in the state of Mississippi, there was gambling going on. And they had what they called juice joints. These places had an electromagnetic device planted underneath craps tables, and the owners used that device to determine the roll of the dice. These machines were brought in from out of state, shipped in from Chicago. So there was an interstate angle there, and the FBI had full jurisdiction.

One morning, two FBI agents came in to my office and identified themselves. They said they'd like to have somebody help them, go and gamble at one of these juice joints to gather evidentiary information for the successful prosecution. They needed someone who was a local person and had no connection with law enforcement whatsoever. So they

promptly lost it all, because I didn't know a thing about gambling. But I went there for two or three nights, and I saw exactly what they were doing, how they were operating. I was able to give them the information they needed, and then testify during the trial. And it turned out to be a successful prosecution for them.

About 60 days later those same agents came by and thanked me for my help. And then they asked me, "Would you like to be an FBI agent?"

I said, "Well, I don't know anything about it. But that was fun, you know, what we did."

So I went to New Orleans and took a test, put in my application. And I was accepted. I went to Washington and was sworn in on May 12, 1952. After that, I was assigned to Albany, New York, which was a shock for a boy from Wiggins, Mississippi. One of Hoover's policies was to send a person completely outside of their environment for their first posting. That way, he could get all these errors and things out of the way, in a place where there were no friends, family, or any possible political influence. That first winter was rough, I have to say.

But I served there for two years, and then went to Syracuse, New York, just briefly before I was sent to New Haven, Connecticut. The FBI had a bit of a crisis there, because of the Soviet efforts to gain information regarding the nuclear subs at the Navy Yard there. There was quite a bit of Soviet activity there.

Another policy of Hoover's was that an agent did not specialize in one particular case. We had well over 100 different classifications—bank robbing, kidnapping, espionage—and any agent was expected to be able to handle any complaint that came through the door.

So I handled all kinds of cases, from the beginning to the end. But I think it's the way with most things: If you really like working on a particular thing, and really enjoy your work, naturally you do your best work. And I really liked working the espionage cases. Trying to identify KGB agents, trying to gather intelligence on them; it was most intriguing to me. So I ended up doing my best work in that area, and I began to get more and more espionage cases, and eventually became a supervisor of that squad.

We learned that, in order for a KGB agent to come to this country, to actively participate in gathering what they wanted, they had to have seven years of training. Seven full years. And that was from every angle. Number one, his cover story. Then the mechanics of espionage: how to operate drop boxes, how to obtain information, how to photograph documents, how to microdot them. That sort of thing. And also how to live under an assumed identity, maybe even as an American citizen. These were very intelligent, well-trained people. And getting to the truth in dealing with them was very difficult. But it was the most intriguing thing of all.

I continued to work in this area until 1964. At that point, I was sent back down South as part of the FBI's response to the civil rights problems there. The White Knights of the Ku Klux Klan were really spreading havoc throughout the south, and particularly in Mississippi.

I was proud to do that work. I was brought up in a traditional Southern home. Segregation was believed in, and if you even mentioned interracial marriage or anything like that, my dad would turn red in the face. But there was another side to him, too. He ran a service station, and that's where I worked after school all the time I was growing up. During the war, gasoline was rationed, and money was scarce and all. Time after time, a poor black farmer would come in who really needed gasoline and couldn't afford it, and my dad would give him some out of the ration for one of the businesses who wouldn't use all theirs. Or a family would need medicine but they didn't have money to pay for it. Dad would call across the street to the pharmacist and say, "Somebody's comin' over and he needs some medicine. Put that on my bill."

It was easy to see how hard a time the black families in that area had, how they were mistreated. Then, when I got into the FBI, I saw what was really taking place: not just denying them the right to register to vote, but killings and lynchings and beatings. It just wasn't in my heart to go along

retired. My wife and I moved up here to the Ozarks, where we can just enjoy ourselves. And to this day, I am proud of the work I did with the Bureau.

THE AUTHOR

Most of you probably know my story already from reading Mindhunter. *But for those of you who don't, here's the condensed version.*

I grew up in Hempstead, Long Island. I never had any idea I'd become an FBI Agent; I didn't even know how to spell FBI. My big ambition was to be a veterinarian. For three summers while I was in high school, I went up to Ithaca, New York, and worked for the Cornell Extension Service. So while my buddies were out playing in the sun at Jones Beach, I was shoveling cow manure.

When it came time to apply for college, I sent off my scores and my grades to Cornell, and they wrote back a very nice letter thanking me for my interest and suggesting that maybe Cornell wasn't the right place for me. They said I might be better off at another fine academic institution: Montana State University.

So I packed up and headed out west to Montana, where the men are men and the sheep are nervous. I spent a few semesters there, diligently working on my extracurricular activities. When I bombed out of MSU, I went home to Long Island for a while, then joined the Air Force.

While I was in the Air Force, I finally started getting my act together. I did some volunteer work with mentally disabled kids, and found that to be tremendously rewarding. I was stationed in New Mexico then, and decided I'd get a degree in education. I started taking classes at Eastern New Mexico University, fondly referred to by its students and alumni as Enema U.

I'd met an FBI agent at the gym we both went to, and shortly after I got my degree, he suggested I apply to the Bureau. I still had no burning interest in law enforcement, but this guy seemed to be doing okay. He was making a nice salary, while I was scraping by and living in a basement apartment that was more like a glorified Roach Motel. So I applied, and I got in.

Then, like all the other guys whose stories you've read, I fell in love with the work. After a few years in the Bureau, I ended up in the Behavioral Sciences unit, analyzing the "why" to develop ways of finding out the "who" behind the most brutal crimes. More and more, I kept thinking that we were missing something basic. We had all these ideas about criminal thinking, but they were really just speculation from the outside. I felt we needed to talk to the criminals themselves to get the real story. After all, they're the real experts.

Now, as Doug Rhoads said, this was a time when the first thing a new agent was told was "Don't screw up." That fear of embarrassing the Bureau sometimes translated into a fear of trying anything new, so I had a hard time getting anyone to listen to me.

By 1978, I was giving classes with the Bureau's "road school" for police officers around the country. One day, a colleague and I were on the road in California. We had some time on our hands and I said, "Let's see if there's anyone we can talk to near here." There was: serial killer Ed Kemper.

Kemper was California's Co-Ed Killer. Like most violent criminals, he'd had a troubled childhood. He never got along with his mother, who didn't like him because he looked like his father. His favorite game as a young child was to have his sister tie him up so he could pretend he was dying in a gas chamber. Later, he killed and mutilated the family's two cats. Finally, his mother sent him to live with his grandparents, who lived in northern California.

One day, when Ed was 14, he got irritated with his grandmother. He shot her and stabbed her over and over again with a kitchen knife. He figured his grandfather wouldn't be happy when he discovered what had happened, so Ed shot him too. Kemper told the cops, "I just wondered how it would feel to shoot Grandma." He was sent to a mental hospital, but released when he turned 21.

Kemper then went to live with his mother, who worked at the University of California at Santa Cruz. Not surprisingly, his relationship with her hadn't improved. The rage he felt toward her eventually got expressed. Within two years, Kemper started killing again.

He quickly developed a simple but effective technique. He'd offer a ride to a young woman, kill her in the car, then take her home where he'd sexually assault the body and take photographs of it. Then he'd dump the body by the side of the road.

Kemper eventually killed six women, becoming bolder as he went along. As a condition of his release, he had to keep regular appointments with a state psychiatrist. He reported to one appointment with the head of a 15-year-old girl in the trunk of his car. That day, he was judged no longer a threat to society.

Finally, Kemper went for his real target. One Saturday night, he beat his mother to death with a hammer, decapitated the corpse and raped it. He cut out his mother's larynx and tossed it into the garbage disposal. But when he flipped the switch, the disposal threw the larynx back up at him. Kemper complained later, "Even after she was dead, she was still bitching at me. I couldn't get her to shut up."

The next morning, Kemper called a friend of his mother's and invited her over for lunch. When she arrived, he killed her and fled. Within days, he called police from the road and surrendered.

Kemper turned out to be the perfect guy to begin our interviews with. For one thing, he's very smart—brilliant, really. And he has a lot of insight into himself and his crimes. I actually like Ed. Do I think this intelligent, sensitive man should be let out of prison, under any circumstances? Hell, no. He's dangerous, and he always will be.

Interviewing Kemper confirmed my theory: The criminals themselves had a lot to teach us. We continued our interviews and, with Ann Burgess, eventually wrote *Sexual Homicide: Patterns and Motives*. A few years later, we followed up with the *Crime Classification Manual*, which was the biggest portion of my thesis for my doctoral degree.

Eventually, profiling became accepted as a legitimate investigative technique, and even as a legal, valid way of linking violent crimes. By the time I retired from the Bureau in 1995, the profiling unit had contributed to the capture and prosecution of some of the nation's most dangerous criminals. And that's something I'll always be proud of.

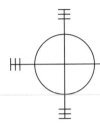

PART TWO

What Applicants Should Know About the FBI

CHAPTER 2
The History of the FBI

The FBI really reflects the country it serves. The crimes under its jurisdiction, the methods used to investigate them—they've changed over the years as the country has changed. To have a real understanding of

HOW IT ALL STARTED

Here's something that might surprise you: The man who founded the FBI apparently had a sense of humor.

In 1892, Charles Bonaparte was a speaker at a meeting of the Baltimore Civil Service Reform Association. The speaker who preceded him was Theodore Roosevelt, then the U.S. Civil Service Commissioner. Roosevelt boasted about his reforms in federal law enforcement, and his moves to replace the patronage system with merit standards in hiring. He went on at some length about one innovation: Border Patrol applicants now were required to take marksmanship tests; the best shooters got the jobs.

When Bonaparte at last took the stage, he suggested an even more effective way to weed out Border Patrol candidates: "Roosevelt should have had the men shoot at each other, and given the jobs to the survivors."

All right, so it's not something you'd hear in Jay Leno's monologue, but it's not bad for a lawman. Apparently Roosevelt was impressed; in 1905, just after his reelection to the presidency, he appointed Bonaparte to the Attorney General post.

At that time, the United States was undergoing huge changes—economically, socially, politically. The Industrial Revolution pulled more and more people away from farms and small towns to the big cities. Railroads, and then automobiles, increased mobility across the country. Americans started looking to the federal government—not the states, the towns, or the counties—for help in dealing with problems such as crime.

This was the background of the Progressive political movement. The Progressives argued that only a strong federal system, run by competent professionals, could provide justice in the new industrial society. Roosevelt was a Progressive; so was his new Attorney General, Charles Bonaparte.

In 1905, when Bonaparte took office, the Department of Justice had no real investigative force: a few Special Agents reported to the Attorney General, and a group of Examiners (trained as accountants) kept an eye on the federal courts' books. If the Department of Justice needed investigators, it hired them from private agencies, or from other government agencies—most often the Secret Service.

Then, in 1908, Congress enacted a law barring the Department of Justice from hiring Secret Service operatives. This was fine with Bonaparte, who preferred to have his investigators reporting to him instead of the Treasury Department, as the Secret Service operatives did. In June 1908, Bonaparte appointed a group of 34 Special Agents within the Department of Justice; on July 26, 1908, he ordered them to report to Chief Examiner Stanley W. Finch. This is marked as the official beginning of the FBI.

On March 16, 1909, Bonaparte's successor, Attorney General George Wickersham, named the force the Bureau of Investigation and changed its leader's title to Chief of the Bureau of Investigation.

The Bureau of Investigation's duties were still fairly vague. At that point, there were few federal crimes. The first Special Agents spent a lot of their time investigating cases of peonage, or involuntary servitude; usually, this happened when someone was forced to "work off" a debt. The Bureau of Investigation also investigated bank fraud cases, antitrust issues, and illegal interstate shipment of liquor. The first major expansion of the Bureau's duties came in 1910, when the Mann Act was passed. This law, also known as the White Slavery Act, made it illegal to transport women across state lines "for immoral purposes."

In 1912, Bureau Chief Finch stepped aside to become Commissioner of White Slavery Act violations, and former Special Examiner A. Bruce Bielaski took his place. Then, as the world lurched toward the Great War, the Bureau's duties really expanded. The Bureau helped the Department of Labor investigate enemy aliens; on its own, the Bureau

ically suspicious of anything considered foreign.

After the war, Americans' xenophobia faded, actual and suspected sabotage disappeared, and the Bureau's duties returned to their prewar scope. In July 1919, William J. Flynn, former head of the Secret Service, became the new Director of the Bureau of Investigation. That October, Congress passed the National Motor Vehicle Theft Act, which soon became the Bureau's major tool in pursuing criminals across state lines.

In 1921, President Warren G. Harding took office, promising to return the country to "normalcy." However, his administration soon became notorious for corruption and graft. Harding's Attorney General replaced Bureau Director Flynn with William J. Burns, an old pal of the AG's who'd operated his own detective agency. The Burns Agency had developed quite a reputation as a strike-breaking organization during the labor wars in the West. Under Burns, the Bureau's ethical standards for hiring and investigations slipped.

Harding died in 1923, in the midst of the Teapot Dome scandal—a case of graft and profiteering that seemed to involve just about everyone in the administration but the president himself. The new president, Calvin Coolidge, was determined to clean house; as part of that cleanup, he demanded the Attorney General's resignation. The new Attorney General, Harlan Fiske Stone, then asked for Burns's resignation as director of the Bureau of Investigation. On May 10, 1924, Stone appointed a new Director—a young Department of Justice employee named J. Edgar Hoover.

THE J. EDGAR HOOVER ERA

Hoover is definitely one of the most controversial figures in American history. I know quite a few former agents from the Hoover days who think he was great. Other current and former agents, and quite a few people outside the Bureau, believe he was overzealous, at best, and diabolical, at worst. This book isn't intended to condemn Hoover or exonerate him, but I want to make my own point of view clear.

I think Hoover did a lot of good for the Bureau, especially in the early days, when it badly needed structure and leadership. However, he did rule with an iron hand. People were scared to death of him. I think that fact, more than anything else, led to the Bureau's well-documented excesses. People were afraid to question him, afraid to deviate from his rules at all, even when the rules didn't make much sense anymore.

For instance, when I first joined the Bureau, there was a rule that agents weren't supposed to be at their desks—ever. They were supposed to be out on the street, working cases. When I got to my second posting, in Milwaukee, I sat down at my desk to get organized. The Special Agent in Charge said, "Douglas, what are you doing? Get out of here!"

I just looked at him and said, "Where am I supposed to go? I don't have a car, I don't have any cases yet."

"I don't care, just get out of here. You're not supposed to be here!"

So I went outside and started wandering around, just window shopping. You could spot all the FBI agents, in their suits and white shirts, walking the streets of downtown Milwaukee. Agents would have to duck into public phone booths to make calls about cases. I don't think we were really doing much good fighting crime that way.

It's that kind of blind obedience to rules that gets people into trouble, and that's what I feel was the worst aspect of the Hoover era. But I do know from personal experience that the Bureau does a damn good job of making improvements when they're needed. Does the Bureau make mistakes? Absolutely. But when they come to light—and I don't mean in the media, I mean internally, too—there's always a serious effort to keep those mistakes from happening again. I honestly feel that whatever excesses and missteps took place in the past, the Bureau has taken steps to safeguard against them in the future.

Okay, that's the end of the sermon; back to the history lesson.

Ness and the Untouchables. (Who, incidentally, were Treasury Agents.) Prohibition opened up new possibilities for crime, and made criminals of many otherwise ordinary Americans. However, even in the middle of a bull market in criminal activity, the Bureau didn't have as much to do as you might think; its jurisdiction was much, much smaller than it is today. The Bureau did investigate Al Capone as a "fugitive federal witness," and it used the Mann Act to bring a philandering Ku Klux Klan "Imperial Kleagle" to justice.

One of J. Edgar Hoover's first projects was a major overhaul in the way the Bureau was run. When he took over, the Bureau of Investigation had approximately 650 employees, including 441 Special Agents. He immediately fired agents he considered unqualified, abolished the seniority rule of promotion, and set up standard performance appraisals. He scheduled regular inspections of Headquarters and field office operations. He developed more stringent standards for hiring and, in January 1928, established a formal training course for new agents. By the end of the decade, the Identification Division was up and running. The Bureau of Investigation was renamed the United States Bureau of Investigation on July 1, 1932.

That same year, the Bureau established its Technical Laboratory. In a story about the new lab, journalist Rex Collier called it "a novel research laboratory where government criminologists will match wits with underworld cunning." Originally the small lab operated strictly as a research facility. Eventually, it offered specialized microscopes for examining forensic evidence, plus an extensive reference collections of guns, watermarks, typefaces, and automobile tire designs. This was the beginning of the Bureau's now-legendary laboratory capability.

THE BUREAU'S JURISDICTION EXPANDS

The Bureau was relegated to the sidelines of one of the century's most spectacular crimes: the 1932 kidnapping and murder of the Lindbergh baby. There were no federal criminal statutes that covered kidnapping, so the Bureau had no jurisdiction; the case was handled by local police. Later that year, Congress passed a kidnapping statute that set the death penalty for transporting a victim across state lines. However, the law had no presumptive clause, which would automatically make kidnapping a federal crime. In 1934, the law was amended, calling for federal intervention if the kidnapping case wasn't solved within seven days. (In the 1950s, that period of time was shortened to 24 hours, after another kidnapping death of an infant. Finally, after more and more of these cases, lawmakers realized that immediate intervention was vital. Today, the FBI is authorized to step in immediately to investigate a kidnapping or any crime involving a child.)

But the Bureau of Investigation did make a name for itself with high-profile shoot-outs with criminals such as John Dillinger, Baby Face Nelson, and Pretty Boy Floyd. In 1934, President Roosevelt used these and other spectacular crimes to push through several laws which expanded the Bureau's jurisdiction. New federal crimes included the killing or assault of a federal officer; extortion involving interstate commerce; kidnapping with no ransom demand; crossing state lines to escape prosecution or avoid giving testimony; robbery of any bank operating under federal rules; and interference with interstate commerce through violence, intimidation or threats. Finally, the Bureau's agents were given full police powers to arrest and apprehend suspects, plus the right to carry firearms at all times while on duty.

The next year, 1935, the agency composed of Department of Justice's investigators got its final name change (so far) and became the Federal Bureau of Investigation. The FBI National Academy started training police officers in modern investigative methods, since states and localities didn't offer formal training for their police and sheriffs.

By 1936, all the major gangsters were either dead or behind bars. But the country was still slogging through a major economic depression, and the world overseas seemed more and more unstable, with the rise of Fascism in Germany and Italy and Communism in the Soviet Union. European Fascists had their counterparts and supporters in the United States—the German-American Bund, the Silver Shirts, and similar

expand membership in the American Communist Party. In 1936 President Roosevelt authorized the FBI to investigate these organizations as threats to national security.

Then, in 1939, war broke out in Europe. A Presidential Directive strengthened the FBI's authority to investigate subversive activity in the United States; subversion, sabotage, and espionage became major targets of FBI investigations. At least one FBI Agent trained in defense plant protection was placed in each of the FBI's 42 field offices. The FBI also developed networks of sources, often relying on fraternal or veterans' organizations. With leads developed by these intelligence networks and through their own work, Special Agents investigated potential threats to national security.

THE FBI AND WORLD WAR II

France fell to the Germans in 1940, and Great Britain became virtually the only opponent to the Axis forces. Under the direction of Russia, the

American Communist Party pushed for U.S. neutrality. But through 1940 and '41, the country increased aid to Great Britain and the Allies. In late 1940, Congress reestablished the draft, and the FBI started tracking down draft evaders and deserters.

The FBI also participated in destroying one of the biggest wartime spy rings discovered; the operation led to the arrest and conviction of 33 people. The key to the case was a man named William Sebold. He was born in Germany, left the country in 1921, settled in the United States, and became a citizen in 1936. He returned to Germany for a visit in 1939; the Gestapo seized him and threatened his family, trying to force him to become a spy.

Sebold agreed, but then contacted the American consulate in Cologne and offered to become a double agent. Sebold returned home to Long Island, and the FBI set up his spy shop. Sebold was given a short-wave radio and a business office fitted with surveillance devices. FBI agents also studied the microfilm Sebold was given in Germany and discovered codes and instructions that led to spies already operating in the United States.

For months, Sebold took instructions from Germany, passed them along to the FBI, and then sent back misleading information carefully designed to seem authentic. In June 1941, the FBI pulled in the net and arrested 33 suspects.

Later that month, on June 22, Hitler's troops attacked Russia—without warning, and in violation of the Nazi-Soviet pact. American Communists became less of a threat, and the FBI focused more and more on potentially dangerous German, Italian, and Japanese nationals, and native-born Americans who worked to assist the Axis. Then, on December 7, 1941, the Japanese bombed the American naval base at Pearl Harbor, Hawaii. President Roosevelt declared the country's entry into World War II the next day.

One of the most shameful episodes of World War II was the internment of Japanese nationals and American citizens of Japanese descent. The FBI had already arrested specific individuals who posed security threats, and Hoover argued that the large-scale internment wasn't necessary. However, President Roosevelt and the Attorney General supported the military's recommendation. Ultimately, the FBI became responsible for arresting curfew and evacuation violators.

In April 1945, President Roosevelt died and Vice President Harry Truman took office as President. Before the end of the month, Hitler committed suicide. In May 1945, Germany's surrender brought peace in Europe, but war raged on through the Pacific. Truman made the decision to use atomic weapons in Japan, and the last Axis power surrendered on August 14, 1945.

THE FBI AND THE COLD WAR

Peace brought prosperity, and anxiety. The United States was the world's

Soviets detonated their own atomic bomb in 1949, counteracting the Communist threat became a paramount focus of government at all levels, as well as the private sector.

While U.S. foreign policy concentrated on defeating Communist expansion abroad, many Americans worried about the Communist threat at home. In 1939 and again in 1943, presidential directives had authorized the FBI to carry out investigations of threats to national security. This role was clarified and expanded under Presidents Truman and Eisenhower. Anyone with information about subversive activities was urged to report it to the FBI. The Bureau distributed a poster on the program to police departments across the country. One of the poster's points, often ignored, warned Americans to "avoid reporting malicious gossip or idle rumors."

During this time, Frank Watts worked in Connecticut, identifying Soviet agents spying at a navy yard there. Here's one story he shared:

Frank Watts: The Case of the Commie Next Door

Often we'd start with surveillance of a Soviet diplomat, and we'd watch him make contact with several other individuals. That's when it became very intriguing, trying to determine who that individual was, why he was contacted, what that individual might furnish as far as secret documents.

I was the Senior Resident Agent in Stamford, covering most all of the Soviet illegal espionage activities in the area. Of course, I was living there in Connecticut. One of my neighbors—I'll call him John Doe—had a son who was the same age as my son, both of them about eight years old. The boys went to Scouts together, so this neighbor and I both became active in Boy Scouts. We got to be pretty close friends; his wife and my wife did things together, and we visited back and forth. I always thought he was a little pushy, maybe overly friendly. But a nice guy. He was the editor and publisher of a technical magazine out of New York.

Well, one day I was working surveillance on one of the diplomatic officials of the Soviet Union. He left the embassy in New York and came up to White Plains, to meet with one of his agents. We covered that site very discreetly, because we had enough information to set it up ahead of time. And we knew this meeting was supposed to be with someone who was passing information.

So the diplomat stepped off the train and went to the telephone booth with his *Life* magazine under his arm, and stood there in the phone booth a minute. And then John Doe, my next-door neighbor, walked right up and made contact with him.

I wanted to go interview John immediately and double him if I could. And I thought I could. But Director Hoover and others in Washington felt it wasn't the time. I had to continue my relationship with him, because we didn't want him to know that we knew what he was up to.

After that, John came in my office at least twice a week for several months. He'd come in with his big briefcase, and sit down, and talk about nothing. We'd sit there and just talk, and talk some more, and then he would leave.

Then one day, John's principal—the diplomat we'd followed—was arrested in New Jersey, clearing a drop box. Of course, this made headlines in the papers, and we knew John would see it and that would have a definite effect on him. So I was told to go ahead and make contact.

John boarded the New Haven–New York commuter train every day. So I got on the train ahead of him. I had a paper folded up under my arm, one of the tabloids with this principal's picture in it. When I saw John sit down, I sat down with him, and we chatted for a minute. Then I opened up the paper. You could see John's reaction—he just got extremely nervous right away.

When we got into Grand Central, John said, "Well, Frank, I'll see you later." And I said, "I'm afraid not. You've got to go with me." He just sighed real big and said, "I knew that was coming."

We went down to the New York office, and we had two, three days of

to confess and become a double agent for us.

What had happened was, he'd been convinced to hand over something pretty minor. And when he did that, they pushed it a step further, then a step further, and started paying him for information. Because he was the publisher and editor of this technical magazine, he had access to places that were off limits to most people. One of those places was the jet propulsion laboratory out in California. He went there and obtained some information that the Soviets wanted, and passed it along for a price. Then he became a fully active agent.

He turned out to be a good double agent. He got a new principal; it took a year or so before they made their contact with him, but they did. John was able to furnish us some valuable information about that principal, and other principals, as well as people who were passing on identity documents to support KGB agents that might be coming in: driver's licenses, marriage licenses, birth certificates, and so forth.

Things were never quite the same in Boy Scout meetings, though.

INVESTIGATIVE ADVANCES

But even in the Cold War '50s, counterespionage and Commie hunting remained a relatively small part of the FBI's work. The Bureau kept pace with scientific and investigative advances in law enforcement, and used the tools at its disposal to assist state and local agencies.

A Bombing above Denver

One of the early tests of the FBI's forensic capabilities came on November 1, 1955. A United Airlines DC-6B exploded 11 minutes after takeoff from Stapleton Airport in Denver. All 44 passengers were killed instantly. (As a measure of how much times have changed, terrorism was never even considered a possibility. Contrast that to the reaction to the TWA 800 disaster 41 years later.)

FBI agents flooded Denver immediately after the crash. Members of the Disaster Squad identified mangled bodies through fingerprints, and other agents began intensive background investigations on the 44 victims. The plane was reconstructed, showing a huge hole in the fuselage. No explosives were listed on the cargo inventory, and investigators quickly realized that a bomb was the most likely cause. Agents sifted through thousands of bits of evidence: airplane parts, pieces of cargo, the passenger's personal effects. Luggage belonging to one passenger, Daisy King, was virtually destroyed; this pointed to her bags as a source of the explosion.

It turned out that Daisy King's son had taken out a substantial life insurance policy on her just minutes before the flight. The son, John Gilbert Graham, also would inherit King's estate. FBI agents spent hours questioning Graham; he finally confessed to placing a bomb in his mother's luggage—25 sticks of dynamite wired to a timer and six-volt battery. Graham later repudiated the confession, but he was convicted and executed a little over a year after the explosion.

Gene Amole, a writer for the *Rocky Mountain News,* covered the Graham trial for a radio station. He and a friend also smuggled a camera into the jail where Graham was held and filmed an interview with the prisoner. In an article marking the fortieth anniversary of the bombing, Amole describes part of the interview:

> "I loved my mother very much," Graham told me. "She meant a lot to me. It's very hard for me to tell exactly how I feel. She left so much of herself behind." When I asked why he had signed a confession, he said the FBI had threatened to involve [his wife] Gloria in the murder. "I was not about to let them touch her in any way, shape, or form."

Like most jailhouse declarations, this one is much more self-serving than truthful. The agents investigating the case knew there was a good chance that Graham would take back his confession, so they gathered and analyzed an enormous amount of forensic evidence linking Graham to the crime. They located and put on the stand the merchants who sold Graham timing devices, blasting caps, and dynamite. The

From a profiling standpoint, I was interested in another detail Amole revealed in his article. While the motive for the bombing is most often assumed to be money, Graham apparently had a troubled relationship with his mother. His father died when he was young; when his mother remarried, she sent him to a charity home. According to Amole, "The final rejection came in November of 1955 when Graham wanted his mother to spend Thanksgiving with him, his wife, and their two infant children. She refused, saying she wanted to go caribou hunting in Alaska."

This just strengthens the case against Graham, as far as I'm concerned. And it fits with Amole's description of Graham's last day on earth: "The night of his execution, he spoke lovingly of his mother. Then he walked confidently into the gas chamber, sat down, inhaled the lethal gas, groaned loudly, and died."

This terrible crime, one of the worst mass murders in United States history, demonstrated the value of immediate, intensive investigation.

DEFENDING CIVIL RIGHTS

Racism, one of the deep-rooted injustices of American society, really came to the fore during the '50s and '60s. After fighting for their country in World War II and Korea, black Americans weren't willing to return to Jim Crow segregation. During most of this time, the FBI had no jurisdiction over civil rights violations, no matter how brutal or blatant. The turning point came in the summer of 1964, when Michael Schwerner, Andrew Goodman, and James Cheney were murdered near Philadelphia, Mississippi. The three young voter-registration workers disappeared shortly after they were released from the city jail; their bodies were found weeks later, buried in a levee.

The Department of Justice ordered an FBI investigation. The case worked its way through the courts for years. In 1966, the Supreme Court broadened its interpretation of civil rights law and made it clear that federal agencies could investigate and prosecute civil rights violations. Seven men were eventually found guilty of the murders of Schwerner, Goodman, and Cheney. In the meantime, the FBI began taking steps to deal with the turmoil in the South, sending in agents to deal specifically with the unrest.

Frank Watts was one of those agents, and he tells an amazing story about one of his encounters with an especially violent racist. (Frank's story, among others, is told in more detail in the book *Terror in the Night: The Klan's Campaign Against the Jews*, by Jack Nelson.)

Frank Watts: Catching the Man from the Klan

I'd been in Connecticut for over ten years at that point, working mostly espionage, when I was sent back to Mississippi. One particular Klan group, the White Knights of the Ku Klux Klan, was really spreading havoc throughout the South, and particularly in Mississippi.

At that time, the FBI did not have an office in Mississippi. The northern part of the state was covered out of Memphis, the southern part out of New Orleans. In 1964, President Johnson instructed Hoover to open up an office in Mississippi, specifically because of this Klan activity. They'd bombed and burned churches and synagogues, disrupted the voter registration activity. Several people had been killed, including three civil rights workers. This was the FBI's major crisis at that time.

So Hoover came down, opened the office, and sent in 100 FBI agents to handle the problem, in Mississippi and several of the southern states. Anything else took a back seat. Of course there wasn't that much else going on in Mississippi, at that point.

Quite a few of us who were sent down were from the South. It was easier to get people to cooperate if you were a Southerner. I think the local people felt that we weren't outsiders, we understood their situation. That made it a little easier to sit down and talk to them and let them see how this violence and bigotry was just not the answer. And that was the most important thing, getting people to cooperate and talk to us. That was how

ated with the FBI. It was difficult for some of these people to do it, to speak to us. They were really putting their lives in danger.

Things shifted when the Bureau solved the murders of those three civil rights workers: Cheney, Goodman, and Schwerner. The Klan leaders were indicted, as well as the ones that actually pulled the triggers. Now, none of them could do anything openly. They knew they were under surveillance, and if they did anything out of the ordinary, any further Klan activity, their bond would be revoked, and they'd go off to jail. They had to get outsiders to do the dirty work.

That's when Tommy Tarrants, this young boy from Mobile, Alabama, came into the picture. He'd attended a few Klan meetings in Alabama, but he'd never been in any trouble with the law. He saw the need of carrying on the Klan activity, so he got in his car and came over to Mississippi to visit with Sam Bowers, the head of the White Knights. Sam was under indictment, and Tommy volunteered his services. Of course, Bowers didn't feel this boy was legitimate, and thought maybe he was an FBI informant. So Sam just thanked him and sent him on his way.

Tommy then went out and did some bombings on his own—burned up some black churches and bombed a rabbi's home. Just to show Bowers that he was really who he said he was, you know. The only injury at this point occurred when he shot into the home of a black civil rights leader, just outside of Jackson, and injured a little girl in the leg. Fortunately, she wasn't badly hurt, but these were significant bombings. Lot of damage, very frightening.

Sam took Tommy seriously at that point, and the Klan set up what they called an underground hit squad. It was composed of six individuals, including Tommy Tarrants, who was the leader of this group. They wouldn't go to meetings or anything; their only contact with the Klan would be through very trusted members. That's how they'd get instructions, monies, and so forth.

This squad started out with bank robberies, in order to get money. They bought ammunition and supplies, and two automobiles. They then began to do the work of casing places to get the information they needed, prior to any bombings or burnings.

At this point, we knew a group existed, but not much else. I was sent to gather intelligence, and that's what we worked on through 1966 and 1967. It was a tough thing to do, but we'd get little tidbits of this, little tidbits of that. That the group was about to do this or that. But we didn't know who was in the group or how it was organized. And we had no idea who the leader was. We had lots and lots of information about the leader's automobile, about his being spotted near violent activity. We were building a file, but the identities of the people involved were just completely unknown to us.

The information we were receiving got more extreme as time went on. The bombings were getting to be more heinous, more focused on actually hurting people instead of just causing property damage. The Klan group started out burning black churches that had someone actively registering voters. It was fairly easy for them to go there in the dark of night and burn those churches.

Then they switched targets and concentrated on Jews. The Klan felt there was a Jewish, Communist conspiracy behind the blacks to support the civil rights work. The squad bombed the Temple Beth Israel synagogue in Jackson, Mississippi, and another synagogue over in Meridien, Mississippi. They burned two rabbis' homes. They were still burning black churches out in the rural areas, but that activity was really reduced.

We were still investigating all these activities, and activities all over Mississippi. We had another killing down in Hattiesburg, Mississippi. Vernon Dahmer was an outstanding individual, a fine man, actively engaged in voter registration. They came in and burned his house and killed him. So we were actively investigating that, and at the same time we were trying to get information to stay a step ahead of this underground hit squad.

That was the real problem, and it was my problem: Trying to stay a

the high-up, trusted ones. We weren't getting the information we really needed, from the inside sources.

And then a Jewish businessman by the name of Meyer Davidson became involved. He had a very outstanding family there in Meridien. They'd done so much for the city, built a baseball complex, and this, that and the other—just a very fine, civic-minded family. It was his synagogue that the Klan had blown up. Meyer Davidson offered a $70,000 payment to anyone who had information that led to a solution and a successful prosecution.

Well, that incensed them, this Klan group. They'd decided they'd bomb his house, murder him and his family. And then they received orders to bomb the Temple Beth Israel synagogue again, this time during the services. You can imagine how many people would be killed then. Women and children and all.

That's what we heard through our sources—this plan was on the drawing board. That was just a little bit too much for us to take, you know.

We didn't know when, or how, or by whom. Just that this underground squad was planning these very violent bombings, designed to kill.

We still didn't know who the leader of the group was, this man we later found out was Tommy Tarrants. The informants didn't know his name, either. They just referred to him as The Man. And so we referred to him as The Man, because we had no other identification. We had a pretty good physical description, but that's all.

We knew we had to have much better information coming from more trusted Klan people, closer to the leaders. We started going to our sources to find out from them who *would* know what we needed to know. And we just had to have that information ahead of time. We could not allow this activity to take place.

We went through all our sources, good ones, bad ones, mediocre ones. We talked to all of them to try to find our targets, and we found two individuals, brothers. They were both in the Klan, and one was reportedly involved in the civil rights murders—Goodman, Cheney and Schwerner. These two brothers were very much in on the Klan's planning and they knew about all the activities.

So we made contact with these brothers and let them know that we had to have this information. I demanded that they come to my house, so we could sit down and have an understanding. Well, they did show up, with their attorney. Even with the attorney there, they laid it on the line— that they did have this information, but their lives were in danger if they divulged it.

We met night after night in a little mobile home out in the woods. Had a real prayer meeting about two or three times a week—the brothers, their attorney, me, a couple of other agents, some of the local detectives. Those brothers would lay their guns out on the table, we'd lay ours out, and then we'd pray.

It was touch-and-go for several weeks. They never would give us the name of The Man; they always claimed didn't know for sure. But they let us know that the Klan decided that before they did the job on the synagogue, making the big splash of killing all these people, they'd take care of Meyer Davidson first. That was really a thorn in their side, this man putting up all this money to stop them.

These brothers knew they might be in a position to get that money, so that was a help. But what really brought them around was, they were convinced that we could take action, and we would take action—action against them, if they didn't cooperate. We had to fight fire with fire. It was completely different from what I had done in New York, with the espionage cases. That was a lot of finesse, trying to match wits with these people who had seven years of training. Any success there came about through careful planning and finesse.

But with the Klan, you were dealing with people who—well, Hoover called them rednecks. And they were. Uneducated, and extremely violent. We saw early on there was no place for finesse. And so they knew that

way out would be to cooperate and prevent these bombings.

So finally they did give us some information, first of all about the targets the Klan had in mind. The Klan had this little code for what they'd do to people—Number One was your basic harassment, like a nasty telephone call. Number Two was throwing a dead chicken on the porch, something of that nature. Number Three was a beating. And Number Four was a killing. Several of us in the FBI were on the list for a Number Four. So was Meyer Davidson, of course, and another Jewish businessman there in town, and the chief of police of Meridien. Of course we were relying on these brothers to let us know who was going to be first.

They did come through on this particular Saturday afternoon, June 30, 1968. They called me and said, "This is it. They're in town, and The Man's here too. He's got a woman with him that's done all the case work, all the preparation for the bombings. They're headed for Meyer Davidson's." Then the brothers said they were going to set up their alibi, which was to go to a nightclub and start a fight so they'd get arrested and be in jail when the bombing happened.

Of course, we were covering all the targeted areas already. I immediately got the Davidson family out of the house, and we set up good roadblocks all over. The people who lived across the street let us take over their house, just moved out for the weekend. And so we were able to set up a good cover.

We knew dynamite was involved, because it had been involved in all the other bombings. We'd called in some dynamite experts from Fort Benning, Georgia, and had them available. So that night we were all set up when they came in.

Tommy Tarrants, he was The Man. Kathy Ainsworth was the woman with him, a married school teacher who'd moved up from Miami. Her husband knew she was in the Klan, but he couldn't get her to leave. She said she'd leave him if he tried to make her leave the Klan. So she kept her activities up, and she did a lot of the preparation work, examining the sites the Klan had picked out.

Shortly after 11:30 that night, they drove up in a nice Buick automobile. This was a little unusual because the Klan used to travel in pickup trucks with shotguns in the back. Turns out this was one of the cars they bought with money from the early bank robberies. Kathy Ainsworth was driving.

Tommy got out of the car, carrying a box. We could tell it was heavy, by the way he was bent down with it. He had 29 sticks of dynamite in there—unstable, highly explosive. In fact, the box was leaking; the dynamite was almost pure nitroglycerine. The bomb experts from Fort Benning said that if that stuff had gone off, it would've blown up seven houses all around, including the house we were in across the street.

So Tommy carried that box over and got under the bedroom window. And he began to place his dynamite on the timing device. It was all set up, except for the wires. All Tommy had to do was attach the wires. He couldn't do that while he was traveling, you know. As he started do that we moved in. We hollered, "FBI! Don't move!" and he turned. He had a .45, and he started firing.

Tommy was an excellent marksman. A lot of the Klan were. They'd go out and practice in a big gravel pit over in Jackson, day after day, for months. But the one thing that they neglected to do was practice at night. Your only light source at night is the sky, so you tend to shoot high.

Well, at Quantico, we had all kinds of firearms training, including how to shoot at night, without a light. We knew how to compensate for that. So Tommy was shooting over our heads, and we were shooting right at him.

We're trained not to shoot to kill, but shoot to capture. The first shot, I got him the leg, just above his knee, and dynamite went all over the place. Tommy hurried back to the car, got to the nearest door. We hit him as he reached the car door, and took a big chunk out of his arm. Kathy was shot in the neck and killed instantly. Tommy got in the car, pushed her over, got behind the wheel and took off.

with an inner tube. You could run over a nail, and it wouldn't go down. We kept shooting at his tires, trying to get him to stop. He went 15 blocks before those tires went down. Finally, he couldn't negotiate a turn and ran up in someone's yard. The police captain was in the car right behind, when Tommy got out of his car and turned his machine gun on him. Tommy hit the captain three times, including once in the heart. And the captain lived.

One of the neighbors there came out on his porch, to see what was going on. Tommy shot him in the stomach, and then went on back behind the house. That man lived, too.

A policeman came up right behind the first car and made his way behind the house, to the field back there. This family was raising German shepherds, and they had the fence electrified. Tommy kept trying to go over the fence, and it kept knocking him down. By the time we got to him, he was laying there, just bleeding. He looked like just a bloody rag, really.

At that point we put him in the ambulance, along with Kathy Ainsworth, although she was already deceased. I sent one agent to the hospital with him, in order to take a dying declaration. I was sure he couldn't live. In case he talked before he died, I wanted someone there to take it down, because dying declarations are admissible in court.

But Tommy never would talk. He got to the hospital, and he lived. There was a real excellent doctor in Meridien who'd made a lot of progress in orthopedic surgery, using pins, that kind of thing. He operated on Tommy's arm and all, and he was able to save the arm. Patched him up pretty well.

Of course Tommy was tried on the state charge, for bombing an occupied dwelling. The FBI cooperated as much as we could, but it was up to the state to handle the prosecution. He was found guilty and sent to the state penitentiary.

Throughout all this, during the investigation and the trial, Tommy Tarrants was totally unrepentant. I interviewed him 36 times and never got anything from him. I really wanted to get him to testify, because if he did, then I felt we could put at least another 28 people in prison. But he never would.

About 16 months after Tommy went to prison, he escaped with the help of the Klan—he and a partner, who wasn't a Klansman. Tommy and his buddy got themselves into the prison hospital, then they knocked a hospital worker over the head with a lead pipe. Then the Klan picked them up behind the prison grounds and they took off down to Jackson, Mississippi. The Klan had set up a little lean-to tent there at the edge of the airport, with food and money and a change of clothes for them. They were ready to hijack an airplane and go to Nova Scotia.

But we were able to surround the tent and move in while they were still inside. They opened fire on us, and we returned fire. Tommy's buddy was killed, but Tommy's life was spared.

Well, Tommy went back to prison, and got two years in solitary confinement for the escape. He was put in a six-by-eight cell, where he could come out twice a week for a shower, and that was it. I continued my interviews with him, kept going to see him there in prison.

I really saw a troubled youth, you know? And he was just about the same age as my older son. I could see how messed up Tommy was. All he wanted was his Bible, so I took that to him. He was using the Bible to justify his Klan activities—completely off-base. We'd argue back and forth. But I was really the only one who could come and talk to him. His family would come, but they weren't allowed to visit with him.

I was just trying to get him to testify. Tommy was really hard at that time. But I believe he came to enjoy me visiting with him. We'd talk about everything—his life in general, and religion. My wife and her church group began a prayer vigil for him. She'd give me little tracts and things to give to Tommy.

And you know, he was appreciative. It was something to do, and

After a while, he really had a born-again experience. He wrote a letter to the *New York Times*, telling people engaged in violent activity that that wasn't the answer. The *Times* published that letter, although they did make a mistake. Tommy had just put "MSU" on the address, which stood for Maximum Security Unit. The article they ran along with the letter said that Tommy had written from Mississippi State University. I got a chuckle out of that.

One of the things we did in the FBI was keep up with the daily papers. You'd clip anything that had thing to do with an FBI case and send it down to Washington, where it would be put in the case file.

When that story hit Hoover's desk, he called me and requested, or demanded, that I get up to the penitentiary and talk with Tommy. Hoover thought this conversion was another ploy to help him escape.

So of course I went right on up. This time, when Tommy came out, I could see that he was completely different. He said, "Frank, I appreciate what you've done for me and all. I want you to know, I'm not the same person I was."

Of course I was leery at first. But I realized it wasn't the jailhouse religion that a lot of people get, because he wasn't wanting anything. That was one of the first things I asked him. What do you want out of this? Are you doing this to get out? And he said, "No, I've accepted Christ. I don't want anything else." I went to the chaplain there, and he then observed Tommy closely, and talked with him. And he felt like I did, that this was a true conversion.

I went to some of the leaders in the Jewish community and the black community and asked them to go visit him, just to find out if they saw what I did. I felt that if he really had changed, he could do more good outside than in. And I was going to do what I could do to get him out.

One of the first people I visited was a prominent Jewish lawyer in Jackson, Mississippi, by the name of Al Binder. He used to bring me the money over to Meridien to pay the informers. He was a target of the Klan, because of his prominence. After a lot of persuasion on my part, he agreed to go see Tommy.

Al Binder sits down and Tommy says, "Let me draw you a picture of your house." He had it right down to pinpoint accuracy: How to get in Al Binder's house, where to place the bomb, and so forth. Al told me later, "It really got my attention." But then Tommy asked him for forgiveness.

Al became convinced Tommy was sincere, and he had a lot more pull than I did in the state of Mississippi. In fact, he was the legal advisor for the governor at the time. He was able to help in getting Tommy paroled. Senator John Stennis, who's deceased now, had a secretary who was a lawyer there in Jackson. The secretary went to interview Tommy and he was able to help. He was convinced. Everybody was convinced except my boss, Hoover. He told me, "If anything happens, I'll hold you personally responsible."

I knew that I was risking my job and everything else, but I was convinced that Tommy really had changed, and he could do some real good on the outside. In the meantime, he was teaching other inmates and reaching out to people who had been in his situation, trying to get them to see that violence was not the answer.

During this whole time, he never gave me the names of the other men who'd been in the underground hit squad with him. Never did. The way he explained it to me, he'd talked so many of these people into doing these things, convinced them to go along, that he felt it wouldn't be right to give me their names. He didn't want to get out of prison by putting other people in.

Well, after this started hitting the papers, we'd start getting phone calls. A Klansman would call up and say, "I know what happened. I read the papers. I know what Tommy was doing, trying to bomb the synagogue and bomb these homes and so forth. I don't want any more part of the Klan. You'll find my robe under an oak tree out on Highway 23."

Tommy wrote a letter to the paper there in Jackson, Mississippi, stat- names to the FBI. He said had no intention of doing so, unless there was more violence. Tommy said the minute the Klan undertook more acts of violence, he'd go to the FBI and cooperate completely. He told me if lives were in danger, he would cooperate with me and put the people responsible in prison. But as long as the people he had worked with stayed away from violence, he wasn't going to give me information just for personal gain.

Well, Tommy was paroled on December 13, 1976. He took classes at Ole Miss for while, then moved up North and worked with Chuck Colson on his prison ministry. Then he and some others there in Washington, D.C. formed an urban school for young ministers. He's been active in that until just this past year. He's taken a year off to get his doctorate.

He's still out there, still doing good work. I'm glad I didn't ever have to go to Mr. Hoover and say, "Sir, I made a mistake. I was wrong about Tommy Tarrants."

TAKING ON THE MOB

With the Klan broken, the FBI turned to another criminal organization—the Mafia.

In 1957, the New York State Police discovered that many of the country's best-known mobsters had met in upstate New York. The FBI collected information on all the individuals identified at the meeting and confirmed the existence of a national organized-crime network. But legal remedies were slow in coming, until an FBI agent convinced mob insider Joseph Valachi to testify before a Senate subcommittee on organized crime. Valachi's testimony, in September 1963, galvanized public opinion. In response, Congress passed two new laws to strengthen existing federal racketeering and gambling statutes.

The Omnibus Crime Control and Safe Streets Act of 1968 provided for the use of court-ordered electronic surveillance in the investigation of certain specified violations. The Racketeer Influenced and Corrupt Organizations (RICO) Statute of 1970 allowed organized groups to be prosecuted for all of their diverse criminal activities, without the crimes being linked by a perpetrator or all-encompassing conspiracy. RICO continues to be a valuable tool in pursuing not only mobsters, but also drug traffickers.

THE SEVENTIES

While the 1960s counterculture was mostly peaceful, there was a violent edge to some protests. In 1970 alone, there were approximately 3,000 bombings and 50,000 bomb threats in the United States. Two of the most violent incidents of the Vietnam War era took place during that same year.

On May 4, 1970, approximately 300 students and activists gathered at Kent State University to stage a demonstration against the Vietnam War. National Guardsmen were on hand, at the governor's request; after the students refused to disperse and began throwing tear gas canisters back at the troops, the Guardsmen opened fire into the crowd. Thirteen students were wounded; four were killed.

Months later, in the very early morning of August 24, 1970, a powerful explosive destroyed a building on campus at the University of Wisconsin at Madison. Sterling Hall housed the Army Math Research Center, the target of the terrorists. A graduate student was killed and three others were injured.

If Kent State had outraged the left, the bombing in Madison showed the horror and futility of violence in retaliation. Draft dodging and property damage seemed tolerable, even reasonable, to many antiwar sympathizers. Deaths were something different, clearly beyond any reasonable boundary.

Even so, a few violent groups such as the Weathermen continued their operations from an increasingly isolated underground. The FBI dealt with these threats as it had those from Communists and the KKK—

gence programs (nicknamed "Cointelpro"). These measures were intended to fight domestic terrorism and gather intelligence on those who threatened terroristic violence. Some of the Cointelpro operations were later found to overstep citizens' right to privacy; this is one reason why wiretapping and other intrusive investigative techniques are now so thoroughly regulated by FBI and Department of Justice guidelines.

On May 2, 1972, J. Edgar Hoover died at the age of 77; he was just a few months away from marking his 48th year as FBI Director. President Nixon appointed L. Patrick Gray as Acting Director the day after Hoover's death.

Not long after that, five men were arrested photographing documents at the Democratic National Headquarters in the Watergate Office Building in Washington, D.C.

The break-in had been authorized by Republican Party officials working to reelect Nixon; within hours, the White House was scrambling to cover up its role. Gray's personal connections to Nixon drew him into the Watergate scandal; he withdrew his name from consideration to be Director and resigned on April 27, 1973.

William Ruckleshaus, a former Congressman and the first head of the Environmental Protection Agency, took over as Acting Director until Clarence Kelley's appointment on July 9, 1973. Kelley was the Kansas City Police Chief at the time of his appointment; he'd been an FBI Agent from 1940 to 1961.

By now, the country was reeling from the Watergate scandal; Americans had become deeply cynical, wary of anything to do with government, including law enforcement. Director Kelley worked to restore public trust in the FBI.

In 1974, he instituted Career Review Boards and programs to identify and train potential managers within the FBI. Through the new National Executive Institute at the FBI National Academy, Kelley also sought to increase professionalism in law enforcement agencies at every level, across the country.

Kelley also had to deal with the fallout from public disclosures of the Cointelpro excesses. A Congressional committee investigated the investigators, examining whether the FBI's programs had violated Constitutional rights.

In response to the hearings, Attorney General Edward Levi established specific guidelines in this area—the first time such guidelines were established. Foreign counterintelligence guidelines went into effect on March 10, 1976; domestic security investigations became effective April 5, 1976. (The domestic guidelines were superseded March 21, 1983.)

Kelley's biggest innovation was "quality over quantity" management. Under Hoover, agents and field offices were expected to handle a certain number of cases each year—a sort of criminal quota. Now, each field office set its own investigative priorities based on the types of crime most prevalent in its territory. The FBI as a whole established three national priorities: foreign counterintelligence, organized crime, and white-collar crime.

In 1978, Director Kelley resigned and was replaced by former federal Judge William H. Webster. In 1982, Webster made counterterrorism a fourth national priority, responding to a rise in international terrorism.

THE EIGHTIES

Another threat that surfaced in the '80s was the illegal drug trade. To meet the challenge, in 1982 the Attorney General gave the FBI concurrent jurisdiction with the Drug Enforcement Administration (DEA) over narcotics violations in the United States. The expanded and coordinated effort led to the seizure of millions of dollars in controlled substances, the arrests of major narcotics figures, and the dismantling of important drug rings.

On another front, Webster strengthened the FBI's response to white-collar crimes. The Bureau investigated corruption in Congress, the judiciary, also handled fraud investigations in the wake of the savings and loan collapse; the investigation grew from ten cases in 1981 to 282 in 1987.

On May 26, 1987, Judge Webster left the FBI to become Director of the Central Intelligence Agency. Executive Assistant Director John E. Otto became Acting Director; during his tenure, he designated drug investigations as the FBI's fifth national priority.

On November 2, 1987, former federal Judge William Steele Sessions was sworn in as FBI Director. He would lead the Bureau through a time of tremendous upheaval across the world.

In 1989, the Berlin Wall fell; the rest of the Iron Curtain soon followed. On Christmas Day 1991, the Soviet Union vanished, and the United States became the world's only superpower.

THE NINETIES

In January 1992, the FBI moved 300 Special Agents from foreign counterintelligence duties to violent crime investigations across the country. This reflected a change in national priorities and problems—including a 40 percent increase in violent crimes over the past decade.

Director Sessions expanded an FBI-Washington, D.C., police program that had proved successful in fighting street crime. "Operation Safe Streets" rolled out nationwide, helping law enforcement agencies across the country target fugitives and gangs in their jurisdictions.

The FBI also fought "crime in the suites," or white-collar crime—large-scale insider bank fraud and financial crimes; complex health care fraud; newly established criminal sanctions enforcing federal environmental laws.

The Bureau expanded its definition of threats to national security, including the proliferation of chemical, biological, and nuclear weapons; the loss of critical technologies; and the improper collection of trade secrets and proprietary information.

On the domestic front, two events of the early 1990s had a major impact on FBI policies and operations.

In August 1992, Deputy U.S. Marshal William Degan was killed at Ruby Ridge, Idaho, while participating in a surveillance of federal fugitive Randall Weaver. During the resulting standoff, Weaver's wife was accidentally shot and killed by an FBI sniper.

In April 1993, outside Waco, Texas, FBI agents tried to end a 51-day standoff with members of a heavily armed religious group who'd killed four officers of the Bureau of Alcohol, Tobacco, and Firearms. As agents watched in horror, the compound burned to the ground; the inferno was touched off by fires lit by members of the group. Eighty people, including children, died in the blaze.

These two events provoked public outcry and congressional inquiries into the FBI's crisis response.

Director Sessions was removed from his post on July 19, 1993, following allegations of ethics violations. President Clinton appointed Deputy Director Floyd I. Clarke as Acting FBI Director. Louis J. Freeh was sworn in as Director of the FBI on September 1, 1993.

Freeh had served as an FBI Agent from 1975 to 1981 in the New York before leaving to join the U.S. Attorney's Office for the Southern District of New York. Freeh prosecuted many major FBI cases, including the notorious "Pizza Connection" case and the "VANPAC" mail bomb case. He was appointed a U.S. District Court Judge for the Southern District of New York in 1991.

Freeh faced both deepening crime problems and a climate of government downsizing. Soon after taking office, he announced a major reorganization. Many management positions were abolished; certain divisions and offices were merged, reorganized, or eliminated; 600 Special Agents in administrative positions were reassigned to investigative posi-

Agents.

During his tenure, Freeh has worked to develop cooperation among law enforcement agencies across the country and around the world through task forces and expanded education programs at the FBI National Academy. Director Freeh has sought to position the Bureau to deal with changing criminal challenges. For example, he began construction of a new, state-of-the-art FBI forensic laboratory; formed the Critical Incident Response Group to deal efficiently with crisis situations; created the Computer Investigations and Infrastructure Threat Assessment Center to respond to attacks against United States infrastructure—in the physical world and in cyberspace.

The FBI has come a long way from that first force of 34 agents. Those guys weren't even authorized to carry guns all the time; today's agents are issued guns *and* laptops. The one thing that's stayed the same, through almost 90 years, is the motivation behind the Bureau's motto—Fidelity, Bravery, and Integrity.

History of the "Top Ten"

I don't know what it is, but there's something about a "Top Ten" list that appeals to us. Over 236 sites on the Internet offer up some kind of Top Ten list, from the Top Ten Bars in Helsinki to the Top Ten Reasons for Whitening Your Teeth. (Not to mention all the official and unofficial sites for David Letterman's Top Ten lists.)

I don't want to claim undue credit for the FBI, but I'm pretty sure the Bureau was one of the first to popularize the decimal delineation, in the form of the Ten Most Wanted Fugitives Program.

The first FBI list was compiled in March 1950, in response to a reporter's question. A writer for International News Service, the predecessor to United Press International, asked the FBI for the names and descriptions of the "toughest guys" they'd targeted. The story was a big hit. J. Edgar Hoover always had a gift for publicizing the Bureau, so he decided to make the list a regular program. On March 14, 1950, the Ten Most Wanted Fugitives Program was implemented. Since then, almost 7,000 of the listed fugitives have been captured.

Over the years, the kinds of crime the FBI focuses on have changed; the kinds of fugitives the FBI pursued have changed, too. During the 1950s, most of the criminals on the list were bank robbers, burglars, and car thieves. During the radical 1960s, the list included leftist revolutionaries, such as the Weathermen. In a criminal reflection of the growing women's movement, Ruth Eisemann-Schier became first woman on the list; she debuted in 1968 for charges including kidnapping and extortion. In the 1970s, the Ten Most Wanted were mainly involved in organized crime and terrorism. Today, serial murderers and drug kingpins have joined the bombers and mobsters.

In May 1998, the first million-dollar reward was offered for information leading to the capture of a Ten-Most-Wanted fugitive; Eric Robert Rudolph is a suspect in the January 29, 1998, bombing of an abortion clinic in Birmingham, Alabama. A Birmingham police officer who had been moonlighting as a security guard was killed in the explosion; a nurse who worked at the clinic was seriously wounded and nearly blinded.

How does the FBI choose the ten fugitives for the list? There are two criteria. First, the fugitive is considered particularly dangerous, which may be reflected either in a long record of serious crimes or involvement in a few extremely heinous incidents. Second, the Bureau believes nationwide publicity will help catch the fugitive. Special Agents of the Criminal Investigative Division (CID), who keep up with all current FBI fugitives, make preliminary recommendations, working with

Congressional Affairs (OPCA) who coordinate fugitive publicity. The FBI's field offices across the country also submit recommendations. The selection is approved by the Assistant Director of CID, the Inspector in Charge of OPCA, and finally, by the Director.

Unless a Top Ten Fugitive is captured, found dead, or surrenders, he or she is removed from the list for only two reasons. Either the criminal charges are dropped or they no longer fit the "top ten" criteria listed above.

Very rarely, the FBI makes "special additions" to the list. James Earl Ray, wanted for the assassination of Dr. Martin Luther King Jr, was the first special addition. Ramzi Ahmed Yousef, wanted for the World Trade Center bombing, was the eleventh and most recent.

Since the 1950s, the media outlets available have grown, and so has the reach of the Ten Most Wanted Fugitives list.

The Fox Television program *America's Most Wanted* featured one of the Top Ten fugitives—David James Roberts. Several citizens who saw Roberts on television contacted the FBI; that information led directly to his arrest. The FBI also posts the Ten Most Wanted list on its Website at www.fbi.gov, where it's viewed by thousands of cybervisitors.

CHAPTER 3
The Organizational Structure of the FBI

In official terms, the FBI is the principal investigative arm of the United States Department of Justice, assigned a four-part mission:

- Uphold the law through investigation of criminal violations

ist activities

- Provide leadership and law enforcement assistance to federal, state, local, and international agencies

- Perform these responsibilities in a manner that is responsive to the needs of the public and is faithful to the Constitution of the United States

That's a pretty big mission, and the FBI has been assigned the budget and resources needed to handle it. The FBI's budget for fiscal year 1997 was $2,837,610,000. As of October 1, 1996, the FBI had approximately 10,500 Special Agents and 14,000 professional support personnel.

Organizationally, the Bureau contains nine divisions and four offices, all directed from headquarters in Washington, D.C.

FBI Headquarters

Federal Bureau of Investigation

J. Edgar Hoover Building

935 Pennsylvania Avenue, N.W.

Washington, D.C. 20535

(202) 324-3000

Web Site: http://www.fbi.gov

Nine FBI Divisions

- Administrative Services Division
- Finance Division
- Criminal Justice Information Services Division
- Information Resources Division
- Criminal Investigative Division
- National Security Division
- Laboratory Division
- Training Division
- Inspection Division

Four FBI Offices

- Office of General Counsel
- Office of Professional Responsibility
- Office of Equal Employment Opportunity Affairs
- Office of Public and Congressional Affairs

From Headquarters, the Bureau's program direction and support are directed to a nationwide network, with outposts around the world:

- Fifty-six field offices
- Over 400 satellite offices, or resident agencies
- Four specialized field installations

The Director is supported by his staff and the Deputy Director. Each division is overseen by an Assistant Director. The offices are headed by an Inspector in Charge or General Counsel. The Assistant Directors, Inspectors in Charge, and General Counsel are supported by Deputies, Section Chiefs, Unit Chiefs, and Supervisors.

Each FBI field office is normally overseen by a Special Agent in Charge (SAC), who's assisted by at least one Assistant Special Agent in Charge (ASAC). Depending on its size, each field office has one or more squads of Special Agents, managed by Supervisory Special Agents. An Office Services Manager administers support operations, such as clerical services. The largest field offices—in Los Angeles, New York City, and Washington, D.C.—are managed by an Assistant Director in Charge (ADIC), who's then supported by multiple SACs and ASACs.

Each of the 400 Resident Agencies is managed by a Resident Agent, or a Supervisory Resident Agent, who reports to the SAC overseeing his or her territory. The ADICs and the SACs report to the Director of the FBI, the Deputy Director, or the Assistant Directors.

Finally, the FBI also maintains four specialized field facilities. Each of these is managed by a Special Agent and professional support personnel, who report to the appropriate division or divisions at FBI Headquarters.

FBI Specialized Field Installations

- **Regional Computer Support Centers:** (Pocatello, Idaho and Fort Monmouth, New Jersey)

- **Information Technology Centers:** Provide information services supporting investigative and administrative operations. There are two; one in Butte, Montana and one in Savannah, Georgia.

- **National Drug Intelligence Center:** Collects and consolidates drug-trafficking intelligence developed by law enforcement. The NDIC receives FBI support, though it's overseen by the DOJ. It's located in Johnstown, Pennsylvania.

- **El Paso Drug Intelligence Center:** Combats drug trafficking. The EPDIC is run by the DEA, with FBI assistance.

International Operations

A lot of people are surprised to learn that the FBI operates overseas. But the Bureau has long believed that good law enforcement doesn't stop at the United States border. The FBI maintains offices, or Legal Attachés, within the United States Embassies in 22 countries around the world. Each Legal Attaché, or "Legat," is headed by a Special Agent with the title of Legal Attaché, supported by one or more Assistant Legal Attachés. The Bureau also operates three Liaison Offices in Honolulu, Hawaii; Miami, Florida; and San Juan, Puerto Rico. Special Agents, or Liaison

Officers, cover designated areas of the Pacific Rim and the Caribbean, and maintain contact with the law enforcement and intelligence services in foreign countries within their jurisdictions.

FBI Special Agents generally don't have arrest authority outside the United States. Likewise, since the Legats exist for liaison purposes, Legal Attachés and Liaison Officers are generally granted no law enforcement powers in foreign countries.

Field Offices

Contact information for the 56 FBI Field Offices is included in the back of this book.

FEDERAL BUREAU OF INVESTIGATION

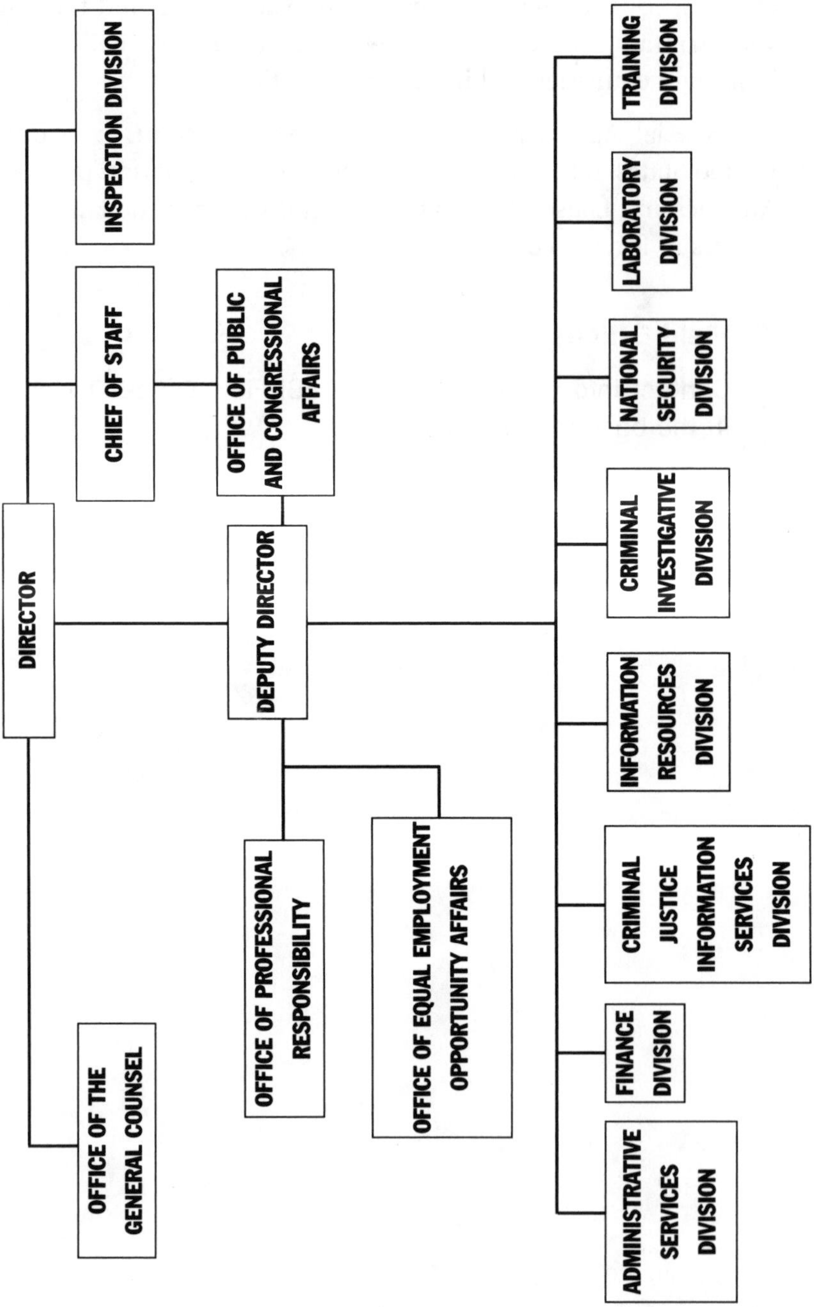

CHAPTER 4
FBI Investigative Programs

The FBI's investigative authority is the broadest of all federal law enforcement agencies. The Bureau is responsible for all criminal violations that aren't specifically assigned to another agency, as well as those in specific areas assigned by Congress, the president, or the attorney

The FBI's strategy has been to stress long-term, complex investigations, emphasizing close relationships and information sharing with other law enforcement and intelligence agencies—federal, state, local, and international. This strategy makes the best use of the FBI's nationwide resources and investigative expertise.

The information and evidence gathered in an FBI investigation are presented to the appropriate U.S. Attorney or Department of Justice official, who then decides whether the case should be prosecuted. If the case does proceed, the U.S. Attorney or DOJ official will handle it.

THE FBI'S ROLE

The bottom line is, the FBI's job is to investigate, not prosecute. That can lead to extremely frustrating situations. The Agent may be absolutely certain who committed a particular crime, but if the evidence doesn't meet certain legal standards, the case doesn't go forward. As with all legal matters, whether the evidence merits prosecution is often open to interpretation. The Agent's interpretation might not match up with the prosecutor's, for any number of reasons.

Jim McFall told me about one particular case he worked early in his career. In 1965, at the height of the civil rights unrest in the South, he was assigned to an FBI "Special"—a team of agents under the supervision of an Inspector from FBI Headquarters, assigned to a particularly sensitive investigation. McFall's Special worked on violent Ku Klux Klan cases. Here's how he tells the story:

> We worked in Natchez, Mississippi, for a while and then the team shifted over into Louisiana. We moved around the state, places covered by Resident Agencies of the New Orleans Division, and we were helping them intensify the investigation of the Klan in those areas. In August of '65 I ended up in a place called Bogalousa, Louisiana. From August till November, I worked on the murder of a deputy sheriff committed by the Klan. The deputy sheriff, Oneal Moore, was killed because he was an African American. That's what I feel the reason was. He'd arrested a white man several weeks before he was killed. The Klan decided somebody needed to teach him a lesson, so they did. They killed him, shot him in an ambush. They wounded his deputy, a white guy, Creed Rogers—shot out his left eye and wounded him in the leg.

> We had to go in and start investigating under pretty hostile conditions. You start by asking questions. You ask questions, you identify potential subjects, you listen to them very carefully, and you try to detect any hint of knowledge that they might have about the crime. You just keep going back and back and back. You don't give up, and you don't let them get away with it.

> And we solved that case. The frustration set in shortly thereafter when it was determined that there was no federal violation. You see, there's no such thing as a federal murder charge, and the U.S. attorney general for that area decided there wasn't enough evidence to warrant any federal charges. We offered to turn the case over to the state as a murder. The people in power at that time were inclined to favor the potential defendants rather than the victim, so they worked a finesse. They demanded

that the FBI identify all the confidential sources that were used in the investigation. We'd have to produce them in court to testify against the three subjects. Of course we couldn't do that. We'd get them killed. The state said if we wouldn't identify the confidential sources, they wouldn't prosecute the case.

The killers are walking around free today. They murdered a police officer by ambush—actually rode up behind the police car and shot him through the window. They murdered Moore and wounded Rogers, and the three of them are walking free today.

You have no idea how frustrating it was. Still is.

I'm willing to bet every Special Agent has at least one story like this—cases that weren't filed, or weren't prosecuted aggressively. Then you have the situations in which an overloaded criminal system seems to undercut the efforts of the Bureau and the police. Bob McGonigel

I remember working a drug case for months, and we finally got the guy. He was arrested, he was convicted—I think he plea-bargained—and we didn't have to testify in the trial.

Just for the heck of it, I drove by his house one day, not long after the trial. He's sitting on the porch with all these girls. Having a great time. I went back to my unit that day, and I said, "Fellas, I wanna tell you what our efforts have gotten." I think he's probably still dealing, to this day.

That kind of thing is frustrating. I mean, this is a dangerous guy, who could have really put a hurting on us. In the course of the investigation, we found out all kinds of things about this guy, his violent activities.

All you can do in a situation like that is say, "Hey, look. We can still do what we do, the best we possibly can. What happens after that—well, we have no control over it." And that's how you keep going out there.

WHAT THE FBI ISN'T

Often, people get confused about the difference between the FBI and all the other federal agencies associated with law enforcement or investigations of various kinds. Doug Rhoads says, "I still get people who ask me, 'What's it like to guard the president?' And I have to say, 'Well, ma'am, I have no idea.'"

For instance, the FBI versus the CIA. The CIA actually has no law enforcement function. The CIA collects and analyzes information needed to develop U.S. policy, especially security policy. The CIA is authorized to gather information on foreign countries and their citizens exclusively; it's specifically prohibited from collecting information concerning "U.S. persons"—a legal term that includes U.S. citizens, resident aliens, legal immigrants, and U.S. corporations, regardless of where they're located. On the other hand, the FBI is all about investigating crimes among and directed at "U.S. persons."

Two other federal agencies involved with law enforcement—the Drug Enforcement Agency (DEA) and the Bureau of Alcohol Tobacco and Firearms (ATF)—are often confused with the FBI. Here are the differences: While the FBI is charged with enforcement of over 300 federal violations, the DEA is a single-mission agency dealing solely with enforcement of drug laws. The ATF also has a relatively restricted area of investigation; its major responsibility is enforcing federal firearms statutes and investigating arsons and bombings that *aren't* related to terrorism.

Obviously, the aims of the Bureau and these other agencies often overlap. The FBI always stresses cooperation and coordination—not competition. The FBI works with all these agencies both on specific cases and ongoing task forces.

So what *does* the FBI do? The FBI's investigative functions fall into the following categories:

- Applicant matters
- Civil rights
- Counterterrorism
- Foreign counterintelligence
- Organized crime and drugs
- Violent crimes and major offenders
- Financial crime

APPLICANT PROGRAM

for a job with the FBI. The FBI also conducts background investigations for certain other government entities—the White House, the Department of Justice, the Administrative Office of the U.S. Courts, and certain House and Senate committees.

Often, retired FBI Special Agents work on contract with the Bureau to carry out these investigations. The investigators take a look at relevant records—credit reports and arrest records—and also conduct interviews with the applicant's references, neighbors, and former employers. This is one reason why former Special Agents make good investigators—they're astute interviewers, experienced in recognizing deception.

Once the investigation is complete, the report is forwarded to the requesting government entity. Under the Freedom of Information/ Privacy Acts, the subject of a background investigation can ask to see the contents of his or her own report. Private citizens can ask to see the contents of other people's reports, but they have to demonstrate a compelling and legitimate reason for access, such as research for a book or a legal proceeding. You can't just flip through someone's file out of idle curiosity. Other government entities may also request the results of a background check, if they need to determine a person's suitability for employment or access to sensitive material.

CIVIL RIGHTS PROGRAM

The FBI investigates all violations of federal civil rights statutes; the Department of Justice determines prosecution. Civil rights violations fall into several categories:

- Racial or religious discrimination
- Abuses "under color of law"—use of excessive force or police misconduct
- Involuntary servitude or slavery
- Violation of the Voting Rights Act of 1965
- Violation of the Civil Rights Act of 1964
- Violation of the Equal Credit Opportunity Act
- Violation of the Freedom of Access to Clinic Entrances Act
- Violation of the Civil Rights of Institutionalized Persons Act

Most civil rights violations investigated by the FBI involve cases of injury or death allegedly caused by the use of excessive force by law enforcement officers. Every year, the FBI investigates hundreds of these cases; on average, about 30 law enforcement personnel are eventually convicted. Another common complaint involves racial violence, such as physical assaults, homicides, verbal or written threats, or desecration of property.

Frank Watts and Jim McFall told some stories about their civil rights work in the 1960s. But the Bureau's efforts in this area are ongoing. One of the biggest civil rights cases in recent years involved a man who was murdered because of what he said on the radio.

The Silent Brotherhood

Just before midnight on June 18, 1984, a quiet residential neighborhood in Denver, Colorado, was disrupted by an unfamiliar sound—a barrage of gunfire.

The target was controversial radio talk show host Alan Berg. He was found in his driveway, sprawled in a pool of blood. He'd been killed instantly by shots to the head and neck. He hadn't even had time to step all the way out of his car.

Berg, who called himself "the last angry man," had helped originate "shock radio." Long before Howard Stern made it big, Berg developed an abrasive style—delivering opinionated diatribes, interrupting callers, insulting and attacking them on the air. Berg's defenders argued that he never indulged in personal attacks, but instead challenging their thinking. Still, Berg had received several death threats, including one a few months before his murder.

Denver police focused immediately on right-wing extremists; Berg's liberal viewpoints and abrasive style had led to run-ins with them before. In 1979, a Ku Klux Klan member burst into the studio while Berg was on the air. Berg said the man had threatened him with a gun. The man denied it, and the issue was later settled out of court.

Over the weeks and months following Berg's murder, Denver police questioned over 200 people and tracked down countless leads. They were sure that right-wing extremists were involved, but they couldn't get any hard evidence.

Then came the shoot-out in Sandpoint, Idaho.

During the early '80s, FBI agents in the northwestern United States came to realize that a group of antigovernment white supremacists had set up operations in the area. The group called themselves the Aryan Nation, and they were suspected of several crimes in the region, including a series of robberies. The agents identified as many of the members of the Aryan Nation as they could, and kept them under surveillance. Slowly, the agents uncovered evidence of an armed and violent group allied with the Aryan Nation—the Order, or the Silent Brotherhood. Agents began keeping track of members of the Silent Brotherhood, as well.

On October 18, 1984, three FBI agents drove down a rutted, rural driveway in Sandpoint, Idaho. They were on their way to visit Gary Lee Yarbrough, known to be a member of the Aryan Nation. Yarbrough also had links to the Order.

Before the Agents reached his house, Yarbrough opened fire. No one was injured in the resulting shoot-out, but Yarbrough escaped. The FBI Agents searched his house and found a cache of explosives and weapons, including a Mac 10 submachine gun—the same kind of gun used to kill Alan Berg. Ballistics tests proved that it was the murder weapon, and investigators had their first major break. (They later found out that Yarbrough wasn't the trigger man. The leader of the Silent Brotherhood had given Yarbrough the Mac 10 and told him to get rid of the weapon by throwing it into one of the thousands of remote mountain lakes in the region. But Yarbrough was too enamored of his new toy, and just couldn't give it up.)

Eventually, the Berg murder became one of a string of major crimes tied to the Order. The group planned an armed overthrow of the U.S. government, a project they knew would be expensive. Their money-making endeavors included counterfeiting and armed robbery, notably a $3.6 million holdup of a Brink's armored car. The Order targeted several prominent people for assassination, including television producer Norman Lear, civil rights lawyer Morris Dees, and Berg.

The FBI's extensive intelligence on right-wing extremist groups proved vital to investigating and prosecuting the case. The Aryan Nation leadership had issued death threats against a former member turned FBI informant; the man's picture and last known address were posted on the

Aryan Liberty Network Website and printed in newsletters, along with threats to "remove his head from his body."

A security officer for the Aryan Nation paid $1,800 for proof of the informant's death—a photograph of the man's decapitated body. The photograph actually was a convincing fake produced in the FBI Lab, and the security officer was arrested for conspiring to kill a government witness.

In September 1985, ten members of the Order were brought to trial in Seattle, Washington, charged under the federal law against conspiring to operate a criminal enterprise. All ten were convicted, and six of the ten were also convicted of separate criminal counts. The prosecution depended on circumstantial evidence—such as hotel, telephone, and airline records—as well as expert fingerprint and ballistics testimony gathered and developed by the FBI. Most of the defendants didn't even try to shake the FBI experts' testimony.

Just over two years later, in October 1997, four members of the Order were brought to trial on federal civil rights charges in Berg's murder. The Denver district attorney declined to file murder charges, saying the circumstantial evidence didn't show a strong enough link to the defendants.

More than 80 witnesses testified in the trial, including the FBI finger-print and ballistics experts who had testified in the racketeering trial. Bruce Pierce was accused of shooting Berg; in his opening statement, Pierce's attorney said, accurately, "There are no eyewitnesses linking him to the scene of the crime, no physical evidence linking him to the scene of the crime." But FBI witnesses linked Pierce to the murder through a fingerprint on a Denver hotel registration and ballistics tests on shells found in a house Pierce rented after Berg's death.

Two of the defendants, Pierce and the getaway driver, were convicted. U.S. District Court Judge Richard Matsch sentenced the two to serve 150 years in prison, on top of their earlier sentences for racketeering. The 150-year sentence requires them to serve at least 50 years before they're eligible for parole. "A life sentence would not be sufficient in this case," Matsch said; a life sentence would have made them eligible for parole sooner. (If Matsch's name seems familiar, there's a reason why. He presided over Timothy McVeigh's trial for the Oklahoma City bombing. That may not be the only link between the two cases. According to some reports, McVeigh closely followed the racketeering and civil rights trials of the Order members.)

The investigation of The Order stretched across most of the western United States; the prosecution lacked eyewitness testimony and needed convincing forensic evidence. It's exactly this kind of complicated case that the FBI was developed to handle.

COUNTERTERRORISM PROGRAM

The FBI is the federal agency charged with protecting the United States and its citizens from the threat of terrorism, here and abroad. The squads assigned to counterterrorism focus on extensive investigation of terrorist incidents—and they work proactively to prevent terrorism through authorized intelligence collection.

Countering terrorism effectively requires the exchange of information and close, daily coordination among U.S. law enforcement, intelligence, and service entities. Also, the overall success in combating international terrorism is directly attributable to a growth of international intelligence sharing and increased international law enforcement efforts.

Generally, the FBI's counterterrorism activities fall into the following categories:

- Domestic terrorism
- Hostage taking
- Overseas homicide and attempted homicide, when the victim(s) are "U.S. persons"
- Protection of foreign officials and guests

- Sabotage

- Domestic security

- Attempted or actual bombings, when the motive is terrorism

- Nuclear extortion

- Sedition, or fostering violent rebellion against the government

Antiterrorism investigations most often involve bombings. When a bombing or bomb threat occurs, either the ATF or the FBI will be given control of the investigation. In general, the ATF investigates violations of the Federal Bombing Statute; however, Department of Justice guidelines give the FBI jurisdiction over separate violations, which the FBI handled before enactment of the Statute.

The FBI's responsibilities cover the deliberate, malicious damage or destruction, by use of an explosive, of property used in interstate or foreign commerce. This includes the bombing or attempted bombing of college or university facilities, and incidents that seem to be the work of terrorist or revolutionary groups. Overseas, the FBI investigates bombings that are an act of terrorism against U.S. persons or interests.

Of course, the investigation of a bombing or bomb threat begins immediately, even before jurisdiction is determined. The FBI and the ATF, plus any local forces, cooperate on the scene, while DOJ makes its determination.

Another common category of the FBI's antiterrorism work is the investigation of domestic hate groups, such as The Order. The Bureau's responsibilities in this area are outlined by the attorney general. Investigations are conducted only when the following three elements exist:

- A threat or advocacy of force

- The apparent ability to carry out the proclaimed act

- The potential violation of a federal law

These guidelines give the FBI a consistent policy for initiating investigations. No one at the FBI can single out a group for surveillance without first making sure the situation meets the attorney general's guidelines. Then, the AG must give the Bureau authorization to begin its investigation. The information uncovered is used to prevent terrorist activity and, whenever possible, to aid in the arrest and prosecution of persons or groups that have violated the law.

The FBI's priority is always to prevent terrorist incidents and to investigate those that do occur. Counterterrorism investigations focus on the group's unlawful activities, not its philosophy or the nationality of its members. When conducting investigations, the FBI collects information that not only serves as the basis for prosecution, but also builds an intelligence base to help prevent terrorist acts.

The successful investigation and prosecution of the World Trade Center bombings is probably the best known of the FBI's counterterrorism cases.

An ongoing counterterrorism case involves the 1996 bombing at the Summer Olympics in Atlanta, which has been linked to bombings at a women's health clinic and a gay bar in Atlanta.

With the Bureau's permission, we've reproduced the letter sent out after the bombings, plus descriptions of the bombs themselves.

The Atlanta Bomb Task Force

The FBI has discovered links among three different bombings in the Atlanta area: the Centennial Olympic Park bombing on July 27, 1996; the bombing at the Sandy Springs Professional Building on January 16, 1997; and the bombing at the Otherside Lounge on February 21, 1997. I'm sure you remember the Olympic Park bombing during the Summer Olympics; one person was killed by the explosion and another suffered a fatal heart attack.

The other two bombings were less spectacular, but intended to be more destructive. Each incident involved two separate explosions, with the second timed to target police and emergency personnel responding to the first.

The following is a list of distinctive bomb components; in each case, this is an unusual quantity or configuration for legitimate use of this particular material. If any of these materials—in this form, by the relevant dates—triggers any recall with you, contact the Atlanta Bomb Task Force at (888) 283-2662. If your information leads to the arrest and conviction of the bomber or bombers, you could be eligible for a $500,000 reward.

Olympic Park Bombing—July 27, 1996

- Steel plate, ⅛" thick (11-gauge), 15" × 12", cut with an oxy-acetylene torch

- Olive-green foam padding, commonly used in military-style sleeping mats, approximately 15" × 12". This section of foam padding was composed of two separate sheets of ⅜" foam laminated together.

- Three metal pipes, each 12" long and 2" in diameter, threaded and capped at both ends

- Three or four pounds of Accurate Arms Brand #7 or #9 smokeless gunpowder

- Six pounds of concrete or masonry nails, 2½" long, size 8d

Sandy Springs Bombing—January 16, 1997

- Two steel plates, each ⅛" thick (11-gauge), 11" × 8", cut with an oxyacetylene torch

- Almost four pounds of flooring nails, 1½" long, size 4d

- Approximately 100 feet of twisted galvanized wire. This wire was manufactured by the bomber, using at least 200 feet of plain wire twisted with something like an electric drill.

- Between 15 and 25 half-pound sticks of dynamite

The Otherside Bombing—February 21, 1997

- Two steel plates, each ¼" thick, cut with a plasma arc cutter

- Almost seven pounds of galvanized wire nails, 2" long, size 6d

- Between 15 and 25 half-pound sticks of dynamite

On the following pages is a reproduction of the letter claiming responsibility for the Sandy Springs and Otherside bombings. Maybe there's something about the handwriting, the distinctive spelling errors, the phrasings, or the ideas expressed that seems familiar to you. If you have any information, call the Atlanta Bomb Task Force at (888) 283-2662.

FOREIGN COUNTERINTELLIGENCE PROGRAM

As the country's lead counterintelligence agency, the FBI works to protect the national interest by lawfully preventing foreign organizations and citizens from gathering sensitive information about the United States—in other words, the Bureau is responsible for preventing spying. As you know from reading the chapter about the FBI's history, you know that the Bureau was deeply involved in Cold War counterespionage. But spy cases didn't end in the '50s.

One of the Bureau's most well-publicized counterespionage cases involved Aldrich Ames, a CIA agent who sold out to the KGB for almost $2 million. The Ames case has been well documented in several books; two of the best are *Confessions of a Spy: The Real Story of Aldrich Ames,* by Pete Earley, and *Killer Spy: The Inside Story of the FBI's Pursuit and Capture of Aldrich Ames, America's Deadliest Spy,* by Peter Maas.

The "Army of God" Letter

THE BOMBING'S IN SANDY SPRINGS
AND MIDTOWN WERE CARRIED-OUT
BY UNITS OF THE ARMY OF GOD.

THE ABORTION WAS THE TARGET
OF THE FIRST DEVICE. THE MURDER
3.5 MILLION CHILDREN EVERY YEAR
WILL NOT BE "TOLERATED". THOSE
WHO PARTICIPATE IN ANYWAY IN
THE MURDER OF CHILDREN MAY
BE TARGETED FOR ATTACK. THE
ATTACK THEREFORE SERVES AS
A WARNING: ANYONE IN OR AROUND
FACILITIES THAT MURDER CHILDREN
MAY BECOME VICTIMS OF
RETRIBUTION. THE NEXT
FACILITY TARGETED MAY NOT
BE EMPTY.
THE SECOND DEVICE WAS
AIMED AT AGENT OF THE
SO-CALLED FEDERAL GOVERNMENT
I.E. A.T.F. F.B.I. MARSHALL'S E.T.C.
WE DECLARE AND WILL WAGE
TOTAL WAR ON THE UNGODLY
COMMUNIST REGIME IN NEW YORK
AND YOUR LEGISLATIVE -
BUREAUCRATIC LACKEY'S IN
WASHINGTON. IT IS YOU WHO ARE
RESPOSIBLE AND PRESIDE OVER

Letter claiming responsibility for the Sandy Springs and Otherside bombings, from the Atlanta Bombing Case Consolidation, June 9, 1997 (continued on next page) (FBI Photo)

The "Army of God" Letter (continued)

+HE MURDER OF CHILDREN AND
ISSUE THE POLICY OF UNGODLY
PREVERSION THATS DESTROYING OUR
PEOPLE. WE WILL TARGET
ALL FACILITIES AND PERSONNEll
OF THE FEDERAL GOVERNMENT.
   THE ATTACK IN MIDTOWN WAS
AIMED AT THE SODOMITE BAR
(THE OTHERSIDE). WE WILL TARGET
SODOMITES, THERE ORGANIZATIONS,
AND ALL THOSE WHO PUSH THERE
AGENDA.
   "DEATH TO THE NEW WORLD ORDER"

Letter claiming responsibility for the Sandy Springs and Otherside bombings (continued from previous page) (FBI Photo)

The Mole

Aldrich Ames apparently never was the brightest bulb on the tree. His bosses gave him mediocre performance evaluations; he drank heavily, and was once found passed out in a gutter; he often napped at his desk after a multiple-martini lunch. Still, in September 1983, he was appointed the CIA's counterintelligence branch chief in Soviet operations. The job gave him access to a wealth of sensitive information, including the identities of Soviets working for the United States.

By early 1985, Rick Ames felt strapped for money. Two years earlier, while posted in Mexico City, he'd become involved with a woman working as a cultural attaché at the Colombian embassy. Rosario Casas Dupuy was an ambitious, forceful woman with a taste for the best—or at least the most expensive—of everything. Ames was in the middle of a divorce, and Rosario had come to live with him in Arlington, Virginia. As a foreign national in the United States on a tourist visa, she couldn't work. She was bored and restless, and complained constantly. Ames had piled up tens of thousands of dollars in debt, and his $45,000-a-year salary seemed pitifully inadequate. Before he married Rosario, Rick felt he needed a solid chunk of money—something to settle his debts and get a fresh start. He thought about a second job at a 7-11; he considered bank robbery. Then he remembered his most valuable asset, something worth a great deal to certain people—information about U.S. espionage.

On April 16, 1985, Ames set up a lunch appointment with an employee at the Soviet embassy, a man he was trying to recruit for the CIA. Ames prepared a note addressed to the KGB *rezident* posted at the Soviet embassy; he was offering to sell the Soviets information about the CIA's spying operations for $50,000 in cash.

Rick Ames got stood up for lunch. But, fortified by several vodka martinis, he decided to forge ahead anyway. He drove straight to the Soviet embassy and handed the security guard an envelope addressed to the KGB *rezident,* using the man's KGB code name. Within a month, Ames had his $50,000, and a new career as a spy. He excelled in his career as a mole in a way he never had while working "above ground."

Over the next five years, Rick Ames sold tremendous amounts of information to the Soviets. He betrayed as many as 20 agents working for the United States; several of these men were promptly executed, leaving their families in the Soviet Union destitute and disgraced. In exchange, Ames received enough money to support himself and Rosario in the manner she wanted to become accustomed to: expensive vacations, live-in servants, designer dresses, custom-tailored silk suits, Rolex and Gucci watches, a Jaguar sports car, cosmetic caps for his unattractive teeth, $5,000-a-month phone bills for chatty calls to her mother in Colombia. When they bought a half-million dollar house in the D.C. suburbs, they paid cash.

This conspicuous consumption didn't go unnoticed; when anyone asked, Ames said Rosario had inherited the money. He told Rosario herself that a friend, "Robert from Chicago," had given him money to invest; Ames had done well, and the free-flowing cash was his percentage of the profits. Rosario never questioned this explanation—why Robert never called, visited, or wrote; why anyone would give Ames so much money to invest; how he managed to do so well after botching his own finances so thoroughly.

While the Ameses spent their blood money, the CIA was trying to discover what had gone wrong. Most of the executions took place in 1985, and the KGB managed to direct suspicion to a disgruntled former employee who'd threatened to expose the Agency's secrets. When the losses seemed to subside, so did the CIA's eagerness to find the mole some suspected was operating in their midst.

But some CIA employees never let the issue drop. In 1988, when the CIA formed a Counterintelligence Center at Langley, one of the investigators assigned to the new unit was Dan Payne. Earlier investigations of the 1985 murders had tried to match the leaked information with those who had access to it. Payne was eager to try a different approach, looking for CIA employees who seemed to be living beyond their means.

Ames's name soon surfaced, but hard proof was lacking. The CIA's Office of Security passed Ames on his regularly scheduled security clearance, despite signs of deception on the polygraph. Payne and his boss, Jeanne Vertefeuille, had to move on to other cases.

Finally, in early 1991, Vertefeuille asked her new boss if she could devote herself full time to the 1985 losses. She was close to retirement, and she really wanted to focus on this project, to try to get some answers before she left the Agency.

At this point, the FBI got involved. In 1985, the Bureau had investigated why two of its Soviet spies had been arrested and executed; by 1987 the investigators concluded they just didn't have enough information to come to a conclusion. But the FBI still wanted answers.

The new dual-agency, mole-hunt task force consisted of Jeanne Vertefueille and CIA investigator Sandy Grimes, plus James P. Milburn, one of the FBI's Soviet experts, and Jim Holt, a veteran FBI agent.

For the first time in this investigation or any other, there was complete cooperation between the two agencies. Vertefueille gave the FBI agents unrestricted access to all the CIA's records, except for medical and psychological files.

Gradually, methodically, the task force narrowed its focus to Ames. Dan Payne was asked to investigate Ames's finances; he was shocked to discover that a man whose salary was barely $70,000 a year was spending $200,000 a year on credit card charges alone. Sandy Grimes constructed a meticulous timeline of events in Rick Ames's life and career; she noticed an interesting pattern. Within a day or two after a visit with a Soviet contact, Ames would deposit several thousand dollars in his checking or savings accounts. These deposits were always just under $10,000—the legal cutoff for federal reporting.

By the end of 1992, Dan Payne had discovered several Swiss bank accounts Ames maintained. Payne calculated that in the past six years, Ames had received $1.3 million from unknown sources. The task force was convinced they'd found their mole.

Once Ames was identified as the chief suspect, the FBI's Washington Field Office organized an investigation, with Special Agent Les Wiser at its head. The full-scale investigation, with round-the-clock surveillance and wiretaps, began in May 1993. FBI agents even "borrowed" Ames's household garbage in the middle of the night, carting it away and sorting through it before returning it to the curb. Agents even took careful notes of the placement of the top layer of trash, so they could duplicate it before bringing back to the Ames home. Everything the agents discovered through the surveillance confirmed their suspicions, but they weren't able to gather enough hard evidence to move forward.

The investigation continued at this plateau for almost four months, and the risk that Ames would realize he was being scrutinized increased every day. Then there was one terrible day in early September 1993, when a series of miscommunications and equipment failures let Ames escape surveillance and make a dead drop.

Wiser and his agents were desperate for a breakthrough. Against explicit orders from Wiser's boss, they made one more trash pickup, on the night of September 15. This time, they hit pay dirt. Buried among the cereal boxes and used paper towels and other household garbage, the Agents found a yellow sticky note torn into bits. When they reassembled the pieces, the note, in Ames's handwriting, read: "I am ready to meet at B on 1 Oct." The agents knew this meant Ames was planning a meeting with his handlers in Bogota, Colombia. Finally, they had hard evidence of Ames's activities. According to Maas, Wiser's boss called his decision to defy direct orders to terminate the trash pickups "a marvelous piece of insubordination."

The October 1 meeting between Ames and his handlers was canceled, but other breakthroughs followed. Wiretaps revealed that Rick and Rosario were planning to attend a wedding out of town in late October; the FBI obtained a search warrant and searched the house while they were away. They found a KBG officer's home phone number scribbled down in Rick's handwriting, and a note rescheduling the Bogota meeting for November 1. On Ames's computer, agents found several letters to his handler, detailing meeting times and places and information that would be passed.

The FBI now had more than enough evidence to demonstrate that Rick was a mole. However, the investigation continued; the Department of Justice wanted to catch Rick in the act.

The FBI staked out Ames at the meeting place in Bogota. However, he again evaded surveillance. There were no contacts between Rick and his handlers for the rest of 1993. However, wiretaps did record conversations between Rick and Rosario that made it clear that she was aware of his spying activities; this evidence would become crucial during the prosecution.

Finally, on February 21, 1994, the move was made to arrest both Ames and his wife. FBI Agents swooped down on Ames's Jaguar as he drove through his neighborhood on that quiet Presidents' Day morning. As he was pushed into a waiting car, Ames muttered to himself, "Think, think, think."

But it was too late for that. Ames was charged with espionage. Rosario Ames was arrested at their home and charged with assisting him.

FBI Agent Julie Johnson had listened to hours and hours of wiretapped conversations between Rick and Rosario; she had real insight into their relationship and their personalities. She advised the agents interviewing Rosario to treat her with respect; try to bully her, and she'll blow up, Johnson warned. But Johnson felt that given a chance, Rosario would turn over on Rick.

Johnson was right. Once the agents interviewing Rosario pointed out her lies and contradictions, she told them she was tired of playing games. "Rick works for the Russians," she said.

The evidence against Ames was devastating—including a letter from his KGB handler listing what Ames had been paid and what was being held for him. The cash total came to $2.7 million; that doesn't count the value of a riverfront dacha set aside for the day when the KGB's valued spy might wish to retire to Russia. Despite the case against him, Ames's attorney, Plato Cacheris, advised him to fight. Cacheris argued that there was only one way to get a deal for himself and for Rosario—Ames had to play hardball, instead of revealing his weakness, his concern for Rosario. (You may recognize Cacheris's name. In June 1998, he became one of the lawyers representing Monica Lewinsky as she was pursued by Special Prosecutor Kenneth Starr, investigating possible sexual misconduct by President Clinton. Just one more example of how "insider" Washington really is.)

But Ames insisted on cooperating. He didn't want Rosario to go through a trial. At first, Rosario wanted to push forward, protesting her innocence in court. Then the prosecutor invited Rosario and her lawyer to listen to wiretap evidence he planned to play in court. As Earley describes them, the tapes capture Rosario "sniveling about money, griping at [their young son] Paul, belittling her friends, and constantly degrading and chiding Rick. She sounded arrogant, contemptuous, totally self-absorbed and, worst of all, greedy." It was also clear from the tapes that she was fully aware of Rick's dealings with the Soviets; while he was in Bogota, she harangued him about putting the documents and cash in his carry-on luggage, rather than entrusting them to airline baggage handlers.

In the end, both Rick and Rosario opted for a plea bargain. Rick received life in prison without possibility of parole; Rosario's sentencing was delayed until Rick was fully debriefed. Rick did cooperate, and Rosario was sentenced to a five-year term. Custody of Paul, their son, was awarded to Rosario's mother while Rosario serves out her sentence.

Without the unprecedented cooperation of investigators from both the FBI and the CIA, without the decision to charge Rosario as well as Rick, this case might never have been untangled. Today, an FBI counterintelligence agent is permanently posted at Langley, a reminder that even government agencies can learn from their mistakes.

The New Espionage

Of course, there's no longer a KGB or a Soviet Union to recruit spies. But the end of the "evil empire" hasn't brought about the end of espionage. Instead, it has brought new threats from new sources—the old Soviet republics, the emerging Asian powers. The threat of espionage hasn't decreased; in fact, in some areas it has grown and become more difficult to assess and predict. And it remains a major problem. According to some estimates, espionage currently costs the United States economy $100 billion per year.

You won't ever hear much in the media about the FBI's ongoing foreign counterintelligence work. Unlike criminal investigations, espionage and espionage-related matters usually don't lead to arrest and prosecution. Instead, the goal is to neutralize the threat; the public never becomes aware of most of the program's activities.

Those activities cover spying on government *and* private industry. Because of our country's technological and business strength, companies and research institutions as well as government entities continue to be prime targets of foreign intelligence services. The FBI investigates wherever and whenever a foreign organization conducts clandestine intelligence activities in the United States.

In fact, there's so much spying directed at business interests that the FBI puts a special focus on *economic espionage*. The Bureau defines economic espionage as follows:

"Foreign power-sponsored or coordinated intelligence activity directed at the U.S. government or U.S. corporations, establishments, or persons designed to unlawfully and clandestinely obtain sensitive financial, trade, or economic policy information; proprietary economic information; critical technologies; or to unlawfully or clandestinely influence sensitive economic policy decisions."

The opportunities for economic espionage, and the value of the information the spies are after, will just continue to grow. As multinational companies expand their operations, and as technology connects individuals and organizations around the globe, information becomes more valuable and harder to protect. And information doesn't have to be "classified" to be valuable. Patents, technical plans, drafts of public policy documents—anything that deals with sensitive economic, technological, or governmental matters, on any level, can catch a spy's eye.

Think about Microsoft, or Java, or any other software company. A significant percentage of the company's budget consists of R&D—research and development into better, more efficient computer applications. If a foreign company can get its hands on the end product, leapfrogging over the expensive R&D process, they'll be that much further ahead.

And software is just one example; the United States leads the world in intellectual property development—software, technological innovations, manufacturing improvements, all sorts of ideas and discoveries with economic value. The theft or misappropriation of this intellectual property can save foreign companies and governments billions of dollars; saving all that money allows those companies and governments to sell their products at a lower cost, increasing their market share and profit margins. In a global market, that costs the United States economy even more money.

You can't spot a spy by his trench coat and shifty eyes. Recent surveys show that corporate insiders account for up to 75 percent of U.S. technology loss. Often, these spies are American citizens acting on their own to sell information to foreign intelligence services.

Just as most of us have had our image of a spy shaped by movies and novels, we think of James Bond–ish technology as part of the spy's arsenal. Yes, new satellite technology, new listening devices, and new microcircuitry advances present new dangers. Those same advances and others—retinal scans, holographic watermarks—can help safeguard information, as well. But espionage comes down to people. The human factor is always crucial.

You can be part of that human factor. Raise your security awareness. Report any suspected espionage activity to the FBI. This doesn't mean you should play spy-counterspy with the guy in the cubicle down the way. But look out for the following:

- Unauthorized attempts to view records or plans

- Scavenging through trash

- Eavesdropping on live or telephone conversations

- Questions from persons who have no need to know certain information to do their job

- Persons found outside their normal work areas or at unusual hours

A recent study by the American Society for Industrial Security has put the cost of the theft of trade secrets from U.S. business at $2 billion a month. The Economic Espionage Act of 1996 was signed into law by President Clinton on October 11, 1996. This created federal criminal jurisdiction regarding both state-sponsored and the commercial theft of trade secrets. Misappropriation or theft of both intangible and tangible property is a crime under the Act. The FBI is currently involved in investigations in both state-sponsored and commercial theft of trade secrets.

Operation Counter Copy

The FBI's efforts regarding the investigation of Intellectual Property Right (IPR) criminal investigations centers on locating and identifying the producers, principal distributors, and publishers of unauthorized trademarks and/or copyrighted products in order to eliminate the sources of illicit productions. These cases typically involve major manufacturers of illegally produced goods that lead to either significant financial losses to victim companies or potential risks to the health and welfare of the general public.

The FBI investigates the illegal manufacturing and distribution trademarked items and copyrightable work. This covers, among other things, motion pictures, sound recordings (tapes and records), audiovisual works (video games), computer software, musical compositions (sheet music), television shows, books, and art objects. The FBI is also seeing more investigations regarding thefts of trade secrets.

The FBI's investigative experience has shown that the most effective way to identify manufacturers and distributors is to buy copies of suspicious items and confirm that the items are unauthorized duplications. Using the counterfeits as evidence, investigators can then request a search warrant to seize the contraband and related duplication equipment. Prosecution of retailers usually depends on two things: their awareness of the illegal counterfeiting, and the extent of their cooperation with the investigation and prosecution of major suppliers.

In April 1996, the U.S. Trade Representative confronted Chinese representatives about China's widespread piracy of American movies, records, and computer software. FBI Director Freeh later met with the

Acting U.S. Trade Representative and discussed the global problem of IPR infringement. In a followup measure, the FBI initiated Operation Counter Copy to further identify and address the growing IPR infringement problem.

Operation Counter Copy has brought together IPR investigations from eleven FBI offices across the country. The cases involve copyright infringement of motion pictures, sound recordings, and computer software, as well as trademark infringement matters. The FBI works closely with the various related industries including the Motion Picture Association, Business Software Alliance, and the Recording Industry Association of America in order to better address this crime problem. This is an ongoing initiative that will be expanding internationally through cooperation with foreign law enforcement authorities.

ORGANIZED CRIME AND DRUG PROGRAM

The Organized Crime and Drug Program investigates the following federal violations:

- Drug matters
- Racketeer Influenced and Corrupt Organizations (RICO) matters
- Criminal enterprise investigations
- Labor racketeering
- Money laundering
- Organized crime/Drug Enforcement Task Force matters

The FBI has an arsenal of weapons at its disposal: asset forfeiture laws, sophisticated investigative techniques, a nationwide and international law enforcement network. The most significant tool used in fighting organized crime passed in 1970: the Racketeer Influenced and Corrupt

Organizations (RICO) statute. Under the criminal and civil RICO provisions, FBI Special Agents and other law enforcement officials are authorized to use undercover operations, court-ordered electronic surveillance (such as wiretaps), informants and cooperating witnesses, and consensual monitoring (or "wearing a wire").

I just mentioned a couple of fairly controversial issues: use of wiretapping and use of informants.

First, contrary to what you may have seen in the movies, wiretapping is not used that often, and it's used only in fighting serious crimes such as major drug dealing, terrorism and, as you saw in the Ames case, espionage. No FBI Special Agent—or anyone else in the Bureau—can install a wiretap on his own. Before a wiretap can be put in place, the FBI has to show probable cause that the wiretap is likely to provide evidence of a felony violation of federal law. A federal judge—someone who has no stake in the outcome—evaluates the agent's evidence; based on that evidence, the judge either authorizes the wiretap, or tells the agent to come back with a more convincing legal argument. While the wiretap is operating, the judge monitors how it's used, and he or she can shut it down at any time if it's being abused. Anyone—including a Special Agent—who installs a wiretap without following these rules commits a serious felony.

Second, I feel that the use of informants has gotten a bad rap in the media. Informants are "rats" and "snitches," while the people who don't give up any information are "stand-up guys." People become informants for all kinds of reasons—they want money, they're looking for revenge, they've got a troubled conscience. Of course some informants are sleazy. Most law-abiding, clean-living citizens don't hang out with chronic law breakers. The fact is, when you're trying to gather intelligence about law-breaking groups, closed societies that isolate themselves from the larger culture, you're going to need informants to get the job done.

When Jim McFall worked in the South during the civil rights era, he relied heavily on informants to break the Klan. "When I started, I had five Klaverns in my territory. When I got transferred back to New Orleans there was only one Klavern, consolidated from all the others. It had 25 members, and of those 25 members, five were my informants. None of these informants knew the others were informants. That was good, because I could validate the information I got from each of them."

U.S. courts recognize the use of informants as lawful, even essential. But the courts also realize that use of informants can involve serious issues: deception, privacy violations, involvement with people who have questionable motives or reliability. To handle these issues, the Attorney General developed specific guidelines regulating the FBI's use of informants. Agents carefully supervise the informants' activities and evaluate their information to make sure nothing about the investigation violates the legal rights of individuals under investigation.

Informants don't become FBI employees, even if they're paid by the FBI. They're not hired or trained by the FBI, and the FBI won't necessarily intervene in any criminal cases pending against the informant.

Okay, back to the Organized Crime and Drug Program. Drug trafficking is closely allied with organized crime, which is why the two areas are combined in one program. Over years of working against an ever-changing drug trade, the FBI developed the Enterprise Theory of Investigation, which focuses investigations and prosecutions on entire criminal enterprises rather than on individuals. Pursuit and prosecution of individual dealers—those are intermediate goals on the way to the ultimate objective, which is to cripple the entire criminal enterprise.

One of the most successful operations in FBI history unfolded over years and years of frustrating work, and relied on both those controversial investigation methods—wiretaps and informants.

The Teflon Don

For decades, New York City was the epicenter of organized crime activity. Five families had a stranglehold on several vital industries: construction, garbage disposal, and garment manufacturing, among others.

They also controlled shipping through New York's airports and docks. The mob set their own prices for their services; anyone who tried undercut them, or interfere with their business in any way, faced threats and intimidation, beatings, destruction of their property, even murder. Organized crime may look glamorous and exciting in the movies, but it's pretty ugly in real life; plenty of people lost their livelihood, and their lives, trying to go up against the mob.

By 1980, the FBI's New York Field Office had organized five squads focusing on the five major organized crime families. This was intensive, dedicated work. Jim McGonigel worked on several cases with these guys. "The agents who've dedicated a major portion of their careers to organized crime—they find out all the family and so forth, memorize names and relationships. It's not something you can just pick up in a year or two and call yourself an expert. These guys can name birthdays, anniversaries, all the relationships—it's like they're a part of the family."

The most powerful of New York's five families was the Gambino family, led for years by Paul Castellano. On December 16, 1985, Castellano was murdered, shot to death in front of a Manhattan steak house. A relatively minor mobster named John Gotti took over the Gambinos, and ushered in a new era of organized crime.

Earlier bosses kept a low profile, but Gotti seemed to thrive on attention. He got the nickname "Dapper Don" in honor of his expensive tailored suits, expensive Italian shoes, and expensive, blow-dried coiffure—not exactly a look favored by most plumbers, which was Gotti's declared profession. He appeared on the cover of *TIME* magazine. He hosted lavish, and blatantly illegal, Fourth of July fireworks displays in his Queens neighborhood.

Over the years, FBI wiretap recordings had helped convict the heads of four Mafia families, but Gotti was more cautious. Agents installed bugs in Gotti's headquarters, the Ravenite Social Club in Manhattan's Little Italy. Even though 20 or 30 associates visited the Ravenite almost every day, Gotti never discussed any sensitive issues within range of the listening devices. In December 1988, the squad pulled back to review their operations.

The agents scrutinized videotapes, watching everyone who entered and exited the Ravenite. They reread all the surveillance reports. They listened again and again to the audiotapes they'd recorded. They pumped their informants for information. Finally, they realized that Gotti seemed to be holding his most sensitive conversations in four places: a hallway at the back of the club, a vacant second-floor apartment above it, the sidewalk just outside, and an office a mile or so away, in Manhattan's garment district.

The squad got authorization to plant new bugs in those locations, and within a week the FBI had the information they needed. In an interview with New York *Newsday,* J. Bruce Mouw, head of the FBI's Gambino squad, described the haul: "They were getting dynamite conversations. Now, we were on the right track. Gotti felt totally secure. He thought he had fooled everyone, so he wasn't as careful as with his conversation."

While the investigations were continuing, Gotti was earning another nickname—"The Teflon Don." In 1986, the New York District Attorney brought an assault case against Gotti, but the case was dismissed when the plaintiff refused to press charges. In 1987, Gotti was acquitted of federal racketeering charges; five years later, a juror in that trial would be convicted of accepting $60,000 in exchange for his vote for acquittal. In 1990, Gotti was acquitted on state assault charges. Finally, in 1992, armed with the "dynamite" audiotapes and the testimony of a mob turncoat, Sammy Gravano, the prosecutors won. Gotti was convicted of thirteen counts of murder and racketeering. He was sentenced to life in prison without possibility of parole.

The head of the FBI's New York office, James M. Fox, was exultant. After the conviction, he said, "Today is another milestone in the fight against organized crime. The Teflon is gone. The Don is covered with Velcro. Every charge in the indictment stuck."

Gotti's conviction was a major blow to organized crime in New York, and the FBI kept up the pressure on the crime families. In 1997, a major sting operation captured 47 alleged thieves and gangsters. The sting involved intensive undercover work by a Special Agent posing as a well-connected fence. A mob informant introduced the agent to high-placed mobsters, including the Gambino boss who'd replaced Gotti. The agent spent months ingratiating himself with the gangsters, until he finally got permission to open a Brooklyn social club and fencing operation. He handled truckloads of stolen goods, ranging from computers to perfume to firearms to featherbeds.

After almost two years of operation, the fencing operation was rolled up, catching 19 Gambino associates and six soldiers from three other Mafia families.

From all indications, the mob's grip on New York is now seriously weakened. Former strongholds, such as the garbage disposal industry and the historic Fulton Fish Market, now operate without mob influence. For the first time in 60 years—since Lucky Luciano first organized the underworld in the 1930s—the leaders of the five organized crime families no longer meet to coordinate their activities. According to informants and wiretaps, the meetings have been suspended for two reasons: leadership squabbles within the families, and fear of exposure to those same informants and wiretaps.

VIOLENT CRIMES AND MAJOR OFFENDERS PROGRAM

This is the FBI's broadest investigative program, and probably its most visible. It covers the following crimes, among others:

- Kidnapping and extortion
- Sexual exploitation of children
- Tampering with consumer products
- Fugitives wanted as a result of FBI investigations
- Escaped federal prisoners (some instances)

- Probation/parole violations (some instances)
- Unlawful flight to avoid prosecution (including parental-kidnapping fugitives)
- Crime on Indian reservations
- Theft of government property
- Interstate transportation of stolen motor vehicles
- Interstate transportation of stolen property
- Theft from interstate shipments
- Assaulting, kidnapping or killing the president, vice president, or a member of congress
- Bank robbery, burglary, or larceny
- Crime aboard aircraft

Just as the FBI has marshaled its forces to combat organized crime, it has developed specific strategies to fight street gangs and the other loosely knit groups that are responsible for much of the increase in violent crime in the United States. By applying the same methods that are used against organized crime, violent crime task forces are developing racketeering and continuing criminal enterprise cases against the highest-ranking or most dangerous members and seizing their assets. The task forces operate under the Safe Streets Violent Crime Initiative—one of the many support programs the FBI participates in.

By definition, most of the cases brought to the profiling unit fall under Violent Crimes and Major Offenders program. It's one of the reasons why the pressure is so intense: If you make a mistake, you can cost someone her life. The case I'm going to tell you about illustrates several aspects of investigating violent crimes: the devastation encountered; the confusing, contradictory evidence; how the preconceptions of a primary investigator can affect the accuracy of a profile; how the determination of one law enforcement officer can ensure that justice does prevail.

We described this case in *Journey into Darkness;* there's also a fascinating book about it, *Stalking Justice,* by Paul Mones.

The Wrong Guy

When I came across this case, it was a murder. One horrible murder.

In late January 1984, two police detectives from Arlington, Virginia—Robert Carrig and Chuck Shelton—asked for a profile on the perpetrator in Carolyn Hamm's murder. Sometime on January 23, Hamm had been raped and killed. The killer entered her home through a basement window and surprised her when she returned home. Police found a knife the perpetrator used to control her. He'd then stripped her, bound her with cords found in the house, raped her, and strangled her to death. Carrig and Shelton brought us crime scene photos and autopsy reports to work with—no other case linkages, little forensic evidence.

Roy Hazelwood and I talked to the detectives; Roy came up with a profile I agreed with. There were elements of both organized and disorganized behavior at the crime scene; this could point to two killers, or to one killer with two divergent aspects to his personality. Because Hamm was white, we predicted that the killer was white. This kind of crime rarely crossed racial boundaries.

Meanwhile, Arlington Detective Joe Horgas was looking at the case, too. Horgas had been up for the next murder investigation in the department rotation, but when Hamm was murdered, he was away on vacation. The case went to Carrig and Shelton.

Still, Horgas felt a connection to the case; he decided to just take a look at reports of break-ins and sexual assaults near the time of the murder. He discovered two break-ins reported within days of Hamm's murder, within blocks of her home. Elements of both crimes seemed to reflect elements in the killing, and they also seemed to be related to a series of rapes in the Arlington area—nine reported rapes since 1983. Witnesses described the perpetrator as a black male, about five-ten, slight, wearing a mask.

When Horgas approached his supervisor with his theory that the break-ins, the rapes, and Hamm's murder were all linked, his supervisor reminded him that the murder case wasn't his—but he gave Horgas the okay to continue investigating the break-in connection. Horgas sent out a teletype to police departments in the area, describing the "black masked rapist" and hoping someone had spotted him.

On February 6, 1984, Arlington police arrested David Vasquez for Hamm's murder. Vasquez had recently moved out of the area, but witnesses reported seeing him near Hamm's home around the time of the murder. When they searched the room where Vasquez had lived, investigators found *Penthouse*-type magazines, along with peeping-Tom photographs of various women in their homes. One of the magazines contained a photograph showing a woman tied up in a way similar to the way Hamm had been bound.

After an interrogation that took place over several days, Vasquez confessed to Carolyn Hamm's murder.

There were problems with the case. Hair samples from the scene were similar to Vasquez's pubic hair, but semen samples couldn't be matched to him. Vasquez didn't drive, and at the time of Hamm's murder, he lived at least an hour away. He was smaller than Hamm and would have had trouble controlling her physically; he wasn't nearly as intelligent as Hamm and couldn't have dominated her mentally.

Based partly on our profile, Arlington police figured that Vasquez had been the less mature, less organized, of two perpetrators. They pushed Vasquez to name his accomplice, but Vasquez insisted there *was* no accomplice. He accepted a plea bargain and was sentenced to 35 years in prison. Hamm's murder was solved.

Almost four years later, on December 1, 1987, the body of Susan Tucker was discovered in her bedroom, nude and bound. Detective Joe Horgas was assigned to the case.

Looking at the scene, Horgas immediately thought of Carolyn Hamm's murder. There were similarities in the method of entry, the binding, the killing itself, the victimology. The women's homes were only blocks apart.

Horgas drove to Buckingham Correction Center to interview David Vasquez. The interview was disturbing, in ways Horgas never expected.

Vasquez desperately wanted out. He cried while talking to Horgas; he'd been assaulted over and over in the prison, and Horgas was his very first visitor. But as miserable as Vasquez was, he didn't give up the name of his accomplice. He couldn't give Horgas any useful information at all.

Horgas left the prison worried about two terrible possibilities. One, Vasquez had been locked up for a crime he didn't commit. Two, the real perpetrator was still out there, still killing.

When Horgas took a look at the Hamm investigation, he became even more convinced that Vasquez was the wrong guy. Vasquez had been interrogated in a way that was sure to confuse and overwhelm his limited mental abilities; his confession hadn't contained any information the investigators didn't already know. To Horgas, the indicators of a second partner now seemed to point to another perpetrator altogether.

Horgas went back to his original theory: a link between the rapes committed by the "black masked rapist," the break-ins, Hamm's murder, and now Tucker's murder. He found a couple of promising leads, but the real breakthrough came when Horgas came across a teletype from the Richmond, Virginia PD, describing a murder strikingly similar to Tucker's. This killing had taken place on October 6, 1987, just two months before.

When Horgas called the Richmond cops, he found out there were even more similarities than described in the teletype—and another rape-murder, possibly related, had happened since. The Richmond cops were dubious about Horgas's theory, but they invited him to a task force meeting anyway.

That openness, and Horgas's determination, would be the keys to solving the case.

Richmond detectives Glen Williams and Ray Williams were in charge of the Tucker investigation. (They aren't related, but everyone in the department calls them "the Williams boys.") They were under a tremendous amount of pressure. Murders are relatively uncommon in Richmond, and a serial rapist-murderer was almost unheard of. Richmond residents were panicking, and there was a lot of media scrutiny. The department poured resources into the investigation.

The Williams boys asked for help from the FBI's profiling unit; Jud Ray and Tom Salp drove down to meet with them. The police presented information on their two murders and, based on that presentation, Jud and Tom came up with a profile.

Those of you who read *Mindhunter* may remember Jud Ray. For those of you who aren't familiar with him, let me just put in a word here. Jud's a fine agent, and an excellent profiler. He also brings a couple of unusual viewpoints to his work. Unlike most members of the profiling unit—at least when I was there—Jud is a black man from the rural South. He's also the survivor of a murder attempt; his wife very nearly succeeded in having him shot to death. That experience, among other things, gives him real empathy for victims, and an uncanny ability to "read" a scene from the victim's point of view.

Jud and Tom pointed out that the killer was somewhat sophisticated, leaving no prints or obvious clues; this indicated he had some experience with the criminal system and had learned from the experience—which meant the perpetrator was reasonably intelligent. The killings took place on Friday nights; he probably had a full-time job. The binding and control of the victims required real physical strength. Petecchial hemorrhages and other evidence indicated that in each case, the killer had strangled the woman, released the ligature, strangled her again, released her again—over and over, until the woman finally died. This was a clear indication of sexual sadism, and the behavior seemed to be escalating. Other factors indicated a loner, someone probably not in a relationship with a woman and not likely to brag about his crimes. Statistically speaking, the killer was probably a white man.

In November 1987, the killer struck again. His victim, Diane Cho, was much younger than the previous targets, but there were unmistakable similarities. Tests on semen at the scenes linked the Cho, Davis, and Hellams murders.

Meanwhile, Joe Horgas was pursuing his theory. He was convinced that the Hamm and Tucker murders in Arlington and the three murders in Richmond were all committed by a "black masked rapist" reported in both areas. Preliminary serological testing linked the Tucker killer to the Richmond murders. Horgas formed a task force to investigate the Tucker murder and started reinvestigating the Arlington rapes.

He called the Investigative Support Unit and asked for a meeting; on December 29, Steve Mardigian and Jud Ray drove down to Arlington. Horgas's presentation was comprehensive, organized, and thorough. And he finally got some support for his theory.

Steve and Jud agreed that there was good reason to think that the Arlington and Richmond murders were linked, and that all the murders were linked to the "black masked rapist" crimes. There were just too many similarities. Jud and Steve felt that the rapes were rehearsals for the murders; the killer perfected his technique before escalating his crimes.

Finally, Horgas revealed that the Hamm case was closed—a killer had been apprehended and sentenced. He described Vasquez and asked whether the agents thought he could have been the more submissive of two criminal partners.

This put everything in a new light. Jud and Steve stressed that they'd need to do a more intensive review of the case materials to give a more definitive answer, but based on what they'd seen, the answer was no. These crimes seemed to be the work of someone who acted alone, someone who wouldn't want or need a partner.

Finally, the three investigators talked about the issue of the perpetrator's race. Why had the earlier profiles predicted a white man? Well, statistically, it was the right answer. The vast majority of serial killers *are* white men. Black men rarely commit these kinds of crimes, and when they do, as in the case of Wayne Williams, the Atlanta child murderer, their victims are almost always black, too. This may be changing, and Jud has some interesting theories about why that is.

Jud's thinking is based on his experience as a cop and as a profiler, but also as a black man raised in the rural South. "There is a noticeable difference in the psychopathology of black sexual offenders and white sexual offenders regarding the way they each treat the living or dead body," Jud says. Black offenders rarely insert foreign objects, sexually mutilate the body, or commit other kinds of depravity common among white offenders. Jud thinks this will hold true for blacks who remain outside the American mainstream. But as minorities become more integrated into the culture, their criminal signatures will also begin to reflect those of the larger culture.

For instance, George Russell Jr. was an intelligent, middle-class black man who raped and killed several Seattle-area women in 1990. Like the classic white sexual predator, Russell arranged his victims in degrading poses. One woman was left with a rifle shoved into her vagina. Russell was fully integrated into the mainstream culture; he moved easily in predominantly white circles. This seems to confirm Jud's theory that culture, rather than race itself, is the significant factor in determining a killer's signature.

The important point to remember is that profiles are predictions, not descriptions. Investigators shouldn't rely on a profile to the exclusion of other evidence. Horgas saw the similarities in the way the rapes and the murders were carried out; those similarities outweighed the contradiction between the profile prediction and the witness descriptions of a black man. Horgas's instincts were sound.

Jud, Steve and Horgas came up with an investigative strategy. Horgas focused on the rapes, since those cases were open and the victims were still alive and could be interviewed. Because the rapes had stopped about the time of Vasquez's arrest, then resumed in Richmond almost four years later, the perpetrator had probably been sent to jail for a relatively minor offense, such as burglary.

Horgas started sifting through arrest and parole records, but the task was overwhelming. He took a break and searched his own memory for clues. Several years before, he'd worked the section of the city where the first rapes had occurred; maybe he'd run into the rapist then.

He had. Horgas remembered a young man named Timothy Spencer—suspected of burglary, accused of setting fire to his mother's home. One of the rape victims had been locked in the trunk of her car, which was then set on fire.

Horgas called up Spencer's records and found that he'd been convicted of burglary on January 29, 1984, and released to a halfway house in Richmond on September 4, 1987. Details of the burglary matched up with details of the murders.

Horgas conferred with Richmond police, who set up surveillance on Spencer. But after a week, when they saw nothing suspicious, they discontinued the surveillance. On January 20, 1988, Horgas obtained an arrest warrant for Spencer and brought him in.

Though Spencer never confessed, DNA and other forensic evidence clinched the case against him. On July 16, 1988, he was found guilty of Susan Tucker's murder; three other murder convictions followed, for the killings of Debbie Davis, Susan Hellams, and Diane Cho in Richmond. He was executed on April 27, 1994.

But what about David Vasquez? Steve Mardigian created a detailed chart that sorted out all the information known about the Hamm case, as well as the rapes, burglaries, and the other murders. He brought the chart to me and each of us analyzed it independently before we conferred. We came to the same conclusion: There was no way two people had committed these crimes. There was no way David Vasquez committed them, either. He didn't have the mental or physical capacity to handle them; nothing in his history or current behavior indicated he was a sexual sadist, as the killer definitely was.

On October 18, 1988, we sent a five-page report to the Arlington County Commonwealth Attorney, presenting our conclusion that the

125

man who'd murdered Tucker, Hellams, and Cho had also murdered Carolyn Hamm. We supported the request from Joe Horgas and the Arlington Police Department that David Vasquez receive a pardon from the governor.

David Vasquez was finally released from prison on January 4, 1989. He might still be there, if Joe Horgas hadn't been so astute and so determined to see real justice done.

WHITE-COLLAR CRIME PROGRAM

A reporter once asked Willie Sutton, a bank robber in the 1940s, why he robbed banks. His reply: "That's where the money is." That little story illustrates a basic fact about white-collar criminals: They go where the money is.

Of course there's still a lot of money in banks, but today there's even more money in places Willie Sutton never dreamed about. The booming stock market, telemarketing, cyberselling—for every new and legitimate way of making money, there are a dozen new and illegitimate money scams. The FBI works to stay in front of changes in white-collar crime, and continues to combat its more traditional forms. Some of the major areas of investigation are:

- **Corruption of public officials:** The FBI investigates violations by public officials in federal, state, and local governments. Most violations occur when the official asks, demands, solicits, accepts, receives, or agrees to receive something of value in return for influence in the performance of an official act. The categories of public corruption investigated by the FBI include legislative, judicial, regulatory, contractual, and law enforcement.

- **Health care fraud:** The FBI is the only federal investigative agency with the full authority to investigate all health care fraud offenses. The Bureau is particularly interested in large-scale fraud schemes involving large sums of money or a threat to patients' welfare.

- **Computer-related crimes:** The FBI pursues computer-related crimes involving both criminal acts and national security issues. Examples of criminal acts would be using a computer to commit fraud, or using the Internet to transmit obscene material. In the national security area, the FBI investigates criminal matters involving computerized banking and financial systems; the various 911 emergency networks; and national telecommunications systems.

White-collar crimes run the gamut—small-time to multimillion-dollar. Early in his career, Doug Rhoads had to figure out how to handle a whole series of relatively small swindles:

Shortly after I got to Lubbock, there was a huge tornado. Flattened half the town, killed I don't know how many people. After anything like that, you get federal agencies coming in to help. So the Small Business Administration gets set up to loan money to the mom-and-pop type businesses that were wiped out. About half the people looking for money were legitimate and needed the money, and half of them were frauds. For instance, a guy said he had a dry-cleaning business with millions of dollars in equipment and clothing in there, when he had a tenth of that. Another guy has a used car lot, he says he had 20 cars destroyed when he had three.

All of a sudden, I've got about 20 of these SBA fraud cases to deal with. Had no clue where to start, no idea what the SBA statute even said. So I got hold of the assistant U.S. attorney, and we looked up the statute. Then I just started interviewing people. If I had a question, I'd get with a veteran agent. It isn't brain surgery, it's just work. Talking to people. That's 90 percent of what the bureau does. That's how you learn, get a bunch of cases and just start doing them.

Doug's right—most of what an agent does is talk to people. And you never know when or where you're going to come across some relevant information. Jim McFall tells a story about one particular case he worked on that covers not just white-collar crime but also corruption of public officials. And it all started with one phone call.

I was at the New Orleans Field Office then. I was sitting at my desk, putting together a report. The switchboard operator called back and said, "Mr. McFall, I've got a gentleman on the line, and he says he wants to talk to an agent, not a clerk. He has some important information but he has to give it to an agent, and you're the only one in the office right now."

I figure the guy's probably some crackpot, but as I said, I'm just working on reports, nothing pressing, so I get on the phone. The guy on the other end is really upset—saying there's a situation that could lead to the deaths of a lot of people if it wasn't looked into right away. I finally got him to calm down and start talking to me so I could get some information about just what it was I was supposed to be looking into.

That one phone call initiated a huge investigation. There was a company in New Orleans that got the contract to do an overlay of the surfaces at the airport, including the runways. The guy was defrauding the government. The specifications called for four inches of new asphalt on the runways. This guy was falsifying delivery tickets and what have you— the paperwork showed the right amount, but in some areas we found less than half an inch of new asphalt on the runway. Imagine a 707 coming in and landing on a runway with a surface that thin. The wheels would go right through it.

By the time the case was wrapped up, we got 17 people convicted, seized the paving company, seized the guy's house, his boat, an airplane. Then from the spinoffs of *that* investigation, we got nine or ten Louisiana state employees for fraud against the government, taking bribes and kickbacks. I was interviewing one guy, and I said, "I don't understand— here you are soliciting bribes, and then cutting other people in and paying them off. Doesn't that bother you?" He looked at me and said, "Boy, don't you understand? That's how things get done in Louisiana." And that's exactly how he felt.

I never identified the guy who started it all. He'd call in periodically, and I'd gather bits and pieces of information, but he'd never give me his name. I'm pretty sure he was a pilot, flying in and out of the New Orleans International Airport—not a commercial pilot, a private pilot.

When the case got to trial, I was on the stand and the defense attorney was cross-examining me. He said, "Now, Agent McFall, just exactly what initiated this investigation?"

"Well, I was in the office working on a report and I got a phone call."

"Who made this phone call?"

"It was an anonymous phone call." Which, in that setting, sounds bogus. Kind of like registering at a hotel as Mr. and Mrs. John Smith. The judge was just shaking his head, laughing. But it was absolutely true.

The defense attorney kept trying to get me say it was some so-called sleazy informant, but I couldn't help him out. It's an anonymous phone call to this day.

While all FBI offices handle isolated instances of white-collar crime, the Bureau also investigates large-scale fraud by organized groups. The FBI also concentrates on mortgage loan fraud, an investigation aimed at loan brokers, appraisers, accountants, and attorneys engaged in conspiracies to defraud lending institutions. Another big investigative area targets telemarketers who conspire to sell worthless goods, investments, or services.

The following investigations are two examples of the FBI's commitment to fighting white-collar crime.

The Fight Against Telemarketing Fraud

I've always thought that telemarketing has got to be a tough way to make a living. Not too many people are thrilled to get calls from telemarketers, and you're probably not going to have a lot of time to make your pitch before the potential customer hangs up and goes back to dinner.

Even so, there are over 3.4 million people nationwide employed in the telemarketing industry. According to telemarketers' estimates, consumer spending through telemarketing tops out at over $500 billion per year. Based on industry surveys and congressional testimony, telemarketing fraud accounts for an estimated $40 billion annually. Both those figures are expected to increase.

Most telemarketers, like most people in any business, are just trying to make an honest living. But because of particular aspects of the telemarketing business, the unscrupulous companies—and they are out there—can be especially hard to catch. The lines between legitimate and illegal telemarketing are usually pretty blurry; fraud schemes are designed to closely resemble legitimate marketing efforts, both to lure customers and to thwart prosecution.

Fraudulent telemarketers also take advantage of the fluidity of their business, using multiples of everything: business names, solicitor names, telephone numbers, mail drops, and business locations. Everything about the business scheme itself—the solicitation method, the product line, prizes offered, any other recognizable traits—can be changed overnight to escape law enforcement or meet changing consumer demands.

This quick-change aspect, the vast number of telemarketers, their mobility across legal jurisdictions and state lines, the complexity of the schemes, and the huge number of victims, who are often embarrassed and reluctant to come forward—all these factors make telemarketing fraud a real challenge to white-collar crime investigators and prosecutors.

These very same aspects call for a federal response. The FBI pursues illegal telemarketing aggressively; the Senior Sentinel project is an outstanding example of proactive and effective investigation.

Senior Sentinel

Unscrupulous telemarketers often target senior citizens, preying on those who seem vulnerable to their fast-talking schemes. In 1993, the San Diego Division of the FBI responded to complaints of telemarketing fraud aimed at seniors by training potential victims to help combat the problem.

Senior Sentinel used citizen volunteers, many referred to the Bureau by the American Association of Retired Persons (AARP). These volunteers had a special monitored phone line installed in their homes, with installation and maintenance costs covered by the FBI. The volunteers were trained in how to respond to telemarketers' pitches, which were recorded. In response to a fraudulent-sounding pitch, the volunteers provided money orders or "sight drafts" (a kind of electronic transfer). Once the volunteer sent in money, his or her name and phone number were "reloaded" and sold to other telemarketers. Soon, the volunteer would be fielding a stream of calls from other shady telemarketers—and the cycle would begin again.

This innovative program resulted in exceptionally strong prosecutions. The recording became direct evidence be used in court; the "prize"— usually a cheap gadget worth a lot less than promised—was additional evidence. I'm sure it made a real impression on the juries, hearing the lavish description of the prize and then seeing the shoddy reality.

Senior Sentinel was so successful that the FBI rolled it out nationwide in 1995. It's currently operated as a joint effort of the FBI, the U.S. Attorney's Office, the Internal Revenue Service, the Federal Trade Commission, and local, state and federal law enforcement.

The FBI "franchised" the citizen volunteer technique, which has been adopted by 38 Field Offices across the country. In each region, copies of the tape recordings are forwarded to a central location, where they're organized according to type of scheme, the company's name and location, and the phone name of the individual solicitor. Thousands of fraudulent pitches have been recorded as a result of Senior Sentinel; the tapes are available to any law enforcement agencies conducting tele-marketing investigations.

Over the last several years, Senior Sentinel has provided the FBI and other law enforcement agencies with vast amounts of information about the structure and functioning of illegal telemarketing operations. This intelligence continues to be invaluable in combating this crime problem.

Operation Rogue Brokers

The stock-market boom has led to cigar bars, Land Rover–mania—and unprecedented opportunities for fraud. In keeping with Willie Sutton's Law, that's because there's more money in the stock market than ever before, and more Americans with a stake in it. A New York Stock Exchange (NYSE) study showed that, by the mid-1990s, about 51 million individuals owned publicly traded stock. An additional 200 million people owned securities indirectly—through retirement plans, insurance policies, savings banks, mutual funds, and other financial instruments.

The large majority of brokerage firms and financial professionals are ethical and aboveboard, careful to follow the regulations set up to pro-tect investors. But some people can't resist the lure of a quick buck, and they take advantage of individuals, businesses, even government agen-cies. And, as new and legal investment methods are developed, new and illegal ways of separating you from your money will keep pace. Stock trading over the Internet is just one example of the challenges facing those who regulate the financial industry.

Like the telemarketing industry, the brokerage industry is flexible and fast-moving, operating easily across state lines. These qualities appeal to unethical brokers, and make some sort of Federal oversight essential. The FBI's Rogue Brokers operation has become one of the major inves-tigative tools for combating unscrupulous and fraudulent financial professionals.

Rogue Brokers grew out of a meeting held in April 1995, chaired by the Department of Justice. At the meeting were representatives from the Department of Justice (DOJ) Criminal Division-Fraud Section, the National Association of Securities Dealers (NASD), the Securities and Exchange Commission (SEC), and the FBI.

The SEC is the regulatory arm of the financial industry, charged with monitoring individuals and firms. In 1994, SEC examiners scrutinized several big brokerage firms for evidence of dishonest or illegal activity; they found potential wrongdoing in 25 percent of the examinations. However, the SEC has no criminal enforcement options; it can only file civil charges, which may lead, at most, to fines or license revocation. But all too often, unethical brokers found ways around the fines, or just got new jobs at new firms where they continued their shady practices. And, with the explosive growth in the stock market, the SEC was stretched thin.

The group reviewed the situation, then developed and initiated an action plan to identify and prosecute fraudulent financial professionals. This action plan eventually took the name Rogue Brokers.

NASD and SEC reviewed their databases and selected a number of cases that involved disciplinary actions against brokers. After review, several cases were identified for further investigation and possible prosecution, and were assigned to the appropriate FBI field offices and United States Attorney's offices. Eleven cases were found to have prosecutive merit.

On November 30, 1995, Rogue Brokers was revealed to the public through a national press conference. Attorney General Janet Reno announced that felony charges had been filed against 11 stockbrokers. The specific charges included stealing money from customer accounts, forging clients' signatures on checks, unauthorized transfer of funds, falsifying account statements, and selling counterfeit certificates of deposit. One broker was charged with stealing $114,000 from his clients; another defrauded 42 clients, mostly elderly women, of more than $950,000. Both men later pleaded guilty.

At the news conference, Reno said that the prosecutions demonstrated that "brokers who seldom risked more than dismissal and restitution [of stolen money] can now expect to be criminally prosecuted and indicted if they cheat their customers."

Because this first phase of Rogue Brokers was so successful, plans were developed for Phase II. Since then, 13 broker-embezzlement cases have identified for inclusion in Phase II of Rogue Brokers. This initiative has forged a continuous working relationship between the FBI, the DOJ and several industry regulatory groups in addressing an ongoing crime problem.

CHAPTER 5
Laboratory Services

The FBI's Laboratory Division, one of the largest and most comprehensive crime labs in the world, conducts scientific examinations on physical evidence submitted in connection with criminal, counterterrorism, and espionage investigations. Forensic disciplines within the lab include chemistry, DNA, trace evidence, photography, document examinations, firearms, and latent fingerprints.

Of course the Lab handles evidence for the Bureau, but when asked, it also will conduct examinations, free of charge, for any federal, state, or local law enforcement organization in the country. Under a special agreement between the attorney general and the secretary of state, the Lab also examines evidence for foreign law enforcement agencies.

Besides forensic evaluations, the Laboratory Division offers two important services: preparation of trial evidence, and identification of casualties through the Disaster Squad.

PREPARATION OF EVIDENCE

Forensic evidence is, by its nature, complicated and detailed. It can be incredibly effective in the courtroom, but only if the jurors can understand it and grasp its significance. Lab specialists develop clear and compelling visuals for courtroom use—such as comparisons of DNA samples—and come up with understandable but accurate summaries of their findings for presentation.

Often good preparation makes a real difference in how the jury perceives the evidence presented. Bruce Koenig describes one case:

> The defense brought in a guy from a recording studio to say this particular piece of evidence, an audiotape, had been altered. He testified that the tape recorder had been turned off at a particular point. The prosecution said, no, it wasn't.
>
> So we look at the tape and found very quickly that the recorder hadn't been turned off. The sounds they were pointing out sounded as if somebody had tapped the microphone. But it was clear from the magnetic and wave forms that it was a continuous recording.
>
> What we did was show pictures. We made big blowups of the magnetic development, where you show the magnetic impulses on the tape, and the waveform, the sound itself. We showed pictures of the recorder starting at one point and stopping at another, in both magnetic and wave form. And then we showed the area in question, in magnetic and wave form. It was very clear visually, the difference between the sounds of the recorder being turned off and the sounds they were pointing to.
>
> The defense attorney was a total idiot. He got up and said, "Well, Mr. Koenig, that's just your opinion."
>
> I said, "No. Anybody looking at these charts can see that the tape didn't stop and start at this point." That just gave me another opportunity to demonstrate the evidence to the jury.
>
> The prosecution won that case.

THE DISASTER SQUAD

The FBI's Disaster Squad, set up in 1940, is made up of highly skilled Special Agents and Latent Fingerprint Specialists assigned to the FBI's

Laboratory Division. From 1940 to April 1996, the Squad has assisted in examining almost 7,262 victims in over 176 disasters. Of these, 4,150 were positively identified through fingerprints, palm prints, and footprints.

Recently, the Disaster Squad assisted in investigating three airplane crashes, the accidental downing of two military aircraft, and overseas military conflict, and the unearthing of grave sites at two cemeteries due to flooding.

History of Fingerprinting

Back in the 1880s, when a criminal was arrested, he wasn't fingerprinted. He was measured—more carefully and more thoroughly than a guy being fitted for a custom-made suit—according to the principles of the Bertillon method.

Alphonse Bertillon, a French police officer, is considered the father of forensics. In the late 1800s, he developed an elaborate identification system based on 243 body measurements, including height, arm span, length of the torso, and length of the right ear. Sounds wacky now, but this was a time when "doctors of phrenology" claimed to analyze your character by feeling the bumps on your head.

The Bertillon method was the first attempt to apply scientific principles and techniques, such as measurement, to the job of criminal investigation—which is the foundation of forensics. But there were serious practical problems with Bertillon's system. The large number of measurements made record keeping and cross-comparison (especially in that precomputer era) very tedious and time-consuming; police often weren't as precise with their measurements as the system demanded; ambitious criminals had the bad habit of beginning their careers before they'd finished growing and their measurements had stabilized. And despite the unwieldy number of figures, a Bertillon profile wasn't unique;

investigators soon discovered that more than one person could fit one profile.

At the same time Bertillon was developing his system, fingerprints were becoming more accepted as a means of identification. One of the pioneers of fingerprinting was Sir William Herschel, a British chief magistrate in Jungipoor, India. In July 1858, he started requiring the locals to put a handprint on the back of contracts, as a way of discouraging them from denying their signature later. According to the New York State Division of Criminal Justice Services (DCJS), the system accomplished its goal—not because the Indians believed in the effectiveness of the identification, but because personal contact with the document made the contract more binding. A superstitious beginning for a forensics technique, but it worked.

In the 1870s, a countryman of Herschel's developed a comprehensive system of categorizing fingerprints. Again according to DCJS, Dr. Henry Faulds, surgeon-superintendent of a hospital in Tokyo, began studying what he called "skin-furrows" after he found impressions of them in old Japanese pottery. He knew his system of classifying and comparing fingerprints could be useful in many scientific areas, especially identification. He offered his data to Scotland Yard, but they weren't interested; in 1880, Faulds sent a description of his system to the leading scientist of the day, Charles Darwin.

Darwin, old and ill by then, forwarded the information to his cousin and fellow scientific researcher, Sir Francis Galton. Galton didn't take up the project until 1888, when the Royal Institute invited him to give a lecture on personal identification.

Galton planned to focus on the Bertillon method, but "wishing to treat the subject generally, and having a vague knowledge of the value sometimes assigned to finger marks,"

Galton also started researching this new-fangled technique, beginning with data collected by Faulds and Herschel.

At first, Galton believed fingerprints might offer a way to trace heredity and racial background—a particular interest of that era. But Galton soon realized that the real value of fingerprints lay in their possibilities for identification. As both Faulds and Herschel had suspected, a person's fingerprints were both unique and permanent. Unless deliberately erased or altered, they remained the same throughout a lifetime.

Galton identified three basic classifications of fingerprints: *loops,* which bend back on themselves like a loop of string; *whorls,* or tiny spirals; and *arches,* anything that isn't a loop or a whorl. Galton's system assigned a numerical position to each fingertip and then classified the general characteristics of each fingertip; this created a ten-letter sequence that was easily recorded, easily compared, and almost infallible. (Galton's system has since been updated and simplified, but the loops, whorls, and arches terminology is still used.)

Dr. Faulds accused Galton of plagiarizing his own system, and the two recording methods are remarkably similar. But Galton remains the official originator of fingerprinting.

For the rest of the nineteenth century, fingerprinting and Bertillonage coexisted as state-of-the-art identification techniques, but the practical benefits of fingerprinting soon won out. During the 1900s, police departments in almost every major metropolitan city in the United States converted to fingerprinting. Some departments, such as New York State's, sent representatives to Scotland Yard to pick the brains of the experts—an early example of international cooperation between law enforcement agencies.

In 1905, the Department of Justice created a Bureau of Criminal Identification (BCI) to provide a centralized archive of fingerprint cards. Two years later, the collection was moved to Kansas to take advantage of a large supply of cheap labor—convicts at Leavenworth Federal Penitentiary.

Understandably enough, police officers were dubious about this misguided effort to save money. They formed their own centralized bureau, which flat out refused to share data with the BCI.

In 1924, Congress merged the two collections and put them under Bureau of Investigation administration. By 1926, law enforcement agencies across the country were contributing fingerprint cards to the Bureau of Investigation. The FBI's identification division soon became, and remains, the most comprehensive archive in the country.

CHAPTER

Criminal Justice Information Services

The Criminal Justice Information Services Division serves as the FBI's focal point and central repository for criminal justice. Major functions include the following:

- *Developing and implementing the Integrated Automated Fingerprint Identification System (IAFIS).* This new system will replace the current paper-based system for identifying and searching criminal history records. It will support a law enforcement agency's ability to digitally record fingerprints and electronically exchange information with the FBI. Reducing the amount of work that must be done manually will increase processing speed.

- *Operating the National Crime Information Center (NCIC).* One component of the NCIC is the National Crime Information Center database, which includes a missing-persons file. The information in this file is available to authorized criminal justice personnel. Currently, there are about 104,000 missing persons on record.

- *Providing identification services such as fingerprint identifications and criminal history information.* The FBI Criminal Justice Information Division handles identification requests from federal, state, or local law enforcement agencies, or any agency directly engaged in criminal justice activity. This information can also be disclosed to foreign or international law enforcement agencies, consistent with international treaties, conventions, and executive agreements. The division won't release this information to private citizens—unless you want a copy of your own arrest record.

Believe it or not, I've been asked whether the FBI will examine fingerprint evidence for private citizens. The answer, not surprisingly, is no. The FBI will conduct fingerprint checks for private companies in certain situations, such as licensing and employment.

- *Converting the summary-based Uniform Crime Reporting (UCR) Program to the National Incident-Based Reporting System (NIBRS).* The FBI's current means of collecting information about criminal activity is the Uniform Crime Reporting (UCR) Program, which began in 1929. Law enforcement agencies across the country submit information on serious crimes in eight categories:

  - Murder and nonnegligent manslaughter

  - Forcible rape

  - Robbery

  - Aggravated assault

  - Burglary

  - Larceny and theft

  - Motor vehicle theft

  - Arson

UCR also collects information on arrests for 21 other less serious crime categories. In 1995, over 16,000 law enforcement agencies, covering 96 percent of the United States population, submitted crime data to the UCR Program.

Participation in UCR is strictly voluntary. The idea is to create a picture of the current problems facing law enforcement, so the data collected only reflects known offenses and arrests. Findings of a court, coroner, jury, or the decision of a prosecutor aren't included. The eight major offenses were selected because of their serious nature, their frequency, or both. For instance, embezzlement rarely becomes a police matter; companies usually handle it on their own. Kidnapping is a relatively uncommon crime. Neither crime is included in UCR figures.

The numbers reported are used to calculate the Crime Index, which can be compared year-to-year to gauge fluctuations in the overall volume and rate of reported crime.

To help keep track of unreported crime, the Department of Justice administers the National Crime Victimization Survey (NCVS), designed to complement the UCR. The NCVS was established to obtain and provide previously unavailable information about victims, offenders, and crime (including crime not reported to the police). While the two programs tabulate their numbers in different ways, they measure a similar subset of serious crimes.

While the UCR has provided valuable information over the years, the system can be improved. This is why the FBI is working to convert the UCR to the the National Incident-Based Reporting System (NIBRS). NIBRS will collect data in 22 crime categories, made up of 46 specific crimes. Unlike the UCR, which is used to create a nationwide summary of offenses and arrests, the NIBRS will collect data on each crime and its components. NIBRS will have several advantages over the UCR:

- Investigators can quantify drug seizures in relation to drug arrests.

- Emerging "trends," such as hate crimes, can be measured.

- Age, sex, race, and other information about the victims and witnesses of all crimes will be recorded.

CHAPTER

Training Programs

Good training is the backbone of the FBI. New agents receive intensive training before they go in the field, and they're expected to return to the Academy for in-service training throughout their careers. The FBI also shares its research and expertise with law enforcement agencies throughout the country and around the world, through classes at the FBI Academy.

Jim O'Connor, as you'll recall from chapter one, was a member of the team who designed the training programs at the FBI Academy. Here's how he describes what his team hoped to achieve in setting up advanced training programs for law enforcement professionals:

> We believed that we could expand investigative techniques using a variety of disciplines, including the behavioral sciences and the forensic sciences.
>
> Because we were designing a law enforcement curriculum, we felt that the philosophy underpinning the curriculum should be the Constitution of the United States and the legal process. Every American officer was required to take law courses. And eventually we settled on four other core disciplines, and each student would have to take at least one course in each discipline. Behavioral science, and communication arts; forensic science, because things were changing, we thought, and rising managers and executives should be aware of what's going on; management science, because of course the trainees were all advancing as managers.

We wanted to find agents who were good investigators, and get them back to study for doctorates, so we can pass along what they learn to police officers here in the United States and elsewhere in the world. Because we felt that while we could educate a great investigator, we can't necessarily make an educated person an investigator. So we were looking for people who had been successful as investigators, to give them the education and the discipline that we felt would be significant.

TRAINING FOR STATE AND LOCAL POLICE

The FBI has a tremendous stake in making sure every law enforcement office in the country operates at maximum effectiveness. Through training classes and road schools, local and state police, sheriff's departments, and other law enforcement personnel from around the world gain the benefit of the Bureau's expertise and advances.

Here's Jim O'Connor's philosophy:

It's essential that the people at the Academy stay on the cutting edge. That's one of the reasons I always encouraged the guys to go out and assist in investigations, keep involved, because they needed to know what was going on. And they needed to have some credibility with the guys they're teaching. Some cop is going to say, "You're one of those academics. When's the last time you worked a case?" That's a legitimate question, if you're not actively investigating cases.

Of course, we also have to cover a huge range of backgrounds—we're bringing in between 1,000 and 1,200 police officers a year, with educational backgrounds ranging from GEDs to PhDs. We had to make sure everybody would be challenged, everybody could take a course in every discipline, and no one would get lost.

FBI NATIONAL ACADEMY

In 1935, the FBI began offering a curriculum for law enforcement officers from around the country. Since then, over 28,000 U.S. and international officers have come to Quantico for classes at the National Academy. The 11-week program is designed to provide advanced professional instruction for midlevel law enforcement officers—a sort of "graduate school" for officers, who will implement the methods and techniques when they return home. The curriculum at the National Academy consists of courses in management science, behavioral science, law enforcement communication, forensic science, and physical training. Leadership development is stressed throughout the curriculum; the FBI encourages strong leadership at all levels of law enforcement.

NATIONAL EXECUTIVE INSTITUTE

The men and women who run the nation's largest law enforcement agencies face problems and challenges that few people can imagine, let alone help with. The FBI set up the National Executive Institute to offer assistance to these hard-working individuals. Each year, up to five federal law enforcement officials, and an equal number of internationally known officers, are invited to attend this 15-day training program at Quantico. The curriculum varies from session to session, but it's always developed with two goals in mind: to enhance cooperation and coordination of policing throughout the law enforcement community, and to promote individual learning and leadership.

LAW ENFORCEMENT EXECUTIVE DEVELOPMENT SEMINAR

Because of the success of the National Executive Institute, the FBI set up a program for the benefit of executives who head up medium-sized law enforcement agencies. This two-week seminar is offered twice a year, and provides instruction on a variety of subjects useful to this audience. Again, the emphasis is on cooperation, individual learning, and leadership development.

FIELD POLICE TRAINING PROGRAM

The men and women on the street are the real front line of any law enforcement effort. To provide support for law enforcement officers in the field, the Bureau instituted an ongoing program of training development. FBI police instructors provide assistance at law enforcement training facilities—local, county, and state, throughout the United States—to improve the investigative, managerial, administrative, and technical skills of local officers. This training program strengthens the cooperative effort between the FBI and local agencies in protecting the public.

FBI/LOCAL POLICE VIOLENT CRIME TASK FORCE TRAINING

This is a component of the Safe Streets Program, which promotes coordinated efforts between FBI field offices and their local counterparts to locate and apprehend violent fugitives and to attack street gang- and drug-related violence. Training is designed to enhance street survival of FBI Agents and local law enforcement officers involved in the associated task forces. These task forces face some of the most violent and dangerous criminals out there, so the training consists of firearms, survival, and tactical movements.

SPECIALIZED COURSES, ROAD SCHOOLS

Specialized courses for police officers are held at the FBI Academy and at police facilities around the country. Instruction includes firearms, latent fingerprints, street survival, hostage negotiation, computer crime, death investigation, DNA analysis, and criminal psychology. In 1995, the FBI trained 4,000 police officers in specialized courses at Quantico and over 114,000 officers in 3,500 road schools.

I taught at road schools early on, when profiling techniques were still new and kind of controversial. I remember standing in front of a bunch of cops, 20 or 25 years older than I was, and thinking, "Who the hell am I to tell them how to do their jobs?" I'm sure they were thinking the same thing. But I had something that worked, and that's what came through. And the experience of meeting those people, talking to them about their cases, hashing out strategies and following up on results—all of that helped me hone this new technique.

INTERNATIONAL TRAINING

The world is becoming a smaller place, and it's more important than ever to create connections between law enforcement agencies around the globe. The FBI's been a proponent of this for years.

International Law Enforcement Academy (ILEA)

As we've all seen by now, the end of the Cold War and the collapse of the Soviet Union created unimagined opportunities, and unanticipated problems. Because effective, fair law enforcement is vital to the well-being of any society, the United States has a special stake in fostering a healthy system of justice in all emerging democracies. The ILEA, located in Budapest, Hungary, is a multinational effort organized by the United States, the Hungarian government, and other international training partners. The Academy brings together representatives from U.S. federal law enforcement agencies and the Department of State to provide training and leadership development to police officers in the emerging democracies. Countries throughout the world actively support this initiative, providing instructors and participants.

The ILEA's curriculum is modeled on the FBI National Academy's, with a focus on topics of particular interest to the attendees: organized crime, economic crime, and nuclear nonproliferation. Up to 50 students attend each eight-week session; at least five sessions are held each year.

Other Training Initiatives

Beyond the ILEA, the FBI conducts extensive police training in foreign countries. I can't say it often enough—this helps police in foreign countries, and also helps law enforcement here at home by building connections that help fight international crime aimed at U.S. citizens and interests. In one recent year, 2,000 international students took part in 32 international training initiatives. Approximately 870 students received training from FBI instructors who traveled outside the United States.

Just to give you an example of what one of these training initiatives involves, here's a description of one recent effort:

A Typical International Training Course

In the fall of 1997, five members of the FBI's New York Evidence Response Team (NY/ERT) traveled to Asunción, Paraguay to meet with law enforcement officers from Paraguay and Peru and present a five-day course in collection and preservation of crime scene evidence.

The FBI's Evidence Response Teams handle a tremendous range of forensic evidence, and they've developed very effective techniques for identifying, handling, and preserving that evidence. This course was intended to give the 41 participants an overview of these techniques, as well as practical experience in using them. Also, they were exposed to evidence recognition and handling techniques, as well as to ways process different categories of evidence that may be encountered at a crime scene.

The curriculum offered a balance of lectures and practical exercises each day. The NY/ERT presented a series of videotapes relating to evidence collection and processing, as well as footage of the more unique evidence recovery operations that they had been involved in recently. After each presentation or at the conclusion of the training day, each NY/ERT instructor remained available for further questions.

Day One. Crime scene management on a small and large scale; evidence documentation and packaging procedures; crime scene sketching and diagramming techniques.

Day Two. Latent and patent fingerprint locating and development techniques; fingerprint photography techniques. The afternoon session was dedicated to a technical demonstration and practical problems.

Day Three. Casting techniques (dental stone, mikrosil) and their application; serology. The Paraguayan Police gave the instructors an in-depth tour of their crime laboratory.

Day Four. Homicide investigation; sex crimes; human remains recovery; ballistics; bombings.

Day Five. On the last day the class was divided into four groups. Each group completed a crime scene practical exercise which necessitated the practical application of all the techniques they learned during the week, as well as management of the crime scene and evidence handling and packaging.

NEW AGENT TRAINING

New agents report to Quantico for a 16-week course intended to give them the basic equipment to take up their jobs. Jim McFall taught at the Academy for six years, specializing in firearms and less-than-lethal weapons. He says, "We always stress that new agents should be taught by agents. These are agents with academic credentials, with other professional skills, with advanced training, but the bottom line is, they're people with experience on the street, using firearms, conducting investigations, conducting apprehensions. People who could instill in the trainees the pride that goes along with being an FBI agent."

New agent training emphasizes practical application, focusing on law, physical training, firearms and self-defense, and investigative techniques: interviewing, interrogation, collecting and preserving evidence, and gathering intelligence.

Law

As members of the largest U.S. law enforcement organization, Special Agents must thoroughly understand the law. Not every agent is expected to have a law degree, or acquire one during New Agent Training, but they need to know the legal parameters they operate under—how to read a statute and identify a violation, what constitutes a legal search, what are the legal limits of suspect and witness interrogation. The Bureau makes sure its training keeps up with changing legal precedent, and Agents continue their legal training throughout their careers. No one wants to be responsible for a case being thrown out on a technicality.

Physical Training

When I was working as a profiler, there were weeks, even months, when I could have worked 24 hours a day and still not cleared my desk. That's a lot of pressure, and there's not a single Special Agent in the FBI who doesn't face that kind of pressure at some point—usually more than one point—in his or her career. There's no way to make the pressure go away, but if you're in good physical condition, at least you'll be able to deal with it.

Firearms

The reality is that criminals are getting better armed all the time. Law enforcement has to be prepared for what they're likely to face out on the streets. All Special Agents are drilled in firearms use under a wide variety of circumstances. Often, that makes a big difference—as you heard in Frank Watts's story about being able to outshoot Tommy Tarrants because the Bureau trains its agents to shoot under a variety of conditions, including at night.

Throughout their training, FBI Special Agents are taught to use deadly force only in very specific circumstances—when the agent believes that a subject poses an immediate threat of death or serious physical injury to the agent or another person. If possible, the agent must give a verbal warning to submit before deadly force is used.

Jim McFall says, "You have to decide, literally in a split second, whether you should draw a weapon. And again, if you draw a weapon, you have to decide in a split second whether you're going to use it. You teach that by drill, drill, drill, by lecture, by demonstration, by putting them in stressful situations and making them perform."

As in all other areas, the Bureau is always looking for better ways to train Special Agents. McFall describes a training device that comes close to simulating real-life situations.

> These are filmed scenarios, projected on a screen which is sensitized to the impact of a laser beam. The training weapons project a laser beam when the trigger's pulled, and there's small explosive devices fitted into the cylinder, so you get the sound of the shot. There's a particular frame that's supposed to initiate the trainee's reaction. Once the weapon is fired, the sensitized screen registers not just where the laser beam hit, but also the time elapsed between the situation that provokes the response and when the weapon is actually fired. There were lots of these scenarios, with different kinds of appropriate reactions. If you fired in a situation where you shouldn't have, this would come up on the screen immediately as an error.

Less-Than-Lethal Weapons

As Jim McFall points out, there's really no such thing as a "nonlethal" weapon: "I can kill you with anything—a pencil, dental floss. Anything." But certain weapons, when used properly, can disable a subject without causing permanent injury. Pepper spray, Mace, stun guns, Tasers—Special Agents are taught not only how to use them effectively and safely, but also how to respond and protect themselves when these weapons are directed at them.

As with everything else, experience is the key to good teaching. McFall has tested out each weapon and each technique on the most logical guinea pig—himself.

> The only thing I didn't do was the Taser. A Taser shoots two barbed darts that are connected to very fine wires. Those darts impact on a

subject and when you depress an activator switch, 50,000 volts of electricity are discharged into that individual. Well, I wouldn't let them shoot me with the darts. There's a telescoping antennae set you fit onto a Taser, so that when you extend the antennae, you can touch the person with the tips and get the voltage discharge that way. I've taken that. I've had pepper spray, I've had tear gas, I've had the Nova XR-5000 stun gun—that's a winner, that'll knock you silly. When I taught the police officers, I could stand there and look every one of them right in the eye and say, "I know this stuff works, I know its effects, because I've had it done to me." That makes a big difference in terms of your credibility.

Hogan's Alley

This little "town" has the highest crime rate in the country. There isn't a day that goes by without a bank robbery, a kidnapping, a shoot-out—all of it unfolding literally in Quantico's backyard.

Everything that happens in Hogan's Alley is carefully scripted, designed to test the Special Agent trainees in a particular situation. At one time, the "lawbreakers" were Special Agents, but for the past several years, the Academy has hired role-players. "These people are very thoroughly briefed as to the role they're to play, how to respond, whether they're supposed be aggressive or cooperative or whatever," says McFall. "The new agents have to go in and handle them just as if they weren't actors. And it's amazing how quickly it starts to seem real."

CHAPTER 8

Helping Other Agencies

I've mentioned over and over how much the FBI stresses cooperation among law enforcement agencies, and that's absolutely true. The FBI doesn't "take over" investigations from state or local police. State and local law enforcement agencies aren't subordinate to the FBI, and the FBI doesn't supervise or usurp their investigations.

Here's how Bob McGonigel puts it: "I've worked with police departments all over the country, and it was a great experience for me. We complemented each other. I was aware of people's sensitivities, and I'd try to put them at ease and let them know that I'm just there to do the job. Don't want my picture taken, and don't want the credit. I just want to work toward a solution of the case. Once they realize that, they put away those petty differences. I was never one who was opposed to learning a more effective way, or a more sensible way to do it. I don't have all the answers."

However, the FBI does have resources and experience that most other law enforcement agencies can't match. The Bureau strengthens the fight against crime on all levels by providing those resources to other agencies.

For instance, the FBI's centralized information databases help apprehend fugitives. When local agencies report a fugitive to the Bureau, a stop is placed against the fugitive's fingerprints in the FBI's Criminal Justice Information Services Division. If any additional fingerprints are turned into the FBI, local police will be notified immediately. The fugitive's name and identifying data also will be entered into the National Crime Information Center, a computerized database that is accessible to law enforcement agencies nationwide. Any agency requesting information about this individual will be informed of his or her fugitive status. If there's reason to believe a fugitive has traveled across a state line or left the United States, the FBI may obtain a federal arrest warrant and join the investigation.

Through the National Name Check Program, specific information from the FBI's central records system is made available to other entities lawfully authorized to receive it—other federal agencies in the Executive Branch, congressional committees, the federal judiciary, some foreign police and intelligence agencies, and state and local agencies within the criminal justice system. The individual's rights are safeguarded, as well; information is released only in accordance with the provisions of the federal Privacy Act, and other applicable federal orders and directives.

One of the FBI's most effective cooperative means of fighting criminal activity is through its range of multiagency task forces. These have proven to be a very effective way for the FBI and state and local law enforcement to join together to address specific crime problems. Criminals generally don't pay a lot of attention to jurisdictional matters—a crime may be a local, state, and federal violation all at the same time. Task forces organize the law enforcement response and represent the best use of scarce resources.

Here's a brief rundown of the major task forces the FBI participates in:

Evidence Response Team (ERT)

Each FBI field office supports an ERT, which specializes in recovery of physical evidence and the execution of search warrants. The ERTs are called out in cases with complicated or multiple crime scenes, in multijurisdictional cases, and in cases requiring the most sophisticated forensic analyses. Seventeen ERTs from across the country participated in evidence recovery at the bombing of the Oklahoma City federal building. ERTs also train local and international police in evidence recovery procedures—as the New York ERT (NY/ERT) recently did in Paraguay.

The 36–member NY/ERT is one of the most active teams in the country, providing most of the New York Office's forensic capability. Participating in the task force is strictly voluntary; everyone on the team has to balance training and operational requirements with everyday squad duties. And these people do work hard. The NY/ERT—and all members of special task forces—put pressure on themselves to make sure their operational, training, and administrative standards are not only met, but improved upon.

A coordinator heads up the three NY/ERT teams—Red, White, and Blue. Each 12-person team rotates "on duty" status every two weeks. In the case of a major disaster, such as TWA 800, everyone on the task force is called out.

Staff Duties

The coordinator serves as the overall program manager with other team members handling organizational responsibilities, as outlined below:

- The Operations/Training Officer coordinates the training activities, researches new training programs, and acts as the NY/ERT's liaison with the FBI and outside agencies.

- The Equipment/Logistics Officer maintains adequate supplies for operational missions, keeps records of equipment issued to each ERT member, and coordinates logistical support for the NY/ERT during missions outside the team's jurisdiction.

- The Medical Officer coordinates medical training, keeps on top of members' inoculations, and makes sure any injuries are documented and referred to the Health Services Unit.

- The Team Leader communicates training and operation requirements to the team and keeps track of the day-to-day availability and accountability of team members.

- The Assistant Team Leader steps in as the Team Leader in his or her absence, and performs major assignments as directed by the Team leader.

- The Administrative Officer maintains accurate and current records on team personnel and administration.

Equipment

Besides the usual equipment any crime scene unit would have—evidence vacuums, latent fingerprinting equipment, laptop computers, alternative light sources—the NY/ERT operates two vehicles outfitted with emergency light package and state-of-the-art communications equipment. These vehicles can operate over radio frequencies in the VHF and UHF range, issue secure communications via cellular telephone, and provide AC power in the field.

The NY/ERT also operates two full-size heavy equipment trucks, a cargo van, and a step van; these are used as needed in major-response situations and for supply purposes. A 14-foot trailer is used in the New York region to transport bulky, specialized equipment not needed on most responses. An 18-foot trailer is stocked with supplies and equipment needed when the team deploys to a major event nationally, or even internationally; this trailer can keep two ERT teams supplied for three days.

Training

Evidence recovery is crucial to the successful investigation and prosecution of a crime. The highly trained Special Agent and support personnel who make up an ERT specialize in organizing and collecting evidence using a variety of technical evidence recovery techniques. ERTs also include personnel with specialized forensic training and unique collection abilities; these skills prove invaluable in unusual searches or crime scenes.

The NY/ERT conducts regular training on the first Wednesday of each month. Each team member also completes at least 80 hours of basic instruction provided by the FBI's Evidence Response Team Unit

(ERTU). The NY/ERT aggressively searches out training opportunities from sources outside the Bureau. And the NY/ERT, along with all the ERTs, establishes partnerships in the law enforcement community to obtain and provide training and operational support wherever needed.

Two Very Special Agents

One of the difficulties of working for the FBI is achieving balance in your life—not letting the job take over. I think we can learn a few lessons in this area from a couple of members of the NY/ERT. These two guys focus completely on the task when they're at work, devoting every ounce of their energy and concentration to the job. But when they're off-duty, they're off. They don't worry about what they should have done last time, or what they might do next time. They give it all they've got, and then they move on. Instead of reacting to stress by boozing it up or snarling at the kids, they just chew on a rawhide and take a nap.

I'm talking, of course, about the canine component of the New York K-9 Program, part of the NY/ERT.

Axel was born in June 1994, of mixed parentage—Rottweiler and German shepherd. He's very well educated; he completed a 400-hour narcotics detection course at the New Jersey State Police Canine Academy. He's certified to detect heroin, cocaine, crack, hashish, marijuana, and methamphetamines; when he sniffs out any of these substances, he scratches and bites at the spot where the odor is strongest. During training, he conducted 160 successful searches at a range of locations—cars, helicopters, boats, trucks, buses, houses, apartments, warehouses, institutions, and open fields. Since starting work for the FBI, he's participated in searches which have resulted in the seizure of over 324.73 kilos of cocaine, 859 grams of crack cocaine, and 361 grams of marijuana, all with an estimated street value of $7,162,290.

Jake is a four-year-old black Labrador Retriever whose specialty is explosive chemical detection. His training, which began at six months, included basic obedience and introduction to explosive residues. He's trained to give a passive response when he detects explosives—biting and scratching could set off the explosives, so instead Jake just sits down. He's been credited with recovery of firearms, fireworks, explosives. He and his handler, a Special Agent bomb technician, assisted in TWA 800 recovery efforts.

Jake

Axel

(FBI Photos)

Safe Streets

This task force targets violent crime and drug trafficking in areas where state or local authorities have identified it as a significant local concern. Participating law enforcement officers work closely with Special Agents at the relevant Field Offices, and receive intensive training in dealing with the specific problems they're likely to face on the streets. As of May 1996, 142 Safe Streets Task Forces had been established in 54 field offices. These task forces include 1,067 state and local officers, 732 FBI Agents, and 150 persons from other federal agencies. Since 1992, over 100,000 criminals have been arrested under the Safe Streets program.

Rapid Start Team

Any law enforcement official knows that the first hours—even the first minutes—of a crime investigation can make or break its success. You have to get a handle on the situation sooner, rather than later. The FBI's Rapid Start task force allows law enforcement to establish and maintain control of complicated cases from the very beginning.

Under Rapid Start, FBI Special Agents and support personnel provide on-site automation for major cases and crises. In the event of a murder, kidnapping, or other task force case, a Rapid Start team travels to the jurisdiction and works with local officials to organize and enter all pertinent facts into one database. The information can then be sorted, filtered, and analyzed instantaneously. This allows for effective lead management, and helps investigators quickly identify the most productive investigative approaches. The Rapid Start Team has been responsible for operating in many investigations, including the bombing of the World Trade Center.

Critical Incident Response Group (CIRG)

This task force was formed to address hostage-taking, barricade situations, terrorist activities, and other critical incidents requiring an emergency response by diverse law enforcement resources. CIRG provides training and operational support crisis management, negotiations, criminal profiling, and special weapons and tactics (SWAT).

SWAT Teams

Nine enhanced SWAT teams are strategically located throughout the United States. They're called into action in the most critical and dangerous situations.

Phil Grivas was on SWAT teams for 17 years, and spent six years as a SWAT team commander. He describes this experience this way: "You can't imagine what it's like to give people an order to go into a situation, knowing that they may not be coming back. It's one thing to go through the door yourself. I never gave it a second thought. But when you're in charge of the team, they become like your kids. You get protective of them.

"When you have to send other people through the front door, that's when you really hope and pray that your plan covers everything. The selection of personnel, the equipment, the weaponry, the communications, all of it—you have to plan and drill and plan and drill some more, to minimize the chance of any more people getting hurt. I've got a lot to be grateful for in my career, and one of the biggest things is the fact that I left without any of my people getting hurt."

Hostage Rescue Team (HRT)

The HRT was created in 1982 as a special counterterrorist unit, offering a tactical option for any extraordinary hostage crisis that might occur within the United States. The team is set up to deploy to any location within four hours of notification by the Director of the FBI or his designated representative. Once there, the team's mission is to conduct a successful rescue of U.S. persons and others who may be held illegally by a hostile force. Team members specialize in communication, command control, use of sophisticated electronic equipment, and handling of explosive devices.

The HRT has been deployed to the scenes of such incidents as prison riots in Georgia and Alabama; the "Freemen" standoff in Jordan, Montana; and the bombing at the 1996 Summer Olympics in Atlanta, Georgia.

Profiling and Behavioral Assessment Unit (PBAU)

I wish there were no need for this unit. This group helps investigate the most brutal, most violent crimes, including child abductions, serial murders, and serial sex crimes. Unfortunately, there's been an increase in all these crimes over the past 20 years. These cases are not only heart-breaking, but they're also complicated and extremely difficult to solve. Investigations of this kind require an immediate all-out response, and a long-term commitment of more personnel and resources than many police departments can spare.

PBAU's primary responsibility is to provide immediate investigative support through violent crime analysis, technical and forensic resource coordination, and application of the most current expertise available. While most cops will never investigate serial killings, mass murders, abductions or mysterious disappearances, PBAU deals with these kinds of crimes all the time. The members of this unit can draw on years of experience in assessing leads, developing strategies, and evaluating evidence. That saves time, which often means saving lives.

The goal is always to support the investigative agencies in first recovering the victim or victims, and then fully resolving the case—ideally, through a conviction.

PBAU Special Agents provide the following services:

- Profiles of unknown subjects (UNSUBs)

- Crime analysis

- Investigative strategies

- Interview and interrogation strategies

- Trial preparation and prosecution strategy

- Expert testimony

- Coordination of other FBI resources, including the use of the Evidence Response Team, Laboratory services, and Rapid Start

PBAU also maintains a close working relationship with the National Center for Missing and Exploited Children and can help in arranging use of their resources, such as widespread poster distribution and age enhancement of photographs.

The Violent Criminal Apprehension Program, (VICAP), a part of the PBAU, is designed to collect, collate and analyze the aspects of violent crimes so that through computer analysis and data processing, violent crimes can be compared, identified and charted. In addition, experienced Major Case Specialists and Crime Analysts review the violent crime cases submitted and are able to provide their investigative and analytical expertise to the submitting law enforcement agencies. Through this process, suspects can be identified, crimes can be linked, and widespread law enforcement agencies can combine their resources to focus on a common criminal.

National Center for the Analysis of Violent Crime (NCAVC)

One of my personal obsessions has been the development of a nationwide resource for fighting particularly vicious crimes. Without a way for law enforcement agencies to compare notes, the most violent, most predatory criminals can escape capture by simply moving from one jurisdiction to another. A killer or rapist vanishes once he leaves the first area, and then appears from nowhere when he begins his crimes somewhere new.

In 1985, NCAVC was formed to combat this problem. Based at the National Academy, NCAVC offers research, training, and investigative and operational support to law enforcement agencies across the country confronted with unusual, high-risk, vicious, or repetitive crimes.

Research activities include the study of serial and violent crimes (such as homicide, rape, child abduction, arson, threats, and computer crimes) as well as hijacking, crisis management, and subjects related to hostage negotiation and SWAT team operations. Investigative support is also offered through the Violent Criminal Apprehension Program (VICAP) to alert law enforcement agencies that may be seeking the same offender for crimes in different jurisdictions.

Regional Drug Intelligence Squads (RDIs)

These multiagency information-gathering groups are based in eight geographic regions—all identified as key trans-shipment centers for illegal drugs. Intelligence information uncovered by RDIs often triggers major drug investigations. Using the Racketeering Enterprise Investigation concept, team members focus on getting information about the most serious drug-trafficking organizations operating in their areas—including their composition, scope, magnitude, internal and external dynamics, and drug-trafficking patterns. Once collected, this information is analyzed and provided to the federal, state, or local law enforcement agency best suited to handle the case.

DRUGX

This joint FBI-DEA drug index database became operational in 1995. It merges over 4.4 million FBI drug records (culled from case index information) with more than 4.1 million DEA records. When the FBI considers opening an investigation on a subject, it can first check to see if the DEA has an investigation on the same subject (or vice versa). This preliminary check saves valuable resources and man-hours by reducing duplicate efforts.

National Drug Intelligence Center (NDIC)

NDIC was established in 1993 to provide a strategic picture of drug-distribution organizations as they evolve in response to the market and law-enforcement efforts. Participating agencies include the FBI and the DEA, along with other federal law enforcement, intelligence and military agencies. NDIC analysts gather information from the field and from the participating agencies' headquarters, then prepare reports, studies, and other research on requested topics.

The NDIC is in the process of developing an electronic library which would enable participating agencies to research specific topics. These services should eventually be available to state and local law enforcement as well.

El Paso Intelligence Center (EPIC)

This multiagency, 24-hour electronic monitoring post keeps tabs on drug trafficking organizations operating across the U.S./Mexico border. EPIC's primary focus is on drug-trafficking activities in the Southwest, but EPIC investigators and analysts from the 15 or so participating agencies also collect and analyze tactical drug intelligence from other areas—including foreign countries—whose drug activities impact on the United States EPIC also prepares periodic assessments of the threat posed by drug-trafficking organizations worldwide. EPIC also acts as an information clearinghouse, regularly sharing automated drug data among participating agencies. This results in better coordinated, more effective investigations.

International Activities

In the course of their operations, the FBI's Legal Attaché Offices sometimes receive information relevant to FBI organized crime and drug cases in the United States and pass on certain information that may help the law enforcement agencies with jurisdiction in the region. In 1995, FBI Legats handled over 11,200 investigative matters.

The FBI regularly participates in international working groups with countries including Italy, Australia, Canada, and Mexico. The Bureau also exchanges midlevel supervisory personnel with police agencies in countries such as Germany, Italy, Australia, and Japan, and with INTER-POL. This regular and ongoing linkage facilitates a rapid exchange of information on drug smuggling and other international crimes.

DNA Technology

The FBI Laboratory, with its extensive technical resources and expertise, has become a world leader in the forensic use of DNA. Currently, the FBI's work with DNA is focused in two areas:

- FBI laboratories now use new DNA casework tests based on a technique for amplifying small quantities of genetic material. This means that the tests can be effective and meaningful, even with there's only a tiny sample of blood or other material available—which is often the case with crime scene evidence.

- The new Combined DNA Index System (CODIS) is a database containing DNA profiles of convicted sex offenders and other violent offenders, as well as missing persons. CODIS allows state and local crime labs to match DNA profiles from UNSUBs in serial rape cases with unknown suspects, helping refocus investigative efforts. When it's deployed nationwide, CODIS will allow law enforcement to review all 20,000 convicted offender DNA records held in 45 DNA crime labs across the country.

National Crime Information Center (NCIC) 2000

NCIC was established in 1967 as a nationwide computerized information system to provide law enforcement with information on fugitives, stolen property, and other information. The enhanced system—NCIC 2000—will incorporate advanced technologies such as capture, transmission, retrieval, and printout of fugitives' photograph and fingerprint images, as well as other improvements.

Integrated Fingerprint Identification System (IFIS)

This program is scheduled to be up and running by early 1999. IFIS will be a rapid-response paperless system that receives and processes electronic fingerprint images, criminal histories, and related information. The new services offered to law enforcement will include remote searches of crime scene fingerprints and remote access to fingerprint images.

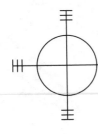

PART THREE

Strategies for Pursuing a Career in the FBI

CHAPTER 9

Career Opportunities in the FBI

Unlike most government agencies, the FBI does its own hiring. But the pay and promotion standards correspond to government guidelines. In the descriptions of specific job requirements, I'll mention levels on government pay scales, such as *GS 14*. Take a look at the pay scale chart included at the end of this chapter. It will show you what the levels mean.

The FBI has a strong commitment to equal opportunity employment, and as you'll see, the Bureau has developed a very strict, but very fair, selection process. All applicants are given an equal opportunity, consistent with established rules and procedures, to compete for vacancies within the Bureau. There's not a lot of turnover in the Bureau—the overall attrition rate for FBI employees, including retirements, is approximately five percent.

The role of the FBI's Office of Equal Employment Opportunity Affairs is to provide equal opportunity in employment for all persons; to prohibit discrimination in employment because of race, color, religion, sex, national origin, sexual orientation, age, or handicap; and to promote the full realization of equal employment opportunity through a continuing affirmative action program.

The following chart shows a breakdown of FBI employees by gender and race:

EMPLOYEE STATISTICS

Special Agent Employment Statistics as of 1/31/98

	No. of Men	% of Total	No. of Women	% of Total	Total Group	% of Total
Am. Indian	45	.4	10	.1	55	.5
Asian	233	2.1	41	.4	274	2.4
Black	526	4.7	114	1.0	640	5.7
Hispanic	676	6.0	111	1.0	787	7.0
White	8,014	71.1	1,501	13.3	9,515	84.4
TOTALS	9,494	84.2	1,777	15.8	11,271	100
ALL MINORITIES	1,480	13.1	276	2.4	1,756	15.6

Support Personnel Employment Statistics as of 1/31/98

	No. of Men	% of Total	No. of Women	% of Total	Total Group	% of Total
Am. Indian	25	.2	46	.3	71	.4
Asian	134	.8	168	1.0	302	1.9
Black	660	4.0	2,926	17.9	3,586	22.0
Hispanic	227	1.4	530	3.2	757	4.6
White	4,174	25.6	7,422	45.5	11,596	71.1
TOTALS	5,220	32.1	11,092	67.9	16,312	100
ALL MINORITIES	1,046	6.4	3,670	22.5	4,716	28.9

Note: Due to rounding of figures, these totals might not be exact to the tenth.

The FBI has recently set up an Employment Home Page as part of its Web site. The address is http://www.fbi.gov. There, you can look up job postings in all areas of the Bureau, check out job requirements, even download an application form.

SPECIAL AGENTS

The FBI Special Agents are without a doubt the most visible members of the FBI. While it's always been pretty tough to get into the training program, it's become really competitive over the past few years. I'm saying this not to be discouraging, but to be realistic. "When I came in, one in 400 was appointed to the Academy," says Jim McFall. "Now it's one in a thousand. The winnowing process is very, very thorough. Very objective, but very thorough."

These are the minimum qualifications for Special Agents, and I stress minimum. If you don't meet *all* these criteria, there's no way you'll get into the Bureau as a Special Agent. That's just a fact.

- You must be a U.S. citizen, or a citizen of Northern Mariana Islands.

- You must be at least 23 years old and no more than 37 years old when you apply.

- You must have *uncorrected* vision that's no worse than 20/200; your corrected vision must be 20/20 in one eye and no worse than 20/40 in the other eye. You also must pass a color vision test, to check for color blindness.

- You must hold a valid driver's license.

- You must have a degree from a four-year resident program at an accredited college.

- You must pass a thorough investigation, which includes the following:

❏ *Background check:* This begins with a basic "paper check"—college transcripts, credit record, medical history. They'll check for an arrest record; parking violations and the occasional speeding ticket won't eliminate you, but anything much beyond that probably will. Once you've cleared several other hurdles, the Bureau will send investigators out to interview your friends, neighbors, and former employers.

❏ *Drug test:* This covers recent use of marijuana, cocaine, heroin and other illegal drugs. However, your drug use history is relevant, too. If you've used marijuana in the last three years, or if you've taken any illegal drug within the last ten years, you're out. If you've ever sold illegal drugs, including marijuana, you're out.

❏ *Polygraph examination:* You will be asked about your criminal and drug history, but the Bureau isn't looking for robots. When you're asked about theft, for instance, that doesn't mean taking a pen home from the office. I'll got into more detail about the polygraph examination later. Basically, if you've got a clean record, it's nothing to worry about.

This isn't an official, stated requirement, but I will tell you that the Bureau really doesn't even look at applicants until they have at least three years of work experience.

Special Agent Entry Programs

The FBI puts new Special Agents into four categories, or "entry programs," depending on the qualifications the candidates bring to the job. The mix of entry programs within any one new agents' class varies, depending on what the Bureau needs at a particular time.

Law

Those entering in this program have a J.D. degree from an accredited resident law school. You don't necessarily have to have passed a state bar exam, although it can't hurt.

There are two reason why a law degree is a desirable asset. First, if you're going to enforce the federal laws, you should have an appreciation and understanding of the Federal Rules of Criminal Procedure. Second, the analytical training you get in law school will help you identify the elements of a criminal violation and collect the evidence needed for successful prosecution.

Accounting

Special Agents in the accounting program hold a B.S. degree with a major in accounting or a related discipline, and they must be eligible to take the CPA examination. If you haven't passed the CPA exam before you apply, you must pass the FBI's accounting test.

An accounting degree is a desirable asset because Special Agents often need to trace financial transactions and analyze complex accounting records. Training in accounting and experience with financial systems will help an investigator develop relevant evidence to uncover sophisticated financial crimes. Special Agent Accountants often testify in such white-collar crime cases as expert witnesses, and need to be accredited as financial experts.

Language

Your B.S. or B.A. can be in any discipline, and you must be able to demonstrate proficiency in a language that meets the needs of the FBI. Those languages shift from year to year, depending on factors as varied as international crime patterns and Bureau retirement rates.

By the way, "proficiency" doesn't mean being able to ask directions and order a beer. The tests administered by the FBI require you to be fluent in speaking, writing, and translating.

Diversified

You must hold a B.S. or B.A. in any discipline and have at least three years of full-time work experience. If you have an advanced degree, you need a minimum of two years of full-time work experience.

The diversified entry program covers everyone from police officers to soldiers to psychologists to teachers. It's impossible to tell what specific careers will meet the needs of the FBI at any particular point.

Special Agent Recruiting

I want to put a word in here about the way the FBI recruits for Special Agents. Doug Rhoads, who designed the current program, will describe it in some detail. But I want to just express my own opinion here.

These days, anytime you talk about diversity in the work force, people start thinking—or talking—about quotas and reverse discrimination. I've had people tell me about a nephew of theirs who was a Marine captain and a homicide detective in New York City and has a black belt in karate and wrestles alligators in his spare time and is just all around rough and tough, and *he* couldn't get into the FBI because he's a white male, while they're letting in all these women and minorities who can't do what he can do.

Well, the fact is the Bureau needs more than alligator wrestlers. Take a look at all the different kinds of cases the Bureau handles. You can't tackle a range of investigations that broad without diversity of skills, diversity of approaches, diversity of talents.

Yes, there are going to be intelligent, talented, hard-working white men who don't make it into the FBI. There are also going to be intelligent, talented, hard-working women, Asians, Hispanics, African Americans, and Native Americans who don't make it in. The process is just too competitive to include everyone who might possibly be a good agent. But I honestly believe, and I've seen from my own experience, that the Bureau makes its decisions as fairly and objectively as possible.

I also believe that there's an inherent value in diversity. Remember when Frank Watts talked about how much easier it was for him, as a Southerner, to talk to other Southerners? That holds true for all kinds of groups. You don't have to be a minority to understand or talk to members of a minority, but it doesn't hurt. Often that common ground can help put a nervous or angry witness at ease.

Again, I want to stress that this is just my opinion—*not* official policy. But some of you reading this are going to apply to the FBI, and you aren't going to get in. I don't want you to think it's because someone less qualified took your place.

The Current Program

Since Doug Rhoads spent almost eight years designing and running the recruiting program, I'm going to let him take over. So here's Doug:

> I'll never forget a futurist saying to me, "If you want to see what the country's going to look like in 20 years, go take a look at the first grade right now." Take a look at any elementary school now, and you'll see that by 2010, white males are not going to be the majority. A law enforcement agency as big as the FBI, as visible as the FBI, has to reflect the culture. *Has* to.
>
> I was called back to headquarters in 1983 to work on the recruiting program, because William Webster had taken a look ahead. When my group came in—1969 to 1972—that was the biggest hiring era. Now, a lot of these agents were going to retire after 20 years. The issue was, how are you going to replace half the agent workforce in this six-, eight-year window? And how are you going to do it when you rely on self-recruiting?
>
> The old recruiting method was—well, there was no method. There were fifty-eight different field offices with 58 different systems. When there was a big push to hire agents, the Bureau would drop leaflets over Detroit, and everybody looking for a job would come in the door.

There were two problems with that. First, that approach was so broad that it forced the system to deselect hundreds of people. You made 90 percent of your applicants mad because you didn't give them a job.

Second, with that approach you ended up with an overwhelming majority of white male agents with a modified background. And the fact was, you didn't have to recruit those guys. They grew up like me, always wanting to be a Fed. That group *always* self-recruits. The FBI could do all its hiring out of that group alone and never have to worry.

But I give Director Webster credit for thinking ahead. Whatever other faults he and the people around him may have had, they were very creative in planning for the Bureau's future.

Take a simple thing like keyboard skills. When I joined the Bureau, computers were nowhere. Now you can't function without them. You don't have to be a computer whiz, but you have to have a basic level of comfort, just to get the job done. And you will need some people who are computer whizzes.

So the people at headquarters said, "You know, we're going to need people who know about computers. We're going to need more people with language skills." Fifteen years ago, Farsi wasn't a necessary language. Today it is. Fifteen years ago, Spanish was common, but not like it is today. In five states—California, Florida, Texas, Illinois, and New York—a lot of the language spoken is Spanish. You've got to have Spanish-speaking agents, and not because Spanish speakers are more likely to be criminals. How do you go do a routine background check in Harlingen, Texas, or an investigation in Nogales, New Mexico, when you don't have any Spanish speakers?

We decided we need bilingual agents, we need agents with financial advising skills. We *need* these different skills. Where are we going to find them? I always stress to the recruiters that you've got to get out of your culture.

I did a survey of new agents for about a year. I was trying to see where they were coming from. White males were still a predominant piece of the hiring, and when you asked what attracted them to the Bureau, where did they first learn about the Bureau, all of them said something like "life-long goal," "contact with an onboard Special Agent," "contact with a law enforcement official who knew an onboard agent." Just about 100 percent had personal contact with an agent.

"Now, when you looked at women, that wasn't true. It could have been advertising, it could have been a career day at their college. When you looked at minorities, same thing. They saw an ad in *Black Enterprise Magazine,* or they went to a special minority recruiting event.

That extends to the professions as well. How do you think an electrical engineer knows the Bureau wants him? Or someone who's proficient in Farsi, or Urdu, or any other language the Bureau might need? If you want those kinds of folks to do those diverse kinds of things you need, targeted advertising and targeted outreach is a part of it, like or not.

When I went back to Headquarters in 1983, I was assigned to the administrative services division, on the personnel side. There I was, by myself, one person to design this thing. I just put on a coat and tie and showed up and said, "Well, what are we going to do here?"

As I jumped in I was very impressed with everyone at the Bureau. Even though there's a human resistance to change, nobody—from the highest levels of management to the agents on the street—nobody ever tried to do anything other than a good job. There was resistance to change and yet in the end people like to do the right thing.

From 1983 to 1985 was the planning stage. Eventually my office became a unit, the Personnel Resources Unit, with three or four agents assigned to it along with five or six support personnel. It's evolved so that pure recruitment is the second half of it. The main purpose of the unit is to plan for the future. What do you need? When are you going to need it? How many people are you losing each year? How many retire, how many are fired, how many resign? What were these people doing?

It's the front end, the planning, that makes the recruitment work. If you need computer people next year, don't be dropping those leaflets over

Detroit. Figure out what these people read, put an ad in there, and make the FBI a career option for computer experts. If you think you're going to need computer people in three, four, five years, go to the schools. Talk to your current people, find out where they went, what schools they recommend. You may only need to do that for a couple of years, then you can shift your focus.

As far as recruiting itself, we developed a coherent system across the country. Each division has an applicant coordinator, who's the agent designated to set up the interviews, coordinate the background checks, go to career recruiting events, doing all of this in his or her respective territory. Some of these applicant coordinators were very effective. They enjoyed what they were doing, they got support from their Special Agent in Charge. Others didn't want the job; they wanted to be out working criminal cases, they got stuck with this job, for whatever reason.

Certain divisions did very well, much better than others, based on pure numbers. No one was unhappy with the quality of the agents recruited; it's just that some offices brought you a bigger pool to choose from. Say a big office like Miami brought in five, while a little office like Tampa hired 50. Well, what's Tampa doing that Miami isn't?

I brought together all the Tampas, everyone whose program was working well. Everyone talked about what they were doing, and we analyzed it. Then we had a series of conferences, five around the country, brought all the recruiters together and let these people who were doing it well talk about what they did. Everybody left, then we analyzed the program again, and started to give a national direction. That was Phase I.

Phase II was *get out of your own culture.* I had every recruiter get involved with their own local or regional college placement association. There's an actual structured association in every state and every region of the country that brings together corporate business people who are recruiting college graduates. People would say, "No, you can't do that. The Bureau doesn't hire new graduates. We only hire people with three years' work experience."

Well, the bottom line is, that's a funnel they pass through. How are you going to reach them once they leave the campus? You're back to dropping leaflets over Detroit. Pick 150 colleges, have recruiters go there, and sell the FBI. If you make a good impression, the person that goes to work for a big accounting firm, does well, decides a few years later he wants a career change—he'll remember that guy from the FBI.

Or the top performer at that accounting firm remembers the FBI recruiter at career day. She doesn't want to leave, but she has lunch with a co-worker, someone talented and bright who wants a change. She says, "Why don't you try the FBI?" Each person has a sphere of influence, and you want to intersect as many spheres as you can, whether it's through campus visits, professional associations, just the contacts you make going about your job as an agent.

The Basics: Special Agent Skills

These are taught and stressed in training, and you're expected to work on them in your early years as an agent, and throughout your career. The application process, directly or indirectly, screens for people with talent in these areas. Work on these skills, and you'll be better prepared for the process. These are also good skills you can put to use in any profession.

Interrogation Skills

This can be one of the most interesting, rewarding aspects of the job. Every subject is different, and you have to be able to read the situation and respond on the fly. Like most things, this gets easier with experience, but there are a few guidelines:

• *Do your homework.* Bob McGonigel describes his experience: "At times, particularly in these typical organized crime cases, my supervisor would suggest, 'Well, go see him. He'll talk to you.' And I would just not do it. Because if I didn't know enough about the case, and the individual, and the other play-ers—that would become apparent to the person I was trying to interrogate, and I wouldn't even know enough to call them on a lie. You're just exhibiting your ignorance. And that's the worst thing you can do."

- *Look for the weak spot.* Just as you don't want to reveal a weak-ness to the subject, you're trying to discover and exploit his weaknesses. This is how Phil Grivas describes it: "You have to try to find where they're vulnerable, an Achilles heel. You may say, 'Oh—you got two little kids? How old do you think they're going to be when you see them again? You're never going to be with them through most of their formative years. You're never going to go out and play baseball. You come out, your kids are going to be 20, 25 years old.' You try to find *something.* Sometimes you gotta play a little bit of hardball. 'You ever been in jail before? You know what they do to good-looking guys like you? It's not gonna be fun. You really want to put that many years in there? What do you think you're going to be like when you come out?' Everybody has a chord you can strike, and if you find it, you'll get to them. They'll look at what they've done, and what their prospects really are. And they'll start talking."

- *Look for common ground.* It'll sometimes surprise you, just how much common ground there is. You need to find it and use it to humanize yourself and the victims you're working for. Establishing a connection with the subject can make the difference between getting the information you need and get-ting stonewalled. Phil Grivas says, "The people who commit the most horrendous crimes—I mean rape, and child murder, mutilation, forget about it—when these people are away from that element, away from that crime of opportunity scenario, many of these people are John Q. Average. They like the same teams you do. Or they grew up in the same neighborhood you did. They're very *average.* It's just that they get caught up with these people, and the drugs, and this and that. And next thing you know they're doing things they never dreamed that they could."

- *Control the situation.* Always keep in mind that you are running the show—and run it. Make sure you're in charge of everything that goes on throughout the interrogation. You may, or may not, want to demonstrate that control. That's part of the unpredictability of interrogations. Phil Grivas describes some of his control techniques. "Let's say we've got a subject locked up, and we think he'd respond better to somebody at a higher rank, as opposed to an Agent. I'd have somebody introduce me as the inspector from Washington, up in New York to personally oversee this investigation. I'd be sitting there, with my jacket on, and people would come in and give me these very important documents to sign—just a blank sheet of paper, but *he* doesn't know that. Someone would come in: 'Mr. Grivas, there's a phone call for you from Washington.' I'd say, 'I'm busy with this gentleman now, just give me a minute.' So all of a sudden, the guy looks at you differently. Now, when you tell the subject, 'Look, you want to help yourself? You better talk to me'—well, he might take you a little more seriously."

- *There are no absolutes.* Whatever rules you learn, you have to be prepared to throw them out the window if the situation requires it. In the 1970s, Bob McGonigel got involved in the investigation of a major kidnapping, and had to take over a suspect interview with no preparation. "I was working in the command post when the call came in, that they had retrieved the victim, and they were bringing two subjects in. One of the supervisors asked me to interview one of the subjects. Initially, I felt a little overwhelmed, because I didn't know that much about the details. And the interview lasted, unfortunately, 16 hours. He was lying in the beginning, denying it. And then he gave us a confession that was ridiculous. And we kind of threw that one aside, and kept after him. In the end, he gave us a confession that was enough ultimately to convict him. I was proud of the fact that I was thrown into the gap, with no preparation, and came through."

Surveillance Skills

Bob McGonigel was great at surveillance. Here's what he has to say on the topic:

> The challenge is first, making sure you don't get made, and second, accomplishing the objective—obtaining the information you need. That information could be used to prosecute the subjects, or it could be used to show that these people aren't doing anything illegal. Maybe when a suspect is put under surveillance, you'll find out that they're not involved in it at all. It's a dead end, and you have to redirect.
>
> I loved surveillance. For a while, I was in what they call "Special Operations." Anywhere from four to seven agents who would work together in concert, basically the top-notch cases. We'd start on surveillance, but in the end we doing most of the arrests in those cases also. We had some very unusual vehicles, cars that had been seized by the government, including a Ferrari, which was virtually useless as a surveillance vehicle. When we wanted to go into a neighborhood, we'd send in a female agent in the Ferrari, just have her drive around, and park different places. People would all look toward her, and no one noticed us at all.

Ability to Write Reports

Writing skills are essential in the Bureau. You don't have to be Shakespeare, but you need to have a handle on the basics. Just about any investigation, no matter how minor, almost immediately turns into something that looks like a recycling bin—forensic reports, interview transcripts, crime scene descriptions, background reports, legal briefs, phone messages, more bits of paper than you can believe. You have to be able to assemble all that information, read it and synthesize it, identify the critical points, organize them logically, and present the relevant material and your conclusions clearly and concisely. Clarity, logic, completeness—those are the critical factors in writing up a report.

This is how Jim McFall puts it: "There's an old saying—'You write a report to express, not impress.' Reports are not rated by how much they weigh—although I've seen some that ran several volumes. But if I took one of my reports and handed it to you, you could read it from front to back and know exactly what the case was about. You'd know what the alleged violation was, you'd know who the witnesses were, the subjects, the empirical data that was obtained—it's all there."

Ability to Give Testimony

You're going to have to communicate verbally, as well as on paper. When you're called to give testimony, as an investigator or as an expert witness, you have to be able to express yourself clearly, without letting the opposing counsel rattle you. You also need to make sure your point gets across to the jury, without talking down to them.

Bruce Koenig describes what can happen when you've got someone who thinks a bit too much of himself up on the stand:

> I haven't seen it really in the FBI at all. But I have seen some of these Ph.D.'s get up on the stand and actually laugh at a prosecutor's question. They'll literally laugh and say, "I can't answer that question. There's nobody in this courtroom smart enough to understand my answer." They don't understand what a negative impact that has on the jury. Everyone on that jury thinks, "What a pompous idiot." That just hurts the prosecution.

> I believe part of my job is to give people some understanding of audio tapes. This is my little stage, my chance to get up there and explain to them exactly what a tape is and how the tape recorder works. I give them the basics before we get into the complicated stuff. I can't expect them to know all that I know, but I can certainly educate them enough so they can comprehend what I tell them. That's vital.

Testifying in a trial can also be tremendously rewarding. After all your work, you finally have a chance to face the criminal in court and, you hope, help put him away. Greg Cooper describes one of these experiences:

> I was contacted by one of the people at VICAP, who said, "'I've got these two cases out of North Carolina. Two separate jurisdictions. I've talked to both county attorneys, and they don't feel that they can successfully convict this guy of either case without being able to introduce evidence linking both cases. They want to do it from a behavioral perspective, and I don't think there's anything there."

> Of course, he was looking at it from a different perspective. He wasn't a profiler, which was why he came to our unit. I take a look at the cases, two incredibly vicious murders, and then I call the prosecutors. I say, "I think we can link these cases together by some of the unique behavior here."

> They're very, very excited, because they feel now they might have a shot at getting this guy. I review the cases, analyze them, go to North Carolina to testify. Carl Steven Mosley is the defendant.

> The experience was so dramatic. The courtroom is filled with people, the public, and the media, but everyone's totally silent. Just listening. As I'm testifying, I look eye to eye with Mosley, and he has a look on his face like, "How the hell did you know? How do you *know* all this?"

> He was convicted and sentenced to death. Then, ten months later, I went back and testified in the second trial. One day, one of the deputies told me that he'd escorted Mosely into court that day. When Mosely saw me, he said, "There's the son of a bitch who's gonna try to make them think I did this one, too." I just smiled and told the deputy, "That's exactly right."

> At this point, profiling was still fairly new. I think John was the only person who'd been accepted as an expert witness in this area, so I felt a certain amount of pressure. But there was no doubt in my mind that Mosely had committed both murders.

The defense attorneys were really rattled. They were so overwhelmed, just flustered. They didn't know what questions to ask. They became very, very upset that this evidence was even allowed. They appealed the conviction based specifically on my testimony, saying it shouldn't have been allowed.

The case has gone through two different appeals processes—state and federal level. But the convictions have been upheld.

I'm glad I helped put Mosely away. I just wish they could bring him back to carry out the second execution.

Special Agent Career Paths

The FBI doesn't expect every agent to take an up-or-out career path. You can climb through the ranks, like Phil Grivas, or you can spend your career on the front lines, like Bob McGonigel. The Bureau values experience and expertise, no matter where the individual chooses to exercise it.

All new agents serve a two-year probationary period. After graduation from the Academy, a new Special Agent is assigned to an FBI field office, based on the Bureau's needs. You can ask for a particular posting, but there's no guarantee you'll get it. Generally, new agents stay in their first offices of assignment for four years.

Those years give the new agent a chance to get some real-world experience. You'll probably start out on the more straightforward cases —interstate auto theft and fugitive recovery. This lets you get the hands-on experience you'll need in the basics of investigation. You'll also start to realize what kinds of work you're drawn to—it might be organized crime, or white-collar crime, or forensics. But those first years are a great opportunity to do some frontline, crime-fighting work.

After you've finished up four years, you're considered eligible for what's called "a nonvoluntary rotational transfer," which means you'll be sent to another office, again depending on the needs of the FBI. However, Special Agents who stay in an office for more than ten years generally won't be considered for a nonvoluntary rotational transfer. The FBI isn't the military; the Bureau seems to try not to shift agents around more than they have to.

Specialties

The question I'm asked, over and over, is, "How do I get to be a profiler?" The fact is that profiling, and every other specialty within the FBI, isn't something you just step right into. For any specialty, you have to begin by establishing a good record as an investigator at your first few postings. Attend the relevant in-service classes back at the Academy, and do well at those. There may be particular assignments you need to handle for a few years before you'll be considered. For instance, Greg Cooper had to put in a stint as a NCAVC coordinator before he could apply for the profiling unit.

Once you've met all the requirements for the specialty, you still have to go through at least one year of training. It's fascinating, but it's not easy. Greg describes what is was like when he finally made it back to Quantico as a profiler:

> The first thing that happens is, I'm in training for a year. You have this unbelievable experience, both academically and practically because you are assigned to cases right away. So I'm taking classes at the National Academy in interpersonal violence and death investigations, classes at the Institute of Pathology, Psychology and the Law from the University of Virginia. It's this intensive, intensive immersion—no matter what your experience has been before, this takes it to another level totally. The learning curve is just phenomenal. And it's not quite like any other academic experience because you have an opportunity to immediately apply the things that you're learning. You're working cases right away. *And* you're learning from those you're working with at the same time.
>
> It's unbelievably high-pressure, and unbelievably rewarding. You have the benefit of the academics and you have the benefit of working the case, and then the benefit of working with people who have already developed this ability and are sharing their insight and guidance with you. It's a tremendous experience.

Special Agent Pay Scale

Special Agents enter as GS 10 and can advance to GS 13 in field assignments. Promotions to supervisory, management, and executive positions are available in Grades 14 and 15, as well as in the Senior Executive Service (SES).

In some areas—New York City and Los Angeles, for example—agents receive a "locality adjustment." This is a percentage added to the base pay, to make up for the increased cost of living in those areas.

Special Agents are required to be available for duty 24 hours a day. Therefore, they're also provided with availability pay—equal to 25 percent of an agent's total salary, which includes base salary plus any locality adjustment.

PROFESSIONAL SUPPORT PERSONNEL POSITIONS

The Special Agents couldn't do their jobs without excellent support from all the other employees of the FBI. These people's backgrounds, and the jobs they do, cover a tremendous range.

Jim O'Connor says, "Criminal justice is a multidisciplinary, interdisciplinary field. For instance, investigators learn a lot from journalists. Where do I go for sources? What are the sources of information that are legal? One of the strengths of the FBI is that they don't limit applicants to any one degree. The broader the educational backgrounds in an agency, the more capable the agency is going to be. Say I have a government fraud case, and it happens to involve a highway construction project. I need engineers to understand what the specifications were, whether the construction met those specs. And that's just one example. The FBI specifically recruits and focuses on areas that give investigators support. And so they favor lawyers and accountants, but also linguists, scientists, computer scientists, behavioral scientists, and so forth. You need that broad variety of educational background, and experiential background, supporting the investigative force."

PROFESSIONAL POSITIONS

This category covers job descriptions ranging from attorneys, to personnel psychologists, to contract specialists, and more. A few professional support positions (for instance, Investigative Specialist) require employees to be available both for transfer, temporary duty assignments, or either one, wherever the needs of the FBI dictate. However, most professional support positions don't require this willingness to pick up and go.

Just as an example, here are the job description and minimum requirements for one professional job, that of biologist/forensic examiner:

Sample Job Description: Biologist/Forensic Examiner

General Duties

These folks are responsible for planning, coordinating, directing, and conducting forensic science activities in the FBI Lab. This includes inventory duties on samples; examining and performing comprehensive technical analyses of evidence such as DNA in body tissues, fluids, and body fluid stains; forensic serology of blood and other body fluids; locating, identifying, reconstructing and preserving pertinent items of evidence for examination from crime scenes. As with Special Agents who are forensic specialists, forensic examiners also prepare and furnish oral and written reports and testify in court as necessary.

General Qualifications

Applicants must have at least a bachelor's degree in biochemistry, biological sciences, biotechnology or a related discipline. Your transcript must include a minimum of 24 semester hours in biochemistry or the biological sciences.

The pay for forensic examiners ranges from GS 7 to GS 13, depending on experience.

Qualifications for GS 7: One full year of graduate-level education, or superior academic achievement in one of the above disciplines, or a bachelor's degree and one year of specialized experience in one of the above disciplines.

Qualifications for GS 11: Three full years of progressively higher graduate-level education, or a Ph.D., or an equivalent doctoral degree, or a bachelor's degree and one year of specialized experience equivalent to at least GS 9 in the federal service. (Qualifications for GS 12 and GS 13 are similar.)

Special Working Conditions

- Must successfully complete training necessary for certification as an FBI Forensic Examiner.

- Must be willing to work irregular and odd-hour shifts and weekends when necessary.

- Must be willing to work under hazardous conditions in a laboratory that may include regular, recurring exposure to hazardous materials, toxic substances, and blood-borne pathogens.

- Must be willing to travel frequently, usually on short notice, to conduct crime-scene examinations and to testify in court.

- Must be able to lift heavy objects (50 lbs or more) and have visual acuity to distinguish colors, sizes, and details.

ADMINISTRATIVE SUPPORT POSITIONS

Administrative support positions offer skilled support for investigations. These positions include computer specialists, management analysts, and language specialists.

As an example, we'll take a look at the job description of an intelligence research specialist.

Sample Job Description: Intelligence Research Specialist

General Duties

Employees in this position are responsible for examining and interpreting national security information gathered by the FBI. Intelligence Research Specialists offer support to the counterintelligence, criminal intelligence, counterterrorism, and organized crime missions of the FBI in the following ways: preparing strategic and operational analyses; developing espionage case studies; creating threat assessments. These documents are distributed within the FBI, as well as the law enforcement and U.S. intelligence communities.

General Qualifications

Education: There's no specific degree requirement, but your transcript should show course work in intelligence or intelligence-related disciplines such as history, political science, international affairs, economics, or journalism.

General experience: Your work experience should demonstrate your ability to do the following:

- Analyze problems, identifying significant factors, gathering pertinent data and recognizing solutions
- Plan and organize work
- Use good judgment
- Communicate effectively orally and in writing

Specialized experience: The Bureau will look for experience directly related to the position to be filled. This could include, but isn't limited to, analytical, research or writing duties associated with drug intelligence, or similar experience in a related discipline such as history, political science, international affairs, economics or journalism.

The pay ranges from GS 5 to GS 14.

Qualifications for GS 5: You must have a bachelor's degree, or three years of general experience, including one year equivalent to at least GS 4 in the federal service.

Qualifications for GS 11: This requires three full academic years of graduate-level education, or a Ph.D. or equivalent doctoral degree, or one year of specialized experience equivalent to GS 9 in the federal service.

TECHNICAL POSITIONS

These are computer technicians, evidence technicians, the people with more hands-on jobs. They keep the Bureau running—sometimes literally, as in the case of auto technicians.

Sample Job Description: Automotive Technician

Qualifications

Applicants must have a high school diploma or the equivalent, plus work experience.

Pay ranges from W 6 to GS 12, depending on experience.

Duties at W 6: These are basic automotive tasks; mainly routine repairs and maintenance.

Duties at GS 12: This position is officially referred to as the Automotive Program Manager—responsible for managing the garage, equipment, personnel, budget, and the entire automotive fleet at a particular FBI Field Office. The job requires interactions with FBI Special Agents at all levels.

CLERICAL POSITIONS

Bob McGonigel started out on the support staff; he says, "You know, Hoover had a theory—the support people were there to cut down the agents' time in the office, so they could be out doing their work on the street. Anything you could do in the office, whether it's collating, or alphabetizing, whatever, that's what you did, to get them out doing their job. The Bureau was really run like a computer, before computers existed. We had a highly organized system of filing and indexing, and it really did save the investigators an awful lot of time. You could access information very readily. And now, with computers, the ability to manage information is just tremendous."

That's still the philosophy behind the Bureau's clerical support staff. There's a range of positions available, from personal assistant to file clerk.

SALARIES AND WAGES

Most FBI white-collar employees are paid according to the General Schedule contained in Title 5, U.S. Code, Section 53332(A). Some General Schedule personnel in specialized or competitive job categories are paid at a higher level under a Special Pay Rate System. In addition, special geographic locality rates may apply; therefore, the pay scales used in different parts of the country vary. The highest-ranking FBI personnel are paid under the SES Schedule or the Executive Schedule.

On the following page is a 1997 pay schedule for the Washington, D.C. metropolitan area, which includes a 7.11 percent locality differential. Special Agents are required to be available for duty 24 hours a day. Therefore, they are also provided availability pay. That amount is equal to 25 percent of an agent's total salary, which includes not only his or her base salary, but also any locality adjustment being received.

General Schedule Salary and Wage Chart

Grade	Step 1	2	3	4	5	6	7	8	9	10
1	13570	14022	14473	14923	15376	15640	16085	16533	16553	16971
2	15256	15620	16125	16553	16739	17232	17725	18217	18710	19203
3	16647	17202	17757	18312	18866	19421	19976	20531	21086	21641
4	18687	19311	19934	20558	21181	21804	22428	23051	23675	24298
5	20908	21605	22302	23000	23697	24394	25092	25789	26486	27183
6	23305	24082	24858	25635	26411	27188	27964	28741	29517	30294
7	25897	26760	27624	28487	29350	30214	31077	31940	32804	33677
8	28681	29637	30594	31550	32507	33463	34420	35376	36333	37289
9	31680	32736	33792	34848	35904	36960	38017	39073	40129	41185
10	34887	36050	37213	38376	39540	40703	41866	43029	44193	44356
11	38330	39608	40866	42164	43442	44719	45997	47275	48553	49831
12	45939	47471	49003	50534	52066	53598	55130	56661	58193	59725
13	54629	56450	58271	60092	61913	63734	65555	67375	69196	71017
14	64555	66707	68859	71011	73163	75314	77466	79618	81770	83922
15	75935	78466	80997	83528	86059	88590	91121	93652	96183	98714

CHAPTER
How to Improve Your Chances

When you apply for a job with the FBI, you're going up against thousands of talented, accomplished people. Only a small percentage of those thousands will make it into the Bureau. How does the FBI make its decisions? Can you do anything to better your chances? This is the chapter that's going to answer those questions.

ONE APPLICANT'S STORY

Things have changed a whole lot since I went into the Bureau. To give you an idea of what the entry process is like now, I'm going to introduce you to someone new—new to you, and new to the FBI. He's a recruit under the diversified program, and I'm not going to identify him by name. The FBI is notoriously tight-lipped, and I don't want to take any chance of harming this guy's career—which I think will be an outstanding one. So let's just call him Josh. His story is an example of an application that goes smoothly from start to finish.

> I've always liked to help people. To say that I've always wanted to be in law enforcement from childhood would probably be a lie. It's strange how things worked out—I initially wanted to be a pharmacist. I figured that's a great way help everybody in the community. Everybody goes to the pharmacist for help from time to time. My first job, actually, was

working in a small pharmacy. I quickly learned that the job wasn't all it was made out to be.

Today it's become a lot of the computer spelling out what to do. Then the pharmacist goes back to a shelf and picks out the appropriate pill and puts it in the right bottle. Not what I had in mind. That's when I actually started to look into law enforcement. By the time I finished high school, I'd gotten it figured out. In my yearbook, it says, "Plans to work for the FBI." I always had a knack for problem solving, for helping out people. And what better way to help out people?

My family is from a totally blue-collar background. From the beginning of time, my family's been in construction. I'm the one to basically break the mold, the only one to go on to college. I double-majored in criminal justice and psychology. Finished in four years—no way was I going to delay things, get on the five-year plan.

The summer after my junior year, I interned with the United States Customs Service. I quickly learned the job is definitely not as glamorous as people might think when they see "Special Agent" or "Criminal Investigator" on your business card. There's a lot of long hours. *A lot.* As an intern, I was required to work 30 hours a week. But most of the summer, I stayed there 60 hours a week, for free. I was the only intern to do that.

The Customs people loved it. They absolutely loved it. I mean, why wouldn't they? And because of that dedication, I got to work on quite a few cases that were really, really interesting. And I learned a lot. I helped execute several search warrants, some arrest warrants. I participated in a cover team. There was a shipment of cash coming in from another country, and Customs put together a team watching the shipment and where it traveled. And I was actually part of that team. I saw the subjects picking up the cash, the entire thing.

As an intern, I actually wasn't supposed to go out on these things. But my supervisor noticed how much dedication I had. He saw how hard I was working. Who's gonna work for 60 hours a week for free? And do a good job, too. He let me participate because he saw that I wanted to learn every little bit that I could. I did learn a lot through the experience. I even got a couple of awards from U.S. Customs.

That just intensified my feelings that I wanted to get out and help people, and I wanted to do it in that field. It solidified everything, and made me realize that I'm made for this field. *This* is what I'd be great at.

I remember one case, we'd gotten a search warrant for a subject we were investigating, and I was assigned to look through the subject's garbage. So I'm sitting there in the middle of this room, surrounded by all this trash. I'm thinking, "Geez, I must be a little strange—because I love this. I'm surrounded by trash and I *love* it." Every little piece you find helps solve the puzzle. It adds to the overall case, builds up the prosecution of the case.

I'm still in touch with a lot of the people I worked with that summer. My old boss is retiring from the Customs Service soon, and I'm invited to his retirement party.

There weren't a lot of jobs out there by the time I graduated, in 1994. I knew I didn't have the experience to get into the FBI yet, so I wanted to find something that would give me the background I'd need. I used to go up to the employment center at school just about every day. One day, I saw a posting for criminal investigator at a bank. I figured, "Hey, it's gotta be pretty interesting—white-collar investigation."

The interviews were scheduled for half-hour slots, and the people I knew who interviewed before I did told me they had maybe a 15-minute interview. Well, my interview actually lasted an hour and a half. The people stacked up behind me didn't appreciate that too much.

I wound up getting the job. It was a pretty intensive process, several interviews and a background check. With the information you're exposed to in a bank, if you went bad, you could ruin them. They want to prevent that any way they can.

My first job at that bank, I worked just as hard as I had at Customs. The only difference was, I was getting paid. The money wasn't that great to start out, but everything I learned was payment. Every little bit of information. Every case that I worked. Every case I worked with the FBI. I worked some sensitive cases with them, and built a great rapport with those Agents.

Anyway, I worked hard and did a good job. In fact, that's how I got my next job. I'd worked a really large case that saved my bank and another bank a lot of money. The second bank actually came and recruited me.

I never took any formal accounting. I taught myself the things that I need to know. What you need for this kind of work is great attention to detail—you've got to make sure every penny is accounted for. But you also need to see the big picture, look for overall patterns.

Also, working in such a large corporation, I've got the resources of a corporation to back me up. If I need something really in-depth, say, a heavy audit, I can pull on the audit department. I can pull on our accounts people. Or I can pull on our legal department if I think something's questionable.

That's a skill, too, knowing when to ask for help. Knowing when to go to an expert instead of floundering by yourself. I've actually seen that happen, where certain investigators maybe had too much pride to say, "I don't know what this is, I need some help here." It actually hurt them in the long run. Of course, if you ask for too much, people are going to say, "Hey, this guy doesn't know what he's doin'." But you have to know when to ask. You have to balance everything.

Of course, the whole time I'm still focused on getting into the FBI. And, you know, it's funny, the way it worked out—the first FBI agent I met is actually my recruiter now. He was the head of the white-collar crimes unit in the Philadelphia Field Office. As soon as I got hired by the first bank, I went to a seminar they were giving in one of their large cash areas, where all the large accounts are held, major corporate accounts. Coca Cola, for one.

Anyway, Owen Smith came to that group and posted a discussion about counterfeit checks and trends in counterfeiting. I was so impressed. His presentation was one of the most professional things that

I'd seen. I went up speak with him afterwards, and of course I've talked to him several times since he's recruited me. Every time, I've learned something new—in terms of investigations, in terms of experience. It's great, to be able to draw on someone else's experience, to learn something that's going to help you out in the future.

About a year into my first job, I started applying to other federal agencies, the ones that will accept you with one year of investigative experience. So I applied to those agencies and figured if I got in, it was going to give me that much more experience when I applied for the FBI. I went through several interviews, and I'm actually still going through the process with a couple of them. It takes a long time. The FBI, I have to say, has been the quickest to respond.

November 1997, I came up on my three years' experience. About then, Owen contacted me and asked me if I was interested in applying. The FBI is coming to me and asking me if I'd be interested in applying. Are you kidding?

This was how I'd hoped it was going to be. I figured if the agents that I've worked with realize that I've got talent and I've got what it takes to be an agent, they're gonna mention it to someone. And it turns out that they did.

That means a lot to me, because these are guys who know my work and appreciate it. They see the product. When I turn a case over to them, they thank me. Because when I give them a case, there's nothing more they have to do—just turn it over to the U.S. Attorney. There are some cases, very few, that get sticky, where there are things they have to dig their hands into. But for the most part, when I turn over a case, say a high-level embezzlement, there's nothing missing. They don't have to call me up and say, "Josh, I need this. Josh, where's that document?" It's all in there. Indexed, filed, in a binder, ready to go. They review it, turn it right over to the U.S. Attorney. They can spend their time on other cases.

I feel drawn to the challenge of white-collar crime. The mental challenge. If I were in drug investigations or narcotics, I'd imagine after a while every narcotics organization starts to look the same. Every drug dealer starts to maybe work in the same way. There's not a lot of room for variation there. When you're dealing with white-collar crime, there's tremendous variation. For every way that you can legally get money, someone is going to devise a way to get it illegally. If you shut down one avenue, they'll find another.

There's a Russian hacker, 26 years old. Vladimir Levin. He actually hacked into Citibank's mainframe, wired out $10 million all over the world. It's that kind of challenge. You're going up against the mental giants. And that kind of case didn't even exist ten, 15 years ago. You've always got to develop new investigative techniques. New safeguards. You're always learning. You're not going to come in and have the same humdrum thing every day.

True, you're going have some check cases. Some counterfeit cases that are the same, possibly because it's the same ring working. There's not a lot of room for variance in a check fraud case. But then when you start to work into the other crimes, there's something else to learn.

Besides, I think there's more challenge in terms of who you're dealing with. I worked a couple of embezzlement cases with pretty high-level employees. The banking industry isn't known for making a lot of people rich. To be making six figures a year, you've got to really be intelligent. And to work against that person? I mean, you're dealing with a challenge there. You're not going to bring this person into an interview room, talk to them and have them spill their guts. You've got to build your case from the ground up.

I've conducted many interviews in the course of my job. Both externally—people committing fraud against the bank from the outside—and the internals, people who are stealing money from the inside. It's amazing that everything that you're taught, you see it in the interview. From the time you sit down with somebody, the first couple of questions, you know how it's going to unfold. This person did it, and I know how it's going to work out.

I do quite a few interviews. And the FBI loves it—if I turn over a case where I've got a full confession, who wouldn't love that?

And you know what? I feel good about turning over a case where there is a confession. One, it's making the FBI's job a lot easier. And two, it's making them realize, "He's got something here." Not everybody can walk in and interview a subject and get them to confess. If the interviews were that easy, I wouldn't have so many late nights at work.

What I do is, I assemble as many of the facts, as much of the background, as I can get at that point in time. I don't like to jump into an interview without the facts and just go blind. You know, say we suspect a particular individual took $50,000 from the bank. I want to find out as much about that person as possible. Do they have family problems? Do they have any drug problems, alcohol problems, gambling problems? You look into their financial background, which can tell you a lot about someone's behavior. Where they use the ATMs, what times. I'll check out how do they get along with co-workers. We get surveillance film in some areas, which helps. Although depending on the kind of system, it can be pretty difficult to catch people red-handed on surveillance.

Then I'll start to create a paper trail and see where it takes me. Is it going lead me directly to this person, as I might have thought originally? A lot of times you may think that an investigation's going to lead to one person. But then the paper trail leads you in another direction.

After I've got everything done, I'll go ahead and interview that person. That's an ideal situation. There have been scenarios where it's so sensitive, you've got to get them right away. I've been pretty successful in these situations as well.

But I generally prefer to do as much research, as much background as I possibly can. I like to take a look at the big picture and see where it leads me.

I've taken the written test, and I'm going to get my panel interview next month. And then they're gonna make the final decision.

Just as a point of comparison, I would say that the FBI's written test is much more difficult than the SAT. The time constraints are much tighter; the math, especially, is much more intense. It's a very difficult test.

I spent a lot of time preparing for it. There's a little sample booklet they give you, but if you rely on just that, you're gonna be in serious trouble. I instantly read that book. As soon as I got out of my recruiter's office, I sat down and started reading it. I took the train back home and kept reading. Took every sample question.

The material seemed pretty general, and I wanted to go a little bit more in depth. So I went out, I bought a GMAT prep book, a GRE prep book. I went back and studied my Special Agent book that I used for the Treasury Enforcement exam. And periodically, I kept going back to the book that the FBI gave me. I used all those resources. It must have worked—I passed the test. The preparation didn't make it a stress-free experience, but at least I passed the exam.

Right now, the only thing that I have to go by to prepare for the interview is the Special Agent Selection Process book they gave me. That's all that I have. It goes over the panel interview a little bit.

Fifteen questions about your life experience. The interview measures these skills, it goes into your ability to communicate and work with others, so on and so forth. I've started thinking about every significant experience I've had and what it involved. And I'm writing it down. It's like writing my autobiography. I'm just collecting all of my thoughts now because I don't want to have to be in that panel struggling to collect my thoughts then. I don't want to blank out. I want to go in there with a clear head, knowing what I want to talk about. I've been going back, thinking of anything I've done that might show skills that could be beneficial to the agency.

Can you overcome a conflict? I mean, that's something that an FBI agent has to be able to do. Sometimes they're working phenomenal case loads. Can you plan out your time? Can you do the work? Can you handle the jobs that the FBI is gonna give you? I want to be able to cite examples that will let them know, "Yes, Josh can do this job."

I'm absolutely not arrogant about what I've done. However, I know in my heart that I can do that job. I know I can be a successful FBI agent, and work successful cases. Maybe get to the level of John Douglas. Right now there's no profiling for white-collar criminals. Maybe I'll be the first person to do that.

I really want this, but I realize that nothing is a guarantee. My friends in the FBI, the agents I've worked with, my recruiter—maybe they think that I'm what the FBI needs and what the FBI wants, that I'm qualified to be in. But there might be other people out there that feel that I'm *not* qualified. What if the individuals on the panel think that I'm not good enough? So I'm continually working. Doing the best that I can at that given time.

I haven't slowed up. I've always given 110 percent. And I'm still giving 110 percent at my job. It's just that now, in my free time, I'm not thinking about work as much. I'm thinking about the process I'm going through, and I'm preparing myself for it. Even physically.

One of the things that actually pushes me to go further, even physically, is the competition. When you're at that point where you're so beat that you don't think that you could lift your leg up to run that extra step. But what I think is that there's someone else out there who is in the same shape. There's someone else out there who's at that point where they're so tired that they don't want to lift up their foot to go. But you know what? I'm gonna go past it. I'm gonna do it. If I have to force myself to do it, I'm gonna do it.

There are so many applicants out there. So many excellent applicants. So well qualified. When I went to my test, I was talking to some of the other applicants. And they are so well qualified. I've gotta keep an edge. I've only got a bachelor's degree. I'm only 26 years old. I'm from a blue-collar background—no Ivy League degrees. I've got to keep myself that much more in tune with what I'm doing. I've got to get myself that much better prepared.

At the time this book went to press, Josh had received his conditional acceptance to the FBI and was scheduled for a new agents' class at Quantico.

AN INSIDER'S VIEW

Owen Smith, the Special Agent who recruited Josh, is the applicant coordinator at the Philadelphia Field Office. Here's what he had to say about how Josh and other applicants first come to the attention of the Bureau:

> There are a lot of people who've always wanted to be an FBI agent, and they either take the initiative and call us, or when we're at a recruiting function—career fairs, what have you—when they're presented with the opportunity to approach us, they seize upon it. We also have individuals, such as Josh, whom I hear about through people I work with, people I know professionally. Personally, I like it when people I know, people I respect in the office here guide me to someone, because I feel those people know what the job entails, and what it takes to succeed in this job. When they tell me here's a good candidate, that gives me some encouragement that there is something here. It's an informed judgment, versus someone calling you on the phone, saying, "I want to be an FBI agent."
>
> Of course, I try to look at everybody the same, but it's a little more encouraging when someone I respect has already had dealings with the person. But the process is completely open. Every person who calls in and says "I want to do it" is given the same exposure as someone who's personally recommended.

PRE-APPLICATION STRATEGIES

No matter what stage of your life you're in—finishing up high school, recently graduated from college, looking for a career change—the FBI might well be a valid career goal for you. But there are several things you should keep in mind before you push ahead.

First, there's no foolproof "recipe" for getting into the FBI, especially as a Special Agent. If you've read this far, you know the Bureau needs people with a variety of backgrounds to handle a variety of investigations. But the FBI's specific hiring needs shift from year to year, and so does the pool of applicants. That means no one—not me; not your uncle, the former Special Agent; not even your best friend, the applicant coordinator at the local FBI Field Office—*no one* can guarantee that your specific package of life experience and skills will get you into the Bureau at a particular point in time. Focusing on becoming an FBI Agent is a little like shooting at a moving target from behind a curtain.

So before you say "I want to be an FBI Agent," back up a step. Do some profiling on yourself. What, specifically, are you going to do in the FBI? If all you can come up with is "Hang out with Agent Scully and carry a gun," then you've got some serious thinking to do.

Think about the classes you did well in, the activities that absorb you so thoroughly that you lose track of time. Make that area your first career focus. Develop a stellar work record. Then, if your skills and experience demonstrate that you have what the Bureau needs, you'll have a shot at getting in. And even if you don't get in, you'll still be making a living doing something you enjoy.

This is how Owen Smith puts it: "The kind of analysis that's helpful is this: 'What does the FBI want? Which of these things could I enjoy doing?' If you say, 'I don't like doing any of these things, but I'm going to pick one and do it anyhow, so I can be an FBI Agent'—well, I think you're taking a real chance. It may pay off for you, but it's a long shot. You're spending a good part of your life proceeding in that direction, and if it doesn't work out you're in trouble."

So my first piece of advice to you is this: Make joining the FBI a *secondary* career goal. By all means focus on it, plan for it, let it be one of the factors that determine your educational and life choices. But make sure your primary focus is finding a career that you can enjoy, in or out of the FBI.

With that said, here are some other general pieces of advice for people thinking about a career in the FBI:

Become a Futurist: Make Some Predictions about What the FBI Is Likely to Need

You can start by looking at the four entry programs in the FBI: law, accounting, languages, and diversified (which covers everything else). Those programs demonstrate the Bureau's long-term, continuing interests. Accounting and languages are, from year to year, the most in-demand programs, with law usually coming in third.

Languages

As Doug Rhoads said, Spanish is becoming more and more prevalent in the United States. There's going to be a need for Spanish speakers in the FBI for years to come. But the Bureau will need people with proficiency in other languages as well. Look at immigration figures; right now, there are lots of people coming over from China and the Indian subcontinent. Law enforcement agencies will need people who can communicate in Chinese, Bengali, Hindu, and other languages common in those regions. Look at the places around the globe where the United States has political or economic interests. The Mideast is always a hot spot, and the Balkans have recently heated up.

Keep in mind that the FBI test for entering under the language program is extremely rigorous; you really need to be thoroughly fluent in that second language to qualify. But even if you can't make it in under the language program, some sort of foreign-language proficiency can only help you.

Accounting

Again, the requirements for entering under this specialized program are pretty stringent. You need to have either passed the CPA exam, or have taken enough classes to qualify for it. But experience with accounting and a level of comfort in dealing with numbers can only help you. Look at Josh. He's not an accounting expert, but his experience in working with financial information demonstrated the qualities that the FBI looks for.

Law

All agents need to have a thorough understanding of legal statutes and an ability to read and comprehend legal documents. Obviously, a law degree demonstrates that ability. This specialized entry program does tend to be less emphasized than accounting or languages, mainly because the Bureau takes pains to thoroughly school all agents in this area. But it is an established entry program, and if you can demonstrate expertise in this area, I'm sure you'll be in demand.

Computers

Along with a gun, each new Special Agent is issued his or her own laptop computer. Of course, this is a big change from when I was a new agent; back then, personal computers didn't exist. I realize that for some of you, that's like saying I rode to work in a horse-and-buggy, but it's true—that's how fast technology is changing. The FBI devotes a lot of resources to keeping pace with those changes; people with computer skills will be in demand throughout the foreseeable future. According to Owen Smith, "This is not the Bureau speaking, this is me speaking, but I wouldn't be surprised if at some point the Bureau institutes another entry program, the computer sciences program. Computers are going to become more and more a part of what we do, and our investigations are going to require more and more people with computer skills."

That doesn't mean word-processing skills or using Quark to design a really cool zine. Again, think about the needs of the Bureau. In one year—1996 to 1997—the number of "computer intrusions" (cases where a computer system is the target of a crime) investigated by the FBI more than doubled—from 200 to over 500. These are the cases like that of Vladimir Lenin, the hacker Josh referred to. Using a creaky old 286 computer, Lenin managed to break into Citibank's system and transfer over $10 million to accounts all over the world. Citibank notified the Bureau, which was able to recover all but $400,000.

In response to the explosive growth in this sort of crime, the FBI recently established Criminal Squad 37, operating out of the New York

Field Office and specializing in computer crime. Similar squads have been set up in San Francisco, Boston, Chicago, Dallas, and Los Angeles.

On a more mundane level, every Field Office and Resident Agency in the country could use someone proficient in computerese—someone who's able to retrieve documents from an erased hard drive while maintaining a chain of custody and protecting the subject's legal rights. If your computer skills put you in a position to do that, I'd say you're a good candidate.

Work to Achieve Leadership

The FBI expects applicants to have at least three years of work experience—but of course not all work experience is the same. If you've spent three years folding T-shirts at the Gap, that's not going to be much to draw on. Whatever you do, make a real effort to excel. Volunteer for extra projects; take on more than you're asked to do. Be proactive—create your own opportunities. Naturally, all this is going to be easier if you're doing something you enjoy—another reason to focus on your own talents and abilities.

Hone Your Skills

Think about the basic skills the FBI needs—the ability to communicate, in person and on paper; the ability to analyze and organize information; a certain basic level of physical fitness. How do you measure up in each of these areas? If you're not in great shape, start a fitness program. If you're weak in writing skills, sign up for a class at your local university or community college; if your schedule makes that impractical, colleges all over the country now offer classes via the Internet; check out Kaplan's *Guide to Distance Learning*. You'll probably also find classes that can help build your analytical skills, or you can try any one of dozens of test-prep books designed to help you study for the GRE or the LSAT.

People sometimes ask me about the benefit of other skills—things like self-defense, or CPR, or piloting—that might be related to law enforcement. Are they worth pursuing? Well, if it's something you're interested in, by all means pursue it. But the bottom line is—you're not going to get into the FBI unless your professional skills and experience meet the Bureau's needs. Something like a CPR certification can't hurt, but it's not a make-or-break attribute. It may bump you up a level, but you have to be basically competitive.

Owen Smith says, "Say we're hiring pilots—that may be something they immediately see on the application. They focus right in on it, but then they look at the application as a whole. 'Is everything else in place? Does it meet our requirements in other areas?' Just being a pilot may not get you in, but if you were an officer in the military, if you were a plant manager at Nabisco for the last two years—those are pretty attractive things. That makes you competitive with the current pool. And then we see you're a certified pilot, too. So we'll pull you right out of the group to get an interview."

Become Active in Community Service

Now, this isn't the kind of thing that's going to automatically open doors for you. But for someone who's just starting out in their career, community service organizations can offer an opportunity for leadership that might be hard to get at work. And I can guarantee you that the immediate benefits will be tremendous. When I was in the Air Force, finishing up my undergraduate degree, I worked with mentally handicapped kids. It was one of the most rewarding experiences of my life.

Again, think about your own talents and abilities. Maybe you could put your athletic skills to use by volunteering with the local Police Athletic League. If you're more academically inclined, consider tutoring with a local literacy organization. Call up the local victims'-rights organization and ask if they could use your help. Get involved with Big Brothers or Big Sisters. Whatever it is, make sure it's something you really support, something you won't resent spending your time doing.

Be an Older Sibling

Big Brothers Big Sisters of America matches at-risk children with volunteer adult mentors. The organization has 500 sites nationwide; to find the location nearest you, contact BBSA headquarters:

Big Brothers Big Sisters of America
230 North 13th Street
Philadelphia, PA 19107
(215) 567-7000

Keep It Clean

The FBI maintains pretty high personal standards for its employees. There's a strict antidrug policy; as Owen Smith says, "Once you've done them, you can't go back and undo them. So that's something anyone who's interested in a career with the FBI should stay away from." The FBI also expects applicants to have a clean criminal record, which shouldn't be much of a surprise. According to Smith, "Applicants can't have any felony convictions; they can't have spent one night in jail." And make sure you maintain a good credit record; the FBI checks that, too. It doesn't do any good to focus on all the other areas if you're going to blow it with a stupid lifestyle choice.

*****

The best thing about these basic steps is that they'll give you immediate benefits. Focusing on your own talents and abilities will always lead you in the right direction, and I don't know any employer that won't reward someone who's hard-working, motivated, and always working to develop his or her skills. Community service really is its own reward. And let's face it—life's a lot easier when you've got good health, good credit, and no criminal record. Follow these steps and even if you don't get into the FBI, you'll be doing pretty well.

What to Do If You're in High School

Plan to Go to College Right Away

This won't come as a surprise for most of you. With nothing more than a high school diploma, you're probably not going to be able to get the kind of job that will give you meaningful work experience, and you'll need a college degree anyway, so why wait?

Choose Your Major Carefully

This is most important issue you're facing right now. I'll say it again: *Focus on what you want to do.* Sure, the FBI is always looking for accounting majors, but if you hate accounting, don't torture yourself for the next seven years—four years of college, plus three years of job experience—on the chance that you'll get into the Bureau in the accounting program.

One important note—If you've told your high school guidance counselor that you're interested in the FBI, he or she might have advised you to major in criminal justice. Well, if you're interested in criminal justice, fine. But don't think this degree leads straight to the Bureau. Owen Smith says, "A criminal justice degree is viewed about the same as a history degree. It's a four-year degree—that's all. It does not get our immediate attention. It's amazing how many candidates tell me that they majored in criminal justice because this is what they were told to do. Unfortunately, a lot of these people are telling me this in their fourth year of college."

A criminal justice degree really prepares you for local law enforcement—working in a police or sheriff's department. Obviously, this will give you experience that can be valuable to the FBI. But if you're really not interested in the front-line aspects of law enforcement, you're much better off choosing another area of study.

Focus on the more stringent disciplines. Physics, mathematics, accounting, even a liberal arts degree in philosophy or English will serve you better than a degree in marketing or general studies. Don't opt for an "easy" degree, betting that good grades will help you out. Grades do matter, but not as much as the applicability of your discipline.

Attend the Best School You Can in Your Area of Study

Once you've decided on your major, do some research on the top-ranked schools in that area and apply to those. It can only benefit you. Remember that "name brand," Ivy League schools aren't the only options. Just about every school emphasizes a particular area, and you can save tens of thousands of dollars by doing a little research.

But what if the top school in your discipline is Stanford, and you don't get in? Or you do get in and you can't afford go? Well, don't assume this means you'll never get into the FBI. As far as the Bureau is concerned, your accomplishments mean more than the name of the school on your diploma.

Consider an ROTC Program

This isn't an option for everyone, but it can offer several benefits. First, you'll get help paying for college. Second, service as a military officer demonstrates the kind of leadership ability the FBI looks for. Third, the military offers specialized training that it's difficult or even impossible to get in the private sector. So if you have the slightest inclination in this area, give it some serious thought.

What to Do If You're in College

Get the Best Grades You Can

Yes, the FBI focuses on things other than grades. But that doesn't mean grades are meaningless. They're a pretty good measure of your ability to organize your time, analyze information, complete tasks—all qualities the FBI looks for.

Use Your Summers Wisely

I'm not the best poster boy for this; those three high school summers I spent shoveling cow manure didn't do much to prepare me for my later career. In retrospect, I might as well have spent the time on the beach with my buddies.

Josh handled things better. While he was in college, he went out and got a summer internship with the U.S. Customs Service—and he treated it like a real job, not just a place to spend his time before happy hour. He worked hard, put in long hours, showed real initiative in taking on projects. And look how it paid off. He found out that he really did have an aptitude for federal law enforcement; he made connections with people directly involved in the area he was interested in; he got to dig around in garbage.

If you can't line up a formal internship for the summer, create one. Think about how you could expand your experience, and offer yourself to a relevant business or organization. Even if you can't afford to take an unpaid internship, carve out some room in your schedule for a part-time volunteer stint. The experience and exposure that you'll get will definitely pay off.

Apply for All the Relevant Internships You Can

Most colleges and universities allow students in most disciplines to earn credit for internships. Check out the policy at your particular school, and research the possibilities. Kaplan's *Yale Daily News Guide to Internships* lists thousands of internship opportunities. The career counseling center at your school will have a list of local opportunities. The Internet offers a huge number of resources in this area.

If you qualify, you should definitely apply for the FBI Honors Internship Program. Here are the specifics: At the time they apply, applicants must be undergraduates in their junior year, or graduate students enrolled full-time, and they have to plan to return to school after the internship. You also must have a cumulative GPA of 3.0 or above, and be a U.S. citizen. The Bureau is looking for individuals who've demonstrated academic achievement and an interest in law enforcement; the preferred areas of study are engineering, computer science, foreign languages, political science, law, accounting, and the physical sciences.

If you meet the requirements, call the local FBI Field Office and ask for Application Form FD646a. You will also need a current academic transcript, a personal résumé, a recent photograph, a written recommendation from your dean or department head, and a 500-word essay describing your interest in the program. Applications are due on November 1; internships are announced the following spring.

Some Useful Job and Internships Sites

Here are some Internet sites to get you started.

http://www.jobtrak.com

Among other resources, JOBTRAK has a national internship database as well as listings targeted at individual campuses. To get to the school-related databases, you may need to get a password from your school's career center.

http://www.tripod.com/work/internships

This site provides a database of internships that you can search by field of study or location.

http://www.4work.com

This site includes an internship database that you can search by keyword. It also has a free service called "Job Alert!" that allows you to enter a personal profile. It e-mails you when it finds a match between your profile and the needs of employers who use the service. This site also covers full-time positions and volunteer work.

Source: *Yale Daily News Guide to Internships*

Attend FBI Recruiting Events

Check out the career placement center at your school. Call the nearest FBI Field Office, ask for the applicant coordinator and find out when he or she will be at local career days or other events. Realize that as a college student or soon-to-be graduate, you're not ready to apply to the Bureau. But personal contact with an on-board agent will provide you with the most up-to-date information. And if you're as good a candidate as you think you are, the applicant coordinator will take note of you.

What to Do If You're Ready for a Career Change

Take a Good Look At Your Qualifications

Your big advantage over people who are still in school is that you now have work experience, a list of career accomplishments. Of course, that could be a big disadvantage, too, if your experience doesn't demonstrate the qualities and skills the FBI needs. Before you submit an application, look at your qualifications. Be ruthlessly honest. Does your work experience dovetail with the investigative needs of the Bureau? Can you point to projects you've headed up, specific results you've attained? What would your boss say about you, if he or she knew you wouldn't find out? *Be honest.* We all like to think well of ourselves, but there's a difference between self-confidence and self-delusion. The application process is so stringent, so competitive, that if you really aren't suited, you're better off realizing that up front. Otherwise, you're just wasting your time and setting yourself up for disappointment.

Seek Out the Local Applicant Coordinator

Call the local Field Office and find out where the applicant coordinator is going to be speaking, what career days he or she is going to be attending. Take that opportunity to present yourself and your qualifications—in an abbreviated form. And listen to what he or she says. If you don't get much encouragement, think hard about whether you want to pursue this. The applicant coordinator has no stake in your potential career, one way or another; he or she is trained to be objective. You'll get an honest evaluation of your chances, from the Bureau's point of view. It's worth paying attention to.

Consider Graduate School

Maybe you don't want to change careers as much as you want to change focus. If you love the field you're in, but are just tired of the private sector, maybe graduate school is a good option. Afterwards, if you still want a career in the FBI, you'll be in a better position to compete.

CHAPTER 11

The Application Process

Applying for a job with the FBI isn't like applying for a job at a corporation. For one thing, it takes a whole lot longer. The time it takes will vary from Field Office to Field Office, depending on the pool of applicants at any particular time. But, in general, it'll take at least a year from start to finish. Here's the breakdown:

Once you submit your initial application it will take two to three weeks for the Bureau to notify you whether you've been selected for the next phase. If you have been, your letter will give you the date of your initial round of tests—usually six to eight weeks later. After you've taken the written test, you'll again be notified of the results within two to three weeks. If you're approved for a panel interview, that'll be scheduled for a date four to six months ahead—if you're a very competitive candidate who's selected from the applicant pool right away. You also might remain in the applicant pool for as long as a year, depending on who else is in that pool. If you pass the panel interview and the written test administered that day, and survive the background check, polygraph, and drug test, you'll be assigned to a new agents' class beginning in about six months.

Once you get into the process, you'll have contact with the applicant coordinator at your Field Office who can answer any questions you'll have. Most of the following information will apply to the earlier stages of the process.

INITIAL APPLICATION STRATEGY

1. Identify the Requirements for the Job You Want

- *Special Agent:* The minimum requirements are listed in the Special Agent section of chapter 9.

- *Support Personnel:* Requirements vary tremendously, depending on the job. Call or write the FBI Field Office nearest you and ask for the requirements brochure for the specific job you're interested in. If you're not sure of a specific job title, ask for a general category—forensic support personnel, for example.

2. Obtain the Forms You'll Need

- *Special Agent:* Call the Field Office nearest you to get an application. Or, download the application from the FBI's Web site at www.fbi.gov.

- *Support Personnel:* Again, because there are so many different jobs, you'll need to get the right application for the job you want. Call the Field Office nearest you.

3. Fill Out the Forms Accurately and Truthfully

Whether you're applying for a job as a Special Agent or in the support area, don't try to hide anything on your application. *Tell the truth.* This is how Doug Rhoads puts it: "Candor is always much more productive than evasion. Say you've got a gap on your résumé. You spent six months on the beach at Pensacola, just taking a break. Well, so what? As long as everything else checks out, who cares? But an applicant cannot survive a lack-of-candor issue."

Top-notch skills which match what the Bureau needs might outweigh what seems to be a blemish in your record. On the other hand, if the blemish is significant—"I have a six-month gap in my résumé because I was in jail on a DWI"—the FBI isn't the place for you, no matter *what* your skills are.

4. Submit Your Application—and Wait

You don't get points for following up your application with a phone call; in fact, calling the Field Office to ask about the status of your application could send the wrong signal. Within three weeks of submitting your initial application, you'll receive a response from the FBI. You'll be told one of two things: You've been scheduled for the next stage of the application process, the written test, or you're considered "not competitive" with other current applicants. If you submit an application and don't hear back within three weeks, then go ahead and call, just to confirm that your application was received. Otherwise, just sit tight.

FREQUENTLY ASKED QUESTIONS

If I'm rejected at this stage of the process, will I find out why?

The standard notification simply states that you've been found "not competitive" with the other candidates applying at the same time. If you have some personal connection with an on-board agent, talk to her about what might have happened. You can also ask to speak to the applicant coordinator at the local Field Office, but remember that it's strictly up to him to decide whether to discuss your application with you. And there may not be much information the applicant coordinator can give you. Owen Smith says, "Sometimes it's something the applicant coordinator can articulate because it's a very basic issue. A person who just got out of college, or a college grad who's been working for three years, but he's been working all that time as a clerk in a convenience store—it's very easy to say to him, 'You just don't have the experience that we would even consider in the FBI.' That's a very clear-cut thing. But if someone has three, four, five years of managerial experience, but she's just not competitive with everyone else in the pool—that's really not something an applicant coordinator or anyone else can expand on."

And also keep in mind that even if the applicant coordinator, or your contact in the Bureau, gives you feedback about a specific problem with your application, correcting that problem is no guarantee that you'll get in the next time you apply. Smith says, "By the time you go out and do what you needed to do to make yourself more competitive with the original pool of applicants, you're competing against a whole new pool of people."

Is there a limit to the number of times I can apply?

At this stage, no. But if you apply several times, after making a real effort to correct any deficiencies you've been able to identify, and you still don't succeed, then you should refocus your efforts.

Once you advance to the next stage, limits do go into effect. You're allowed to take the three-part written test twice, and you're allowed to sit for the panel interview twice. But if you can't make it through the process by then, you're out.

Will my application be held on file?

Again, at this stage, no. If you make it through the written test, your application may be held for as long as a year before you're called up for a panel interview. It depends on how competitive you are with the other applicants. The applicant coordinator at the Field Office through which you apply will keep you informed along the way.

THE STANDARDIZED TEST

Once you've made it through the initial cut, you'll be scheduled for a three-part standardized test. When you're notified of the date of your test, you'll also be given a study guide. New recruits, including Josh, strongly recommend that you go beyond this study guide when you're preparing for the test. You will need to demonstrate mathematical ability, so brush up on your algebra. If it's been a while since you've taken a standardized test, refresh yourself on basic test-taking strategy—how to organize your time, what to do if you get stuck.

This test is divided into three sections:

The Biodata Inventory

You're given 45 minutes to answer 47 questions. The test is intended to measure: your ability to organize, plan, and prioritize, your ability to maintain a positive image, your ability to evaluate information and make judgments, your initiative and motivation, your ability to adapt to changing situations, and your ability to meet the physical requirements.

This is a fairly standard personal-assessment test. You're expected to answer questions as they apply to you. Owen Smith provided the following example:

> "In connection with your work, in which of the following have you taken the most pride?
>
> A. Having been able to avoid any major controversies
>
> B. Having gotten where you are on your own
>
> C. Having been able to work smoothly with people
>
> D. Having provided a lot of new ideas, good or bad
>
> E. Having been able to do well, no matter what management requested"

The Cognitive Ability Test

This is where you'll need your algebra. This section of the test, measuring your mathematical ability, is divided into three parts:

- Mathematical reasoning—29 minutes to answer 25 questions

- Ability to interpret data in tables and graphs—24 minutes to answer 25 questions

- Ability to learn mathematical relationships—22 minutes to answer 25 questions

Taken together, the three test areas are designed to measure mathematical reasoning, data and analytical interpretation skills, mathematical knowledge, ability to attend to detail, and ability to evaluate information and make decisions.

The Situational Judgment Test

You're given 33 problem situations and 90 minutes to answer questions about how you'd handle the situations. This section is designed to measure: your ability to organize, plan, and prioritize, your ability to relate to others effectively, your ability to maintain a positive image, your ability to evaluate information and use your judgment to make decisions, your ability to adapt to changing situations, and your integrity.

Here's an example of this type of question that Owen Smith provided:

"You are shopping when you notice a man robbing the store. What would you do?

A. Leave the store as quickly as possible and call the police

B. Try to apprehend the robber yourself

C. Follow the man and call the police as soon as he seems settled somewhere

D. Nothing, as you do not wish to get involved in the situation"

With the situational judgment and biodata inventory sections, you may be tempted to fudge your answers—marking the responses you think the FBI is looking for, rather than the ones that really apply to you. Not a good idea. There's no way to do that kind of second-guessing consistently, and you'll end up with answers that are all over the map. The test won't reflect who you are, and what it seems to show probably won't be all that attractive. Smith says, "You're better off taking your chances with your honest answers than you are trying to out-think the test. You probably have more of a chance of giving yourself a shot at it that way."

THE PANEL INTERVIEW

Once you take the standardized test, the results are analyzed and you're notified whether or not you can proceed to the next phase of the application process. This is where the real pressure kicks in. Owen Smith says, "The three-part test is just a key to open the door; once that door is open, the written test has no bearing on anything. You are then strictly on your own. It's your ability to compete with others on the interview."

Your panel interview could be scheduled as soon as four months after your standardized test, or it could take up to a year. You and several other applicants from the same region will be scheduled for your interviews on the same day.

Each applicant will also take a written exam. Some applicants will be scheduled for the interview first; others will take the exam first. This exam consists of a single problem—a scenario you're expected to analyze and respond to. Unlike the standardized test, this is an open-ended exam. You're expected to read and evaluate the scenario, formulate a response, and write out your answer. You're given a specific length of time in which to respond; that time period may change from test to test. One recent applicant offered this example: "It was something like this: You're a journalist, researching a story. While you're doing your research, you find out all this information about another situation. You have to write a memo to your editor, convincing him that there's a story in this new situation and you need to be able to pursue it."

The panel interview is administered by three assessors, Special Agents who primarily work in the field. The assessors receive training in conducting the interviews and evaluating applicants' answers. They're given 15 questions to ask each applicant; the wording and order of the questions remain the same for each applicant. Those questions are formulated by the recruiting office at FBI Headquarters, and revised about once a year. Each time the questions are revised, the assessors throughout the country go through another training session.

When you walk into the interview room, the assessors know two things about you: your name and your Social Security number. They don't know how you did on the earlier tests, what you do for a living, whom you listed as references. Your performance in that room, on that day, is all the assessors care about. Owen Smith says, "You're always going to have some element of subjectivity, but whole process is designed to be as objective as possible. That's why the assessors receive that training; that's why they're given certain keys to evaluate answers. We really try to take out as much of the subjectivity as possible, realizing there's always the human element. But that's why the applicant has a blank slate when they walk in."

During the interview as a whole, you're going to be evaluated on your ability to communicate orally. Specific questions are designed to test your ability to organize, plan, and prioritize; your ability to relate effectively with others; your ability to maintain a positive image; your ability to evaluate information and make judgment decisions; your initiative and motivation; your ability to adapt to changing situations; your integrity; and your ability to meet physical requirements. Throughout the interview, the assessors take detailed notes; the entire interview is also tape recorded.

After the interview is concluded, the assessors come up with individual ratings for the applicant, then discuss their responses to come up with a consensus rating. Everything from the interview—the assessors' notes, the tape, the rating forms—is sent to FBI Headquarters to become part of the applicant's file.

THE BACKGROUND CHECK

The first step in the FBI's background check involves following up your paper trail. This happens fairly early in the process, just to weed out the obviously unsuitable people. They'll look up your school transcripts, your credit report, your medical history, and any military or arrest record.

The more intensive background check occurs later in the process, after you've already cleared several hurdles. Sending retired Agents like me out on these investigations gets expensive, and the Bureau doesn't want to waste money checking up on people that are just going to wash out on some other point.

The face-to-face interviews begin with the references and employers you've listed. The investigators ask the kinds of questions any employer would ask—how your work performance was, what kind of student you were, that sort of thing. There's nothing especially tricky about the questions. Go ahead and tell your references that you're applying for a job with the FBI, you've listed them as references, and they might be getting a visit from some guys with badges.

Doug Rhoads has conducted a few of these background investigations, and he recommends that you notify your references. "Tell people they're likely to get a visit. It'll make things easier, and it's not like there's anything undercover about the investigation, anyway. When I go see people, I show them my I.D. and my credentials. I say right up front, 'My name's Doug Rhoads, I'm an FBI Special Investigator, and I'm here to conduct a background investigation on So-and-so for employment with the FBI.' Then there's two statements I make very clearly up front. I let them know, 'This is not a criminal matter. So-and-so is being considered for employment as a Special Agent,' or whatever the position is. Then I tell them, 'Under the Freedom of Information Act, if there's anything you say to me that you wish to be treated as confidential, all you have to do is express that wish to me.' That's to elicit candor. The applicant can have access to whatever's in the file, unless the interviewees specifically request confidentiality. And we want the interviewees to feel like they can be honest without having it come back to them."

Of course, the investigators will gather other sources, too. There's no way you can alert every single person the FBI will speak to—which is really the point of a background check. But unless you had significant trouble with former neighbors or employers, you shouldn't have anything to worry about.

This is how Doug describes it: "Painting a complete picture—that's what the background is for. The truth of it is, the biggest reason people are knocked out during the background check isn't because we find out they've been selling drugs or anything like that. It's poor work performance. The former boss says, 'No, this person really wasn't the best employee. There were these incidents where he didn't deliver.' The applicant just wasn't as good as he thought he was.

"It's not the little old lady next door saying, 'Oh, there were all kinds of wild parties over there. They were such heavy drinkers, they'd drink a whole six-pack a week over there.' And you're thinking, 'Oh my God, four people going through a six-pack.' You've got to put it into perspective. 'They were loud twice a month'—that's not going to keep you from getting hired."

Believe it or not, FBI agents were young once, too.

POLYGRAPH FAQs

If you've never had a polygraph, the idea of taking one can be intimidating. How does it work? What are they going to ask about? What if I'm nervous during the test? Can I beat the polygraph? Well, here are the answers:

How does it work?

The polygraph measures several involuntary physiological responses to stress—specifically, the stress involved in lying. When you're actually "hooked up," you'll be seated in a chair near the polygraph. Three sensors will be attached:

- Blood pressure cuff, to measure heart rate

- Convoluted rubber tubes, around the abdomen and chest, to measure respiratory activity

- Two small metal plates, attached to the fingers, to measure sweat gland activity.

The questioning phase also has three parts:

Pretest. Before you're hooked up to the polygraph, the examiner asks you several questions. There are the baseline questions—"Is your name Jane Doe? Were you born in Peoria, Illinois?" Then there are the real questions—questions such as "Have you ever manufactured, transported, or sold illegal drugs?" You're not going to lie about your name or where you were born; even if your heart is beating faster than it normally would because you're nervous, that elevated heart rate is going to register as the baseline for the test.

Chart Collection Phase. You're then hooked up to the polygraph, and the examiner goes through the questions again. Then, there's the follow-up— "Did you lie when you told me you haven't manufactured, transported or sold illegal drugs?" This is the key to the use of the polygraph—the specific questioning and the immediate response.

Test Data Analysis Phase. The examiner reviews the charts and notes areas where deception is indicated. When appropriate, the examiner will ask the subject to explain or clarify unusual physiological responses— something along the lines of, "You seemed to react strongly to the questions about theft. Is there a specific reason for that?"

What are they going to ask about?

The FBI maintains very high ethical standards among its employees. Even so, they're not looking for saints, or robots. Drug use isn't defined as being in the same room as a marijuana cigarette; theft isn't defined as making a few personal phone calls on company time.

The questions on a polygraph are very carefully designed to be limited and specific, and thus useful. Doug Rhoads says, "You're not asked things like, 'Have you ever stolen a pen from work?' Give me a break. The questions also can't be as broad as 'Have you ever. . . ?' That's why the pretest is so important. You'll be asked, 'Did you lie to the examiner when you said you've never significantly defrauded your employer?' It must be specific. The broad, 'have you ever' questions will always show deception because the subject doesn't know exactly what you mean. 'Well, maybe that *box* of pens counts as significant fraud.' You've got to narrow it down to get the meaningful deceptions."

What if the polygraph shows I'm lying when I'm not?

During the pretest, the examiner will assess the subject's emotional state and physical condition and allow for any effect these might have. The control questions help identify subjects who are extremely responsive or extremely nervous; there are specialized tests for use in these circumstances. The examiners make every effort to get an accurate reading from the polygraph.

If you know a deceptive response on your polygraph is inaccurate, you can request a second polygraph with a second examiner, or you can ask to have the first polygraph reviewed by another examiner.

As far as trying to beat the polygraph, forget it. It's not the machine you're trying to fool, it's the examiner—and a skilled, experienced polygraph examiner is almost impossible to fool. Doug Rhoads says, "We've got examiners here in Charlottesville who are so good—say I've got you on the machine, and you lay out six cards in front of you. You pick up one card. It's the six of hearts. Then you rearrange the cards, keeping your eye on the six of hearts. Then I'll rearrange them. Slowly; this is not a trick. You know exactly where the six of hearts is. I'll have you put your hand on each card and the examiner asks you, 'Is that the six of hearts? Is *that* the six of hearts?' You say no to all of them. And he can tell you from the machine which one you lied on. You just can't control your body. You know that's the six of hearts and you're saying no. And that's not even a lie that you care anything about. Your responses are going to be even more obvious on a big lie."

No offense to Doug's examiners down in Charlottesville, but I'm sure the people at the FBI are at least as good.

DRUG TEST

This is a standard urine test that screens for opiates and THC, or marijuana by-products. Along with the polygraph, this test is designed to ensure that applicants adhere to the strict no-drugs policy. Nothing to worry about if you don't indulge.

* * * *

So now you know more about what it takes to become an FBI agent, and what kind of career you could expect to have. If you decide to go for it, I wish you the best of luck. I still believe it's an incredible honor and privilege to be a member of the finest law enforcement agency in the world.

PART FOUR
Appendices

FBI Field Offices

Albany Field Office
Federal Bureau of Investigation
Suite 502, James T. Foley Building
445 Broadway
Albany, New York 12207
(518) 465-7551
www.fbi.gov/fo/alfo/alfohome.htm

Albuquerque Field Office
Federal Bureau of Investigation
Suite 300
415 Silver Avenue, S.W.
Albuquerque, New Mexico 87102
(505) 224-2000
www.fbi.gov/fo/aq/aqhome.htm

Anchorage Field Office
Federal Bureau of Investigation
101 East Sixth Avenue
Anchorage, Alaska 99501
(907) 258-5322

Atlanta Field Office
Federal Bureau of Investigation
Suite 400
2635 Century Parkway, N.E.
Atlanta, Georgia 30345
(404) 679-9000

Baltimore Field Office
Federal Bureau of Investigation
7142 Ambassador Road
Baltimore, Maryland 21244
(410) 265-8080

Birmingham Field Office
Federal Bureau of Investigation
Room 1400
2121 8th Avenue N.
Birmingham, Alabama 35203
(205) 326-6166

Boston Field Office
Federal Bureau of Investigation
Suite 600
One Center Plaza
Boston, Massachusetts 02108
(617) 742-5533

Buffalo Field Office
Federal Bureau of Investigation
One FBI Plaza
Buffalo, New York 14202
(716) 856-7800
www.fbi.gov/fo/bffo/bffohome.htm

Charlotte Field Office
Federal Bureau of Investigation
Suite 900
400 South Tryon Street
Charlotte, North Carolina 28285
(704) 377-9200

Chicago Field Office
Federal Bureau of Investigation
Room 905
E. M. Dirksen Federal Office
Building
219 South Dearborn Street
Chicago, Illinois 60604
(312) 431-1333

Cincinnati Field Office
Federal Bureau of Investigation
Room 9000
550 Main Street
Cincinnati, Ohio 45202
(513) 421-4310
www.fbi.gov/fo/ci/index.htm

Cleveland Field Office
Federal Bureau of Investigation
Room 3005
Federal Office Building
1240 East 9th Street
Cleveland, Ohio 44199
(216) 522-1400
www.fbi.gov/fo/cleveland/
cleveland.htm

Columbia Field Office
Federal Bureau of Investigation
Room 1357
1835 Assembly Street
Columbia, South Carolina 29201
(803) 254-3011

Dallas Field Office
Federal Bureau of Investigation
1801 North Lamar
Dallas, Texas 75202-1795
(214) 720-2200
www.fbi.gov/fo/dl/dallas.htm

Denver Field Office
Federal Bureau of Investigation
Federal Office Building, Suite 1823
1961 Stout Street, 18th Floor
Denver, Colorado 80294
(303) 629-7171

Detroit Field Office
Federal Bureau of Investigation
26th Floor, P. V. McNamara FOB
477 Michigan Avenue
Detroit, Michigan 48226
(313) 965-2323

El Paso Field Office
Federal Bureau of Investigation
660 South Mesa Hills
Suite 3000
El Paso, Texas 79912
(915) 832-5000

Honolulu Field Office
Federal Bureau of Investigation
P.O. Box 50164
Honolulu, Hawaii 96850
(808) 521-1411

Houston Field Office
Federal Bureau of Investigation
Suite 200
2500 East TC Jester
Houston, Texas 77008
(713) 693-5000
www.gbi.gov/fo/ho/houston.htm

Indianapolis Field Office
Federal Bureau of Investigation
Room 679, FOB
575 North Pennsylvania Street
Indianapolis, Indiana 46204
(317) 639-3301

Jackson Field Office
Federal Bureau of Investigation
Room 1553, FOB
100 West Capitol Street
Jackson, Mississippi 39269
(601) 948-5000
www.fbi.gov/fo/jackson/jackson.htm

Jacksonville Field Office
Federal Bureau of Investigation
Suite 200
7820 Arlington Expressway
Jacksonville, Florida 32211
(904) 721-1211

Kansas City Field Office
Federal Bureau of Investigation
1300 Summit
Kansas City, Missouri 64105-1362
(816) 221-6100
www.fbi.gov/fo/kc/kcpage.htm

Knoxville Field Office
Federal Bureau of Investigation
Suite 600, John J. Duncan FOB
710 Locust Street
Knoxville, Tennessee 37902
(423) 544-0751
www.fbi.gov/fo/kx/knoxhome.htm

Las Vegas Field Office
Federal Bureau of Investigation
700 East Charleston Boulevard
Las Vegas, Nevada 89104
(702) 385-1281

Little Rock Field Office
Federal Bureau of Investigation
Suite 200
Two Financial Centre
10825 Financial Centre Parkway
Little Rock, Arkansas 72211
(501) 221-9100
www.fbi.gov/fo/lr/main.htm

Los Angeles Field Office
Federal Bureau of Investigation
Suite 1700, FOB
11000 Wilshire Boulevard
Los Angeles, California 90024
(310) 477-6565

Louisville Field Office
Federal Bureau of Investigation
Room 500
600 Martin Luther King Jr. Place
Louisville, Kentucky 40202
(502) 583-3941

Memphis Field Office
Federal Bureau of Investigation
Suite 3000, Eagle Crest Building
225 North Humphreys Boulevard
Memphis, Tennessee 38120
(901) 747-4300

Miami Field Office
Federal Bureau of Investigation
16320 Northwest Second Avenue
North Miami Beach, Florida 33169
(305) 944-9101
www.fbi.gov/fo/mb/index.htm

Milwaukee Field Office
Federal Bureau of Investigation
Suite 600
330 East Kilbourn Avenue
Milwaukee, Wisconsin 53202-6627
(414) 276-4684

Minneapolis Field Office
Federal Bureau of Investigation
Suite 1100
111 Washington Avenue, South
Minneapolis, Minnesota 55401
(612) 376-3200

Mobile Field Office
Federal Bureau of Investigation
P.O. Box 2128
Mobile, Alabama 36652
(334) 438-3674

Newark Field Office
Federal Bureau of Investigation
P.O. Box 1158
Newark, New Jersey 07101
(973) 622-5613

New Haven Field Office
Federal Bureau of Investigation
150 Court Street, 5th Floor
New Haven, Connecticut 06510
(203) 777-6311

New Orleans Field Office
Federal Bureau of Investigation
Suite 2200
1250 Poydras Street
New Orleans, Louisiana
70113
(504) 522-4671

New York Field Office
Federal Bureau of Investigation
26 Federal Plaza, 23rd Floor
New York, New York 10278
(212) 384-1000
www.fbi.gov/fo/nyfo/nyfohome.
htm

Norfolk Field Office
Federal Bureau of Investigation
150 Corporate Boulevard
Norfolk, Virginia 23502
(757) 455-0100

Oklahoma City Field Office
Federal Bureau of Investigation
P.O. Box 54511
Oklahoma City, Oklahoma 73154
(405) 290-7770

Omaha Field Office
Federal Bureau of Investigation
10755 Burt Street
Omaha, Nebraska 68114
(402) 493-8688

Philadelphia Field Office
Federal Bureau of Investigation
8th Floor
William J. Green Jr. FOB
600 Arch Street
Philadelphia, Pennsylvania 19106
(215) 418-4000

Phoenix Field Office
Federal Bureau of Investigation
Suite 400
201 East Indianola Avenue
Phoenix, Arizona 85012
(602) 279-5511

Pittsburgh Field Office
Federal Bureau of Investigation
Suite 300
U.S. Post Office Building
700 Grant Street
Pittsburgh, Pennsylvania 15219
(412) 471-2000

Portland Field Office
Federal Bureau of Investigation
Suite 400, Crown Plaza Building
1500 Southwest 1st Avenue
Portland, Oregon 97201
(503) 224-4181
www.fbi.gov/fo/pd/portlnd.htm

Richmond Field Office
Federal Bureau of Investigation
111 Greencourt Road
Richmond, Virginia 23228
(804) 261-1044

Sacramento Field Office
Federal Bureau of Investigation
4500 Orange Grove Avenue
Sacramento, California 95841-4205
(916) 481-9110
www.fbi.gov/fo/sc/fbisc.htm

St. Louis Field Office
Federal Bureau of Investigation
Room 2704
L. Douglas Abram Federal
Building
1520 Market Street
St. Louis, Missouri 63103
(314) 241-5357
www.fbi.gov/fo/sl/home.htm

Salt Lake City Field Office
Federal Bureau of Investigation
Suite 1200
257 East, 200 South
Salt Lake City, Utah 84111
(801) 579-1400
www.fbi.gov/fo/saltlake/index.htm

San Antonio Field Office
Federal Bureau of Investigation
Suite 200
U.S. Post Office Courthouse
Building
615 East Houston Street
San Antonio, Texas 78205
(210) 225-6741
www.fbi.gov/fo/sanant/sanant.htm

San Diego Field Office
Federal Bureau of Investigation
Federal Office Building
9797 Aero Drive
San Diego, California 92123-1800
(619) 565-1255

San Francisco Field Office
Federal Bureau of Investigation
450 Golden Gate Avenue
13th Floor
San Francisco, California 94102
(415) 553-7400

San Juan Field Office
Federal Bureau of Investigation
Room 526, U.S. Federal Building
150 Carlos Chardon Avenue
Hato Rey
San Juan, Puerto Rico
00918-1716
(787) 754-6000

Seattle Field Office
Federal Bureau of Investigation
Room 710
915 Second Avenue
Seattle, Washington 98174
(206) 622-0460
www.fbi.gov/fo/seattle/Default.htm

Springfield Field Office
Federal Bureau of Investigation
Suite 400
400 West Monroe Street
Springfield, Illinois 62704
(217) 522-9675
www.fbi.gov/fo/si/spfldfbi.htm

Tampa Field Office
Federal Bureau of Investigation
Suite 510, FOB
500 Zack Street
Tampa, Florida 33602
(813) 273-4566

**Washington Metropolitan
Field Office**
Federal Bureau of Investigation
601 4th Street NW
Washington, D.C. 20535
(202) 278-2000

APPENDIX 2
LSAT Sampler

The LSAT, or Law School Admission Test, is a half-day standardized test required for admission to all schools that are members of the Law School Admission Council.

The LSAT is designed to measure skills that are considered essential for success in law school: comprehending complex written material with accuracy and insight; analyzing arguments and drawing reliable conclusions; organizing and managing information; and writing persuasively.

CONTENT AND STRUCTURE

The LSAT consists of five 35-minute sections (totalling 175 minutes) of multiple-choice questions, a break of 10–15 minutes, and a 30-minute writing sample. A typical LSAT can last five hours or more because of administrative necessities before and after the test. Here's how the test format works:

Section	# of Questions	Time
Logical Reasoning	24–26	35 minutes
Logical Reasoning	24–26	35 minutes
Reading Comprehension	27–28	35 minutes
Logic Games	24	35 minutes
"Experimental"	24–28	30 minutes
Writing Sample	____	30 minutes

The writing sample is always administered last, and the 10–15 minute break is always given between the third and fourth multiple-choice sections. However, the five 35-minute multiple choice sections can appear in any order.

Each of the two scored Logical Reasoning sections is based on short passages. The Reading Comprehension section consists of four passages, each about 450 words long, with five to eight questions per passage. The Logic Games (Analytical Reasoning) section normally contains four games with five to seven questions per game.

The experimental section is unscored and allows the test makers to test questions that they may use on future tests. It will look exactly like a scored section of the same question type, so when you're taking the LSAT, *don't spend time trying to figure out which section is experimental.*

SCORING

The scoring scale for the multiple-choice sections of the LSAT runs from 120–180; 120 is the lowest possible score and 180 the highest. Your score on this 120–180 scale is based on your raw score, the total number of questions that you get right. All questions are weighted equally. Your scaled score also corresponds to a percentile ranking, which allows law schools to compare scores from various LSAT administrations.

If you get about half of the questions on your LSAT right (about 50), you'll score in approximately the 30th percentile. After getting 50 questions right, if you get only one more question right every ten minutes during the exam, you'll jump to the 60th percentile (about 64 questions right). And get this: On most LSATs you can get as many as 28 questions wrong and score above the 80th percentile, and as many as 21 wrong and score above the 90th percentile.

The writing sample is not scored. However, a copy of your essay is sent to every law school to which you apply.

Here's a quick, important tip. Since there's no penalty for wrong answers on the LSAT, select an answer choice for every question.

REGISTRATION

Obtain a copy of the *LSAT/LSDAS Registration and Information Book* from The Law School Admissions Council (LSAC). It's free and available at designated distribution points, such as undergraduate advising offices, law schools, and Kaplan centers. You can also call LSAC at (215) 968-1001 and have them mail you a copy. If you have Internet access, you can order one online at http://www.lsac.org.

PREPARATION

In the *LSAT/LSDAS Registration and Information Book,* LSAC states that very few people achieve their full scoring potential without preparation. LSAC also recommends that you familiarize yourself with test directions, test mechanics, and question types.

Why does preparation make such a difference? Because the LSAT is an extremely predictable test. The skills required for LSAT success are the same from test to test. If you can develop and master these skills, you'll be prepared to do your best on the LSAT. In fact, Kaplan students see average score improvement of 7.2 points (which can equate to an increase of 30 percentile points).

THE SAMPLE QUESTIONS

To introduce you to the LSAT, we've included samples of every type of multiple-choice question* that appears on the LSAT: Logical Reasoning, Logic Games, and Reading Comprehension. We've also included a Writing Sample topic. Answers to the multiple-choice questions are at the end of this section. If you'd like to take a full-length practice test and receive a score, visit any Kaplan center.

Good Luck!

*Instructions for Kaplan LSAT sample questions © Law School Admission Council, Inc. Reprinted by permission.

LOGICAL REASONING

Directions: *The questions in this section are based on the reasoning contained in brief statements or passages. For some questions, more than one of the choices could conceivably answer the question. However, you are to choose the best answer; that is, the response that most accurately and completely answers the question. You should not make assumptions that are by commonsense standards implausible, superfluous, or incompatible with the passage. After you have chosen the best answer, blacken the corresponding space on your answer sheet.*

1. One morning, George Petersen of Petersen's Garage watches as a 1995 Da Volo station wagon is towed onto his lot. Because he knows that nearly 90 percent of the 1995 Da Volo station wagons brought to his garage for work in the past were brought in because of malfunctioning power windows, he reasons that there is an almost 9 to 1 chance that the car he saw this morning has also been brought in to correct its faulty power windows.

    Which one of the following employs flawed reasoning most similar to that employed by George Petersen?

    (A) Mayor Lieberman was reelected by a majority of almost 75 percent. Since Janine Davis voted in that mayoral election, the chances are almost 3 to 1 that she voted for Mayor Lieberman.

    (B) Each week nine out of ten best-selling paperback books at The Reader's Nook are works of fiction. Since Nash's history of World War II was among the ten best-selling paperback books at The Reader's Nook this week, the chances are 9 to 1 that it is a work of fiction.

    (C) Ninety percent of those who attempt to get into Myrmidon Military Academy are turned down. Since the previous ten candidates to the academy were not accepted, Vladimir's application will almost certainly be approved.

    (D) Only one out of 50 applications to bypass zoning regulations and establish a new business in the Gedford residential district is accepted. Since only 12 such applications were made last month, there is virtually no chance that any of them will be accepted.

    (E) Nearly 95 percent of last year's Borough High School graduating class went on to some type of further schooling. Since only a little more than 5 percent of that graduating class took longer than the usual four years to graduate, it is probable that everyone who did graduate within four years went on to further schooling.

Questions 2–3

Bruce: Almost a century ago, country X annexed its neighbor's western province, clearly an unjust act. It is the obligation of country X to return the province to its former possessors, even if doing so would involve great sacrifice on the part of those citizens of country X who are currently living within that province.

Linda: A nation's paramount responsibility is the well being of its own citizens. Country X should make the sacrifice of returning the province only if it can be sure that such an act will provide some tangible benefit to the citizens of country X. The issue of whether the original annexation was just is a secondary consideration.

2. Linda's reply to Bruce most closely conforms to which one of the following principles?

   (A)   A nation is obliged to make sacrifices only in order to fulfill its paramount responsibility.

   (B)   Historical wrongs can properly be redressed only when all interested parties agree that a wrong has been committed.

   (C)   No national sacrifice is too great, provided that it is undertaken in order to ensure the future well being of the nation.

   (D)   The views of the entire nation should be consulted before the nation takes an action that involves considerable sacrifice from any part of the nation.

   (E)   A nation is obligated to redress historical injustices only when such redress would involve minimal sacrifice from that nation.

3. Bruce and Linda are committed to holding opposing points of view in answer to which one of the following questions?

   (A)   Can the original annexation of the neighboring nation's western province accurately be characterized as an unjust act?

   (B)   Would the return of the annexed province to its original possessors involve appreciable sacrifice on the part of the citizens of country X?

   (C)   Would the return of the annexed province to its original possessors confer any benefit on the citizens of country X?

   (D)   Should the citizens of country X who are currently living in the annexed province be consulted in deciding whether or not to return the province to its original possessors?

   (E)   Does country X have the obligation to redress an historic injustice at the risk of providing no benefit to its own citizens?

4. Biologists attached a radio transmitter to one of a number of wolves that had been released earlier in the White River Wilderness Area as part of a relocation project. The biologists hoped to use this wolf to track the movements of the whole pack. Wolves usually range over a wide area in search of prey, and frequently follow the migrations of their prey animals. The biologists were surprised to find that this particular wolf never moved more than five miles away from the location in which it was first tagged.

    Which one of the following, if true, would by itself most help to explain the behavior of the wolf tagged by the biologists?

    (A) The area in which the wolf was released was rocky and mountainous, in contrast to the flat, heavily wooded area from which it was taken.

    (B) The wolf had been tagged and released by the biologists only three miles away from a sheep ranch that provided a large, stable population of prey animals.

    (C) The White River Wilderness Area had supported a population of wolves in past years, but they had been hunted to extinction.

    (D) Although the wolves in the White River Wilderness Area were under government protection, their numbers had been sharply reduced, within a few years of their release, by illegal hunting.

    (E) The wolf captured and tagged by the biologists had split off from the main pack whose movements the biologists had hoped to study, and its movements did not represent those of the main pack.

5. Video arcades, legally defined as video parlors having at least five video games, require a special city license and, in primarily residential areas such as Eastview, a zoning variance. The owners of the Video Zone, popular with Eastview teenagers, have maintained that their establishment requires neither an arcade license nor a zoning variance, because it is really a retail outlet.

    Which one of the following is an assumption on which the argument of the Video Zone's owners is based?

    (A) The existing Eastview zoning regulations are unconstitutionally strict.

    (B) At no time are more than four video games in operation at the Video Zone.

    (C) Stores like the Video Zone perform an important social function.

    (D) Many of the Video Zone's games were developed after the city's zoning laws were written.

    (E) Retail establishments require no special licenses or zoning variances in Eastview.

6. It doesn't surprise me that the critic on our local radio station went off on another tirade today about the city men's choir. This is not the first time that he has criticized the choir. But this time his criticisms were simply inaccurate and unjustified. For ten minutes, he spoke of nothing but the choir's lack of expressiveness. As a professional vocal instructor, I have met with these singers individually; I can state with complete confidence that each of the members of the choir has quite an expressive voice.

Which one of the following is the most serious flaw in the author's reasoning?

(A) He directs his argument against the critic's character rather than against his claims.

(B) He ignores evidence that the critic's remarks might in fact be justified.

(C) He cites his own professional expertise as the sole explanation for his defense of the choir.

(D) He assumes that a group will have a given attribute if each of its parts has that attribute.

(E) He attempts to conclude the truth of a general situation from evidence about one specific situation.

7. Whitley Hospital's much publicized increase in emergency room efficiency due to its new procedures for handling trauma patients does not withstand careful analysis. The average time before treatment for all patients is nearly 40 minutes—the highest in the city. And for trauma victims, who are the specific target of the guidelines, the situation is even worse: The average time before treatment is nearly half an hour—more than twice the city average.

Which of the following, if true, would most seriously weaken the conclusion about the value of the new procedures?

(A) The city hospitals with the most efficient emergency rooms utilize the same procedures for handling trauma patients as does Whitley Hospital.

(B) After the new procedures went into effect, Whitley's average time before treatment for trauma patients and patients in general dropped by nearly 35 percent.

(C) Because trauma patients account for a large percentage of emergency room patients, procedures that hasten their treatment will likely increase overall emergency room efficiency.

(D) Due to differences in location and size of staff, not all emergency rooms can be expected to reach similar levels of efficiency.

(E) The recently hired administrators who instituted the new procedures also increased Whitley's emergency room staff by nearly 15 percent.

LOGIC GAMES

Directions: *Each group of questions in this section is based on a set of conditions. In answering some of the questions, it may be useful to draw a rough diagram. Choose the response that most accurately and completely answers each question.*

Questions 1–6

A zoo curator is selecting animals to import for the zoo's annual summer exhibit. Exactly one male and one female of each of the following types of animal are available: hippo, llama, monkey, ostrich, panther. The following restrictions apply:

> *If no panthers are selected, then both ostriches must be selected.*
>
> *A male panther cannot be selected unless a female llama is selected.*
>
> *If a male monkey is selected, then neither a female ostrich nor a female panther may be selected.*
>
> *At least one hippo must be selected.*

1. Which one of the following is an acceptable selection of animals for the exhibit?
    - (A)   female hippo, female monkey, male monkey, male ostrich, male panther
    - (B)   female hippo, male llama, female monkey, female ostrich, male ostrich
    - (C)   male hippo, female llama, male llama, female monkey, female ostrich
    - (D)   male hippo, female llama, male monkey, female panther, male panther
    - (E)   female llama, male llama, male monkey, female ostrich, male panther

2. Which one of the following must be false?
    - (A)   Both a female hippo and male panther are selected.
    - (B)   Both a male monkey and a female llama are selected.
    - (C)   Both a female ostrich and a male hippo are selected.
    - (D)   All of the animals selected are female.
    - (E)   All of the animals selected are male.

3. If a male monkey is selected, then which one of the following animals must also be selected?

    (A) female hippo
    (B) male hippo
    (C) female llama
    (D) female monkey
    (E) male ostrich

4. If the smallest number of animals is selected, then which one of the following animals must be selected?

    (A) male hippo
    (B) female llama
    (C) male monkey
    (D) female panther
    (E) male panther

5. All of the following could be true EXCEPT:

    (A) A female llama is the only female animal selected.
    (B) A female monkey is the only female animal selected.
    (C) A female ostrich is the only female animal selected.
    (D) A male ostrich is the only male animal selected.
    (E) A male panther is the only male animal selected.

6. If a female llama is not selected, then which one of the following is a pair of animals at least one of which must be selected?

    (A) female hippo, female monkey
    (B) male hippo, male llama
    (C) female ostrich, male ostrich
    (D) male ostrich, female panther
    (E) female panther, male panther

READING COMPREHENSION

Directions: *Each passage in this section is followed by a group of questions to be answered on the basis of what is stated or implied in the passage. For some of the questions, more than one of the choices could conceivably answer the question. However, you are to choose the best answer; that is, the response that most accurately and completely answers the question.*

Since it was proposed in 1980, the Alvarezes' theory that the mass extinction of plant and animal species at the end of the Cretaceous period sixty-five million years ago resulted from a devastating extraterrestrial impact has won increasing
Line support, although even today there is no consensus for it among scientists. In the
(5) Alvarezes' scenario, an asteroid 10 kilometers in diameter struck the earth at high velocity, forming a crater 150 kilometers wide. In addition to the immediate devastation of tidal waves, global fires, and giant storms, impact debris hurled into the atmosphere at high altitude spread around the earth, preventing sunlight from reaching the ground. With photosynthesis blocked, herbivorous and carnivorous
(10) species died as the food chain was snapped at its base.

The Alvarezes' primary evidence is a superabundance of iridium in the "Cretaceous/Tertiary boundary" (KT boundary), a thin rock stratum dividing Cretaceous rocks from those of the later Tertiary period. Iridium, relatively rare in the earth's crust, comes mainly from the slow fall of interplanetary debris; in some
(15) KT boundary strata, iridium is 10–100 times as abundant as normal, suggesting a rapid, massive deposition. Coincident with the boundary, whole species of pollens and unicellular animals vanished from the fossil record, strongly supporting the idea of a catastrophic event. Later studies have shown that some KT boundary samples also contain osmium isotopes typical of meteorites, basalt sphericles that
(20) may have melted on impact and rapidly cooled in the atmosphere, and quartz grains deformed in a manner typical of high velocity impacts.

Initially, paleontologists dismissed the theory, arguing that fossils of large animals such as dinosaurs showed a gradual extinction lasting millions of years. But recent intensive exploration in the Hell Creek formation of North Dakota and
(25) Montana, aimed at collecting all available dinosaur remnants rather than selectively searching for rare or well-preserved fossils, has shown an abundance of dinosaurs right up to the KT boundary. As a result, opposition to catastrophic mass extinction has substantially weakened among paleontologists.

Given the lack of a known impact crater of the necessary age and size, and the
(30) fact that the theory requires the extinctions to have occurred in an extremely short time, some scientists have proposed alternative catastrophe scenarios. Courtillot and others have argued that massive volcanic eruptions, lasting

hundreds of thousands of years, pumped enough debris into the atmosphere to cause the darkness and chemical changes that devastated life on the planet.

(35) Courtillot's evidence includes huge volcanic flows in India that coincide with the KT boundary, and analyses of KT boundary rocks that seem to show that the excess iridium was laid down over 10–100,000 years, too long for the impact hypothesis.

Walter Alvarez and Frank Asaro reply that the shock wave caused by an impact

(40) could have melted mantle rocks, triggering the volcanic activity. They concede, though, that the exact mechanism is unclear. Meanwhile, drillings at a 150-kilometer-wide circular geologic formation in Yucatan, found in 1978 but not carefully examined until 1990, have shown a composition consistent with extraterrestrial impact. However, there is still no conclusive evidence that the

(45) Yucatan formation is the long-sought impact site.

1. Which of the following, if true, would most weaken the theory that the Cretaceous extinctions were caused by the impact of an asteroid?

    (A) The iridium layer was deposited over a period of 10,000 years.
    (B) The dinosaurs flourished up until the KT boundary.
    (C) The extinctions coincided with extensive volcanic activity.
    (D) The location of the impact has yet to be conclusively established.
    (E) The extinction of animal species accompanied the disappearance of plant life.

2. It can be inferred that supporters of the Alvarez and Courtillot theories share which of the following views?

    (A) The iridium layer was deposited over thousands of years.
    (B) Large animals such as the dinosaurs died out gradually over millions of years.
    (C) Mass extinction occurred as an indirect result of debris saturating the atmosphere.
    (D) It is unlikely that the specific cause of the extinctions will ever be determined.
    (E) Volcanic activity may have been triggered by shock waves from the impact of an asteroid.

    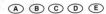

253

3. The author mentions "recent intensive exploration in the Hell Creek formation" (line 24) primarily in order to

(A) point out the benefits of using field research to validate scientific theories

(B) suggest that the asteroid impact theory is not consistent with fossil evidence

(C) discuss new fossil discoveries in North Dakota and Montana

(D) summarize the evidence that led to wide acceptance of catastrophe scenarios of mass extinction

(E) show that dinosaurs survived until the end of the Cretaceous period

4. The author would most likely endorse which of the following statements about the asteroid impact theory?

(A) It is strongly supported by all of the available evidence.

(B) It should not be tested by a search for geologic evidence.

(C) It is supported by substantial but not conclusive evidence.

(D) Paleontologists have not yet realized its importance.

(E) Its main value is that it will eventually lead to a more accurate impact theory.

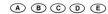

5. In the passage, the author is primarily concerned with doing which one of the following?

(A) describing recent fossil finds in North America

(B) offering a new explanation for a scientific problem

(C) summarizing the history of a geologic era

(D) revising the research methods of paleontologists

(E) comparing two theories about a mass extinction

6. According to the passage, the fossil discoveries at Hell Creek

(A) support the notion that dinosaurs died out gradually over a long period of time

(B) undermined Courtillot's volcanic theory of mass extinction

(C) convinced scientists to investigate the Yucatan geologic formation

(D) caused paleontologists to reassess their views about catastrophic mass extinction

(E) prove that dinosaurs continued to survive into the Tertiary period

254

WRITING SAMPLE

Directions: *You are to write a brief essay on the topic below. You will have 30 minutes in which to plan and write. Read the topic carefully. You will most likely benefit from spending several minutes organizing your response and planning your essay before you begin to write. DO NOT WRITE ON A TOPIC OTHER THAN THE ONE GIVEN. WRITING ON A TOPIC OF YOUR OWN CHOOSING IS NOT ACCEPTABLE.*

There is no "correct" or "incorrect" answer to this question. Law schools are primarily interested to see how clearly and carefully you argue your position. No specialized knowledge is required. Schools are interested in the level of vocabulary, organization, and writing mechanics that you employ. They understand the time constraints and pressured condition under which you will write.

Margaret has received $6,500 in an insurance settlement. The money is an unexpected boon to Margaret, who has taught elementary school for the past six years. She is trying to decide in which of two ways to spend the money. Write an essay explaining why one plan is superior to the other. Two factors should help formulate your decision:

- *Margaret wants to use the money for something that will prove to be of long-range advantage.*

- *Margaret is unable to contribute any of her own funds, so the insurance money must cover the entire cost of the plan she selects.*

Margaret is considering buying her own car. She has been commuting to work by public transportation, but has long desired the personal freedom that having her own car can provide. Since she wants a car that is fully protected under both manufacturer's and dealer's warranties, Margaret has decided against buying a used car, which would have been considerably less expensive. She has also decided against the smaller and less expensive cars because she fears that they would be unsafe in a collision. She has found a midsize car within her price range. The insurance money will leave her with monthly payments only slightly higher than her current transportation costs. Title and insurance will add to the cost, but Margaret feels that by getting two other teachers to join her in a carpool, she can manage the expense. If all goes according to schedule, the car should be paid for within two years.

The insurance money could also be used to pay for a master's degree in psychology. Margaret's ultimate goal is to become a school psychologist, and toward this end she has been working as a volunteer counselor for a hotline serving runaways and troubled teenagers. Margaret would have to give up this volunteer work in order to take classes three nights a week at the state university, but she feels that she can keep her current job while studying. The money would fund tuition, books, and incidental expenses, but would not be sufficient to cover her expenses for the required six-month internship.

ANSWERS ON PAGE 276

APPENDIX 3
GMAT Sampler

The GMAT, or Graduate Management Admission Test, is a standardized test designed to assess skills relevant to graduate studies in business and management. Most schools require submission of GMAT scores with applications to their graduate business programs.

Since October 1997, the GMAT has been administered exclusively as a computer adaptive test, or CAT. The GMAT CAT consists of 150 minutes of multiple-choice testing, plus two 30-minute writing sessions. (Test takers are required to type their essays using a simple word-processing program.)

Here's how the four sections of the GMAT CAT break down.

Section	# of Questions	Time
Analytical Writing Analysis of an Issue topic	1	30 minutes
Analytical Writing Analysis of an Argument topic	1	30 minutes
Verbal Section Reading Comprehension Sentence Correction Critical Reasoning	41	75 minutes
Quantitative Section Data Sufficiency Problem Solving	37	75 minutes

The essay questions are administered first, followed by the multiple-choice sections. The question types within a section appear in random order.

CAT FORMAT

A compter adaptive test (CAT) is very different structurally from a traditional paper and pencil test. On a CAT, the computer will select which questions to administer based on how well you're doing up to that point. The better you do, the harder the questions you see will become.

The CAT is designed to find the level at which you get about 50 percent of the questions correct. Therefore, no matter how good you are at taking standardized tests, you'll probably come out of the test thinking the CAT is difficult.

SCORING

Your GMAT score report will show three scores relating to the multiple-choice sections and a separate score for the Analytical Writing sections. You'll receive an overall scaled score, ranging from 200 to 800, and sub-scores for the Quantitative and Verbal sections, both ranging from 0 to 60. Your score report will show a corresponding percentile ranking for your overall score, your Quantitative subscore, and your Verbal subscore.

The percentile figures are important. They allow business schools to quickly see where you fall in the pool of applicants. An overall score of 590, for instance, corresponds to the 80th percentile, meaning that 80 percent of test takers scored at or below this level.

Experimental questions will be scattered through the test, accounting for about a quarter of all the questions. They will look just like the other multiple-choice questions but won't contribute to your score. There's no way to know which questions are experimental, so it's best to treat every question as if it were scored.

When you start the GMAT CAT, the computer assumes you have an average score and gives you a question of medium difficulty. If you answer the question correctly, your score goes up and you're given a harder question. If you answer incorrectly, your score goes down and you're given an easier question. This continues for the rest of the test as the computer tries to "home in" on your score.

As you get to the end of a section, you will reach a point where you get half the questions of a certain level of difficulty right and half the questions wrong. Once the computer finds this level, it has found what is supposed to be your ability level. Therefore, the most critical part of the CAT is not how many questions you answer correctly, but rather how difficult the questions that you answer correctly are.

REGISTRATION

The GMAT is administered by the Educational Testing Service and costs $125 (domestic)/$160 (international). To register, contact:

GMAT
Educational Testing Service
P.O. Box 6103
Princeton, NJ 08541-6103
Tel. (609) 771-7330
E-mail: gmat@ets.org
Web site: http://www.gmat.org

THE SAMPLE QUESTIONS

To introduce you to the GMAT, we've included sample questions of every type that you will see on the test. The multiple-choice question types are Reading Comprehension, Sentence Correction, Critical Reasoning, Data Sufficiency, and Problem Solving. We've also included sample topics for the two Analytical Writing Assessment sections and an answer key. If you'd like to take a full-length practice test and receive a score, visit any Kaplan center. Good Luck!

READING COMPREHENSION

Directions: *Answer questions 1–4 after reading through the passage below. Base your answers on information that is either stated or implied in the passage.*

An important feature of the labor market in recent years has been the increasing participation of women, particularly married women. Many analysts suggest, however, that women comprise a secondary labor market in which rates of pay and
Line promotion prospects are inferior to those available to men. The principal reason is
(5) that women have, or are assumed to have, domestic responsibilities that compete with paid employment. Such domestic responsibilities are strongly influenced by social values that require women to give priority to home and family over paid employment.

The difficulties that women face in the labor market and in their ability to reach
(10) senior positions in organizations are accentuated by the arrival of children. In order to become full-time employees, women with children must overcome the problems of finding good, affordable child care and the psychological barriers of workplace marginality. Some women balance domestic and workplace commitments by working part time. However, part-time work is a precarious form
(15) of employment. Female part timers are often the first laid off in a difficult economy. These workers are often referred to as the "reserve army" of female labor.

One researcher has found that approximately 80 percent of women in their twenties who have children remain at home. Such women who later return to work represent another sector of the work force facing difficulties. When the
(20) typical houseworker returns to the labor market, she is unsure of herself in her new environment. This doubt is accentuated by her recent immersion in housework, a very private form of work. Without recent employment experience, these women confront a restricted range of opportunities and will almost certainly be offered low-status jobs with poor prospects.
(25) Even women professionals who interrupt their careers to have children experience difficulties. Their technical skills may become rusty or obsolete, important networks of business contacts are broken, and their delayed return to work may mean that they are likely to come up for promotion well after the age that would be otherwise normal. Consequently, women, even those of high ability,
(30) may find themselves blocked in the lower echelons of an organization, overlooked or even "invisible" to senior management.

1. The author of the passage is primarily concerned with
    (A) advocating changes in employers' practices toward women with children
    (B) examining some of the reasons women rarely reach the higher echelons of paid labor
    (C) describing the psychological consequences for women of working outside the home
    (D) taking issue with those who believe women should not work outside the home
    (E) analyzing the contribution of women to industry and business

2. The passage provides information to support which of the following statements about women workers?
    (A) It is the responsibility of employers to provide childcare accommodations for women workers with children.
    (B) Women in high-status positions are easily able to integrate career and children.
    (C) Conditions for working mothers are much better today than 20 years ago.
    (D) The decision to work outside the home is often the source of considerable anxiety for women with children.
    (E) With the expense of child care, it is often not profitable for women with children to work.

3. The author's discussion of women professionals in the last paragraph serves to
    (A) show that the difficulties of integrating career and motherhood can be overcome
    (B) indicate that even women of higher status are not exempt from the difficulties of integrating careers and children
    (C) defend changes in the policies of employers toward working mothers
    (D) modify a hypothesis regarding the increased labor force participation of women
    (E) point out the lack of opportunities for women in business

4. According to the passage, men generally receive higher salaries and have a better chance of being promoted because women

    (A) tend to work in industries that rely almost exclusively on part-time labor
    (B) lack the technical and managerial experience of their male counterparts
    (C) have responsibilities outside of the workplace that demand considerable attention
    (D) are the first to be laid off when the economy grows at a very slow pace
    (E) suffer discrimination in the male-dominated corporate environment

SENTENCE CORRECTION

Directions: *The following questions consist of sentences that are either partly or entirely underlined. Below each sentence are five versions of the underlined portion of the sentence. Choice (A) duplicates the original version. The four other versions revise the underlined portion of the sentence. Read the sentence and the five choices carefully, and select the best version. If the original seems better than any of the revisions, select choice (A). If not, choose one of the revisions.*

These questions test your recognition of correct grammatical usage and your sense of clear and economical writing style. Choose answers according to the norms of standard written English for grammar, word choice, and sentence construction. Your selected answer should express the intended meaning of the original sentence as clearly and precisely as possible, while avoiding ambiguous, awkward, or unnecessarily wordy constructions.

1. Several consumer protection agencies have filed suit, seeking to bar distributors from advertising treatments for baldness, <u>which brings no discernible improvement and may even result in potential harm</u>.

   (A) which brings no discernible improvement and may even result in potential harm
   (B) which bring no discernible improvement and may even prove harmful
   (C) bringing no discernible improvement and even being harmful
   (D) which brings no discernible improvement and may even potentially result in harm being done
   (E) which bring no discernible improvement, maybe even resulting in harm

2. Local reporters investigating the labor dispute reported that only half of the workers in the plant were covered by the union health plan; <u>at least as much as a hundred and more others had not any</u> health insurance whatsoever.

   (A) at least as much as a hundred and more others had not any
   (B) at least as much as more than a hundred others had no
   (C) more than a hundred others had not any
   (D) more than a hundred others had no
   (E) there was at least a hundred or more others without any

263

3. Archaeologists have shown that ingesting lead in drinking water was a significant health hazard for the ancient Romans, <u>like that of modern Americans</u>.
   (A) like that of modern Americans
   (B) as that for modern Americans
   (C) just as modern Americans do
   (D) as do modern Americans
   (E) as it is for modern Americans

4. Born Nathan Weinstein in New York City on October 17, 1903, <u>Nathanael West's first novel, *The Dream Life of Balso Snell* was written during a stay in Paris and published when the author</u> was 28.
   (A) Nathanael West's first novel, *The Dream Life of Balso Snell* was written during a stay in Paris and published when the author
   (B) Nathanael West's first novel, *The Dream Life of Balso Snell*, written while he was staying in Paris, was published when the author
   (C) Nathanael West's *The Dream Life of Balso Snell*, his first novel, was written while the author was staying in Paris and published when he
   (D) Nathanael West wrote his first novel, *The Dream Life of Balso Snell*, during a stay in Paris and published it when he
   (E) when Nathanael West was staying in Paris, he wrote his first novel, *The Dream Life of Balso Snell*, publishing it when he

5. In commercial garment construction, one advantage of serging over single-needle sewing is that the seam allowance is overcast as the seam is sewn <u>instead of</u> a separate process requiring deeper seam allowances.
   (A) instead of
   (B) rather than in
   (C) in contrast with
   (D) as opposed to
   (E) as against being done in

CRITICAL REASONING

Directions: Select the best answer for each question.

A study of 20 overweight men revealed that each man experienced significant weight loss after adding SlimDown, an artificial food supplement, to his daily diet. For three months, each man consumed one SlimDown portion every morning after exercising, and then followed his normal diet for the rest of the day. Clearly, anyone who consumes one portion of SlimDown every day for at least three months will lose weight and will look and feel his best.

1. Which one of the following is an assumption on which the argument depends?

   (A) The men in the study will gain back the weight if they discontinue the SlimDown program.

   (B) No other dietary supplement will have the same effect on overweight men.

   (C) The daily exercise regimen was not responsible for the effects noted in the study.

   (D) Women won't experience similar weight reductions if they adhere to the SlimDown program for three months.

   (E) Overweight men will achieve only partial weight loss if they don't remain on the SlimDown program for a full three months.

   Ⓐ Ⓑ Ⓒ Ⓓ Ⓔ

2. According to a recent study, advertisements in medical journals often contain misleading information about the effectiveness and safety of new prescription drugs. The medical researchers who wrote the study concluded that the advertisements could result in doctors' prescribing inappropriate drugs to their patients.

   The researchers' conclusion would be most strengthened if which of the following were true?

   (A) Advertisements for new prescription drugs are an important source of revenue for medical journals.

   (B) Editors of medical journals are often unable to evaluate the claims made in advertisements for new prescription drugs.

   (C) Doctors rely on the advertisements as a source of information about new prescription drugs.

   (D) Advertisements for new prescription drugs are typically less accurate than medical journal articles evaluating those same drugs.

   (E) The Food and Drug Administration, the government agency responsible for drug regulation, reviews advertisements for new drugs only after the ads have already been printed.

   Ⓐ Ⓑ Ⓒ Ⓓ Ⓔ

265

3. A state legislator argues that her state's ban against casino gambling is inconsistent and impractical, since other forms of gambling such as bingo and the state lottery are legal. She claims that instead of vainly attempting to enforce the ban, the legislature should simply legalize all gambling, and that to do so would also have the positive effect of reducing the crime rate.

Which of the following, if true, most seriously weakens the legislator's argument above?

(A) Since many people enjoy the thrill of participating in illegal practices, legalizing gambling would probably cause a decline rather than an increase in this activity.

(B) Because prosecutors rarely seek prison terms for illegal gamblers, legalizing gambling would not result in a significant savings of money.

(C) Long-term studies have shown that the number of people who participate in the lottery is higher now than it was when the lottery was prohibited.

(D) Legalizing gambling would entice gamblers from states where it is still banned, and many of them are involved in other illegal activities such as drug smuggling.

(E) Many people who participate in illegal gambling claim that they would risk their money on the stock market if they had more disposable income.

4. Aggressive fertility treatments are not responsible for the rise in the incidence of twin births. Rather, this increase can be attributed to the fact that women are waiting longer to become mothers. Statistically, women over 35 are more likely to conceive twins, and these women comprise a greater percentage of women giving birth than ever before.

The argument above is flawed in that it ignores the possibility that

(A) many women over 35 who give birth to twins are not first-time mothers

(B) women over 35 are not the only women who give birth to twins

(C) the correlation between fertility treatments and the increased incidence of multiple births may be a coincidence

(D) on average, women over 35 are no more likely to conceive identical twins than other women are

(E) women over 35 are more likely to resort to the sorts of fertility treatments that tend to yield twin births

5. A researcher studying cats discovered that during the dream state of sleep, the cerebral cortex of a cat's brain fires messages to its body as rapidly as it does during wakefulness. In an effort to determine why the sleeping cat's body does not respond to the messages being fired by the brain, the researcher removed a cluster of neurons from a sleeping cat's brain stem, the part of the brain that connects the cerebral cortex to the spinal cord. After he had done so, the still-sleeping cat got up, pounced as if it were chasing a mouse, and arched its back.

    Which of the following, if true, taken together with the information above, best supports the conclusion that the sleeping cat was acting out its dreams?

    (A) The neurons that were removed from the brain stem normally serve to trigger the dream state of sleep and the rapid brain activity that accompanies it.

    (B) The cerebral cortex is able to receive and transmit sensory information even when the brain is in a sleeping state.

    (C) The neurons that were removed from the brain stem are normally responsible for transmitting messages from the cerebral cortex.

    (D) The neurons that were removed from the brain stem normally prevent messages fired by the cerebral cortex during sleep from being received by the spinal cord.

    (E) The types of brain waves produced by the cerebral cortex during sleep have distinctly different properties from those produced during a wakeful state.

6. Until the Federal government began providing low-cost flood insurance to coastal property owners, construction along beaches was limited by owners' fears that their property would be washed away. Since the insurance was made available, however, beachfront construction has boomed and land erosion has increased at a dangerous rate.

    Which of the following, if feasible, offers the best prospects for the Federal government to put a stop to the problem of land erosion along beaches?

    (A) prohibiting beachfront property owners from embellishing or adding to existing buildings
    (B) utilizing computer science techniques to obtain detailed information on the extent and rapidity of land erosion along beaches
    (C) enacting building codes requiring new beachfront structures in flood-threatened areas to be elevated above the high water level of a storm
    (D) compensating beachfront property owners for moving to a new location off the coast while canceling flood insurance benefits for any new or remaining beachfront construction
    (E) requiring beachfront property owners receiving flood insurance coverage to adopt construction standards that will protect their buildings from inundation

PROBLEM SOLVING

Directions: *Solve the following problems and choose the best answer.*

1. At a certain diner, Joe ordered 3 doughnuts and a cup of coffee and was charged $2.25. Stella ordered 2 doughnuts and a cup of coffee and was charged $1.70. What is the price of two doughnuts?

   (A) $0.55
   (B) $1.00
   (C) $1.10
   (D) $1.30
   (E) $1.80

2. Carol spends $\frac{1}{4}$ of her savings on a stereo and $\frac{1}{3}$ less than she spent on the stereo for a television. What fraction of her savings did she spend on the stereo and television?

   (A) $\frac{1}{4}$

   (B) $\frac{2}{7}$

   (C) $\frac{5}{12}$

   (D) $\frac{1}{2}$

   (E) $\frac{7}{12}$

3. If $a > 1$, what is the value of $\dfrac{2a + 6}{a^2 + 2a - 3}$?

(A) a

(B) $a + 3$

(C) $\dfrac{2}{a - 1}$

(D) $\dfrac{2a}{a - 3}$

(E) $\dfrac{a - 1}{2}$

4. A car rental company charges for mileage as follows: x dollars per mile for the first n miles and $x + 1$ dollars per mile for each mile over n miles. How much will the mileage charge be, in dollars, for a journey of d miles, where $d > n$?
(A) $d(x + 1) - n$
(B) $xn + d$
(C) $xn + d(x + 1)$
(D) $x(n + d) + d$
(E) $(x + 1)(d - n)$

DATA SUFFICIENCY

Directions: *In each of the problems below, a question is followed by two statements containing certain data. You are to determine whether the data provided by the statements are sufficient to answer the question. Choose the correct answer based upon the statements' data, your knowledge of mathematics, and your familiarity with everyday facts (such as the number of minutes in an hour or cents in a dollar).*

A   if statement (1) <u>by itself</u> is sufficient to answer the question, but statement (2) by itself is not;

B   if statement (2) <u>by itself</u> is sufficient to answer the question, but statement (1) by itself is not;

C   if statements (1) and (2) <u>taken together</u> are sufficient to answer the question, even though <u>neither</u> statement <u>by itself</u> is sufficient;

D   if <u>either</u> statement <u>by itself</u> is sufficient to answer the question;

E   if statements (1) and (2) <u>taken together</u> are <u>not</u> sufficient to answer the question, requiring more data pertaining to the problem.

Note: Diagrams accompanying problems agree with information given in the questions, but may not agree with additional information given in statements (1) and (2).

All numbers used are real numbers.

Example:

A B C

What is the length of segment *AC* ?

   (1)   B is the midpoint of AC.

   (2)   AB = 5

Ⓐ Ⓑ ● Ⓓ Ⓔ

Explanation: *Statement (1) tells you that B is the midpoint of AC, so AB = BC and AC = 2AB = 2BC. Since statement (1) does not give a value for AB or BC, you cannot answer the question using statement (1) alone. Statement (2) says that AB = 5. Since statement (2) does not give you a value for BC, the question cannot be answered by statement (2) alone. Using both statements together you can find a value for both AB and BC; therefore you can find AC, so the answer to the problem is C.*

1. Team X won 40 basketball games. What percent of its basketball games did Team X win?

    (1) Team X played the same number of basketball games as Team Y.
    (2) Team Y won 45 games, representing 62.5 percent of the basketball games it played.

    Ⓐ Ⓑ Ⓒ Ⓓ Ⓔ

2. If $2b - 2a^2 = 18$, what is the value of b ?

    (1) $a^2 = 1,156$
    (2) $a > 0$

    Ⓐ Ⓑ Ⓒ Ⓓ Ⓔ

3. A certain company produces exactly three products, X, Y, and Z. In 1990, what was the total income for the company from the sale of its products?

    (1) In 1990, the company sold 8,000 units of product X, 10,000 units of product Y, and 16,000 units of product Z.
    (2) In 1990, the company charged $28 per unit for product X, and twice as much for product Z.

    Ⓐ Ⓑ Ⓒ Ⓓ Ⓔ

4. A number of bacteria were placed in a petri dish at 5:00 A.M. If the number of bacteria in the petri dish grew for 5 days, by doubling every 12 hours, how many bacteria were in the petri dish at 5:00 P.M. on the third day?

    (1) From 5:00 A.M. to 5:00 P.M. on the second day the number of bacteria increased by 100 percent.
    (2) Twenty bacteria were placed in the petri dish at 5:00 A.M. the first day.

    Ⓐ Ⓑ Ⓒ Ⓓ Ⓔ

5. What is the value of x ?

    (1) $x^2 - 9 = 16$
    (2) $3x(x - 5) = 0$

    Ⓐ Ⓑ Ⓒ Ⓓ Ⓔ

6. If a and b are positive integers, what is the value of a ?

    (1) $a = \dfrac{3}{5}b$

    (2) $b = 75$

    Ⓐ Ⓑ Ⓒ Ⓓ Ⓔ

ANALYSIS OF AN ISSUE

Directions: Analyze and present your point of view on the issue described below. There is no "right" point of view. In developing your point of view, you should consider the issue from a number of different viewpoints. Read the statement below and the directions that follow it. Write your response on separate pieces of paper. Allow yourself 30 minutes to plan and write your response.

"Some people argue that those who do not send their children to public schools should not have to fund these schools through taxes, since neither parents nor children benefit from these schools. They ignore the fact that everyone benefits from the strong economy that a well-educated populace generates."

Which argument do you find more compelling, the case for forcing everyone to fund public schools or the opposing viewpoint? Explain your position using relevant reasons or examples taken from your own experience, observations, or reading.

ANALYSIS OF AN ARGUMENT

Directions: Provide a critique of the argument below. Focus on one or all of the following, depending upon your considered opinion of the argument: questionable assumptions underlying the reasoning, alternative explanations or evidence that would weaken the reasoning, additional information that would support or weaken the argument. Read the statement below and the directions that follow it. Write your response on seperate pieces of paper. Allow yourself 30 minutes to plan and write your response.

"The placement of telescopes on orbiting space stations will allow us to see planets in other solar systems. At present, the earth's atmosphere distorts the images telescopes provide of far-off stars, making it nearly impossible to see any orbiting planets."

Explain how logically persuasive you find this argument. In discussing your viewpoint, analyze the argument's line of reasoning and its use of evidence. Also explain what, if anything, would make the argument more valid and convincing or help you to better evaluate its conclusion.